Competing Memories

Other books written or edited by Mark K. Christ:

Rugged and Sublime:
The Civil War in Arkansas (1994)

"Getting Used to Being Shot At":
The Spence Family Civil War Letters (2002)

"All Cut to Pieces and Gone to Hell":
The Civil War, Race Relations, and the Battle of Poison Spring (2003)

"The Earth Reeled and Trees Trembled":
Civil War Arkansas 1863–1864 (2007)

"Ready, Booted, and Spurred":
Arkansas in the U.S.–Mexican War (2009)

The Die Is Cast:
Arkansas Goes to War, 1861 (2010)

Civil War Arkansas, 1863:
The Battle for a State (2010)

"This Day We Marched Again":
A Union Soldier's Account of War
in Arkansas and the Trans-Mississippi (2014)

I Do Wish This Cruel War Was Over:
First-Person Accounts of Civil War Arkansas
from the Arkansas Historical Quarterly (2014)

Competing Memories

The Legacy of Arkansas's Civil War

Edited by
Mark K. Christ

Contributors:

Mark K. Christ

Thomas A. DeBlack

Kelly Houston Jones

Cherisse Jones-Branch

Carl Moneyhon

Mary Jane Warde

Elliott West

Jeannie Whayne

BUTLER CENTER BOOKS
Little Rock, Arkansas

BUTLER CENTER BOOKS

The Butler Center for Arkansas Studies
Central Arkansas Library System
100 Rock Street
Little Rock, Arkansas 72201
www.butlercenter.org

First edition: September 2016

ISBN 978-1-935106-96-8

Manager: Rod Lorenzen
Book and cover design: H. K. Stewart
Copyeditor: Ali Welky

Publication of this book was made possible by the generous financial support of the Arkansas Civil War Sesquicentennial Commission.

ARKANSAS CIVIL WAR
Sesquicentennial Commission

Front cover image courtesy of the Old State House Museum, Little Rock, AR

Library of Congress Cataloging-in-Publication Data

Names: Christ, Mark K., editor. | DeBlack, Thomas A., 1951- author. | Whayne, Jeannie M., author. | West, Elliott, 1945- author. | Jones-Branch, Cherisse, author. | Warde, Mary Jane, 1944- author. | Jones, Kelly Houston, author. | Moneyhon, Carl H., 1944- author.
Title: Competing memories : the legacy of Arkansas's Civil War / edited by Mark K. Christ; contributing writers: Thomas A. DeBlack, Jeannie Whayne, Elliott West, Cherisse Jones-Branch, Mary Jane Warde, Kelly Houston Jones, Carl Moneyhon.
Description: First edition. | Little Rock, Arkansas : Butler Center Books, [2016] | Includes bibliographical references and index.
Identifiers: LCCN 2016030017 | ISBN 9781935106968 (hardcover : alk. paper)
Subjects: LCSH: Reconstruction (U.S. history, 1865-1877)--Arkansas. | Arkansas--History. | Arkansas--Economic conditions. | Arkansas--History--Civil War, 1861-1865.
Classification: LCC F411 .C73 2016 | DDC 976.7/04--dc23 LC record available at https://lccn.loc.gov/2016030017

Printed in the United States of America.
This book is printed on archival-quality paper that meets requirements of the American National Standard for Information Sciences, Permanence of Paper, Printed Library Materials, ANSI Z39.48-1984.

Butler Center Books, the publishing division of the Butler Center for Arkansas Studies, was made possible by the generosity of Dora Johnson Ragsdale and John G. Ragsdale Jr.

In memory of

Archie Lee Moore Jr.

Arkansas Civil War Sesquicentennial Commissioner,

colleague, and friend.

Table of Contents

Contributors

Mark K. Christ is community outreach director for the Arkansas Historic Preservation Program, an agency of the Department of Arkansas Heritage. A 1982 graduate of the University of Arkansas at Little Rock, he received his master's degree in 2000 from the University of Oklahoma. The Arkansas Historical Association presented him with its Lifetime Achievement Award in 2015, and the Civil War Trust awarded him the 2013 State Preservation Leadership Award. He has written, edited, and co-edited several books of Civil War history, including *Getting Used to Being Shot At: The Spence Family Civil War Letters*; *Civil War Arkansas, 1863: The Battle for a State*, which won the Military Order of the Stars and Bars' 2010 Douglas Southall Freeman Award and the Central Arkansas Library System's 2013 Booker Worthen Literary Prize; *"This Day We Marched Again": A Union Soldier's Account of War in Arkansas and the Trans-Mississippi*; and *I Do Wish This Cruel War Was Over: First-Person Accounts of Civil War Arkansas from the* Arkansas Historical Quarterly.

Thomas A. DeBlack, professor of history at Arkansas Tech University in Russellville, received his bachelor's degree at Southern Methodist University, his master's degree at Ouachita Baptist University, and his doctorate at the University of Arkansas in Fayetteville. Winner of a 2015 Lifetime Achievement Award from the Arkansas Historical Association, he is the author of *With Fire and Sword: Arkansas, 1861–1874*; co-author of *Arkansas: A Narrative History*; and co-editor of *The Southern Elite and Social Change: Essays in Honor of Willard B. Gatewood Jr.*

Kelly Houston Jones is an assistant professor of history at Austin Peay State University in Clarksville, Tennessee. She received her doctorate from the University of Arkansas in Fayetteville in 2014 under the direction of Jeannie Whayne. Her research is published in the journals *Agricultural History* and the *Arkansas Historical Quarterly*, and in the volume *Race and Ethnicity in Arkansas: New Perspectives*, edited by John Kirk. Among other projects on Arkansas history, she is currently at work on a book manuscript based on her dissertation, "The Peculiar Institution on the Periphery: Slavery in Arkansas."

Cherisse Jones-Branch is professor of history at Arkansas State University in Jonesboro, where she teaches courses in U.S. history, women's history, civil rights and African American history, and heritage studies. She received her bachelor's and master's degrees from the College of Charleston, South Carolina, and a doctorate in history from Ohio State University in Columbus. She is the author of numerous articles on women's civil rights activism. In 2014, she published *Crossing the Line: Women and Interracial Activism in South Carolina during and after World War II* with the University Press of Florida and is the co-editor of the forthcoming *Arkansas Women: Their Lives and Times*, which will be published by the University of Georgia Press. She is also working on a second monograph, *Better Living by Their Own Bootstraps: Rural Black Women's Activism in Arkansas*, which is under contract with the University of Arkansas Press.

Carl H. Moneyhon is a professor in the history department at the University of Arkansas at Little Rock. With BA and MA degrees from the University of Texas in Austin and a PhD from the University of

Chicago, he is a specialist in the history of the American South and the Civil War and Reconstruction. Among his works on Arkansas are *The Impact of the Civil War and Reconstruction in Arkansas: Persistence in the Midst of Ruin* (1994), *Arkansas and the New South* (1997), and *Portraits of Conflict: A Photographic History of the Civil War in Arkansas* (1987). He also is the author of numerous articles and book chapters on the Civil War in Arkansas.

Mary Jane Warde of Stillwater, Oklahoma, earned a BA at the University of Tennessee at Martin and an MA and a PhD in history at Oklahoma State University (OSU). She was Indian historian/Indian archivist at the Oklahoma Historical Society for eight years. Her work there included collecting nearly eighty oral histories, mostly from Native Americans, and helping design the Indian Gallery in the new Oklahoma Museum of History. Although she retired in 2006, subsequent projects include exhibit research for the American Indian Cultural Center and Museum in Oklahoma City and historic preservation projects for Indian tribal governments, Oklahoma's State Historic Preservation Office, the National Park Service, and private clients. She wrote the National Historic Landmark nomination for Honey Springs Battlefield in Oklahoma and has taught at five universities and for the Osher Lifelong Learning Institute at OSU. Her third book, *When the Wolf Came: The Civil War and the Indian Territory*, won the 2014 United Daughters of the Confederacy's Jefferson Davis Gold Medal, the 2014 Oklahoma Book Award for nonfiction, and the 2014 Pate Award from the Fort Worth Civil War Round Table. In April 2014, she was inducted into the Oklahoma Historical Society's Oklahoma Historians Hall of Fame.

Elliott West is Alumni Distinguished Professor of History at the University of Arkansas in Fayetteville. He has particular interest in the social and environmental history of the American West and in Native American history. He has published eight books, most recently *The Last Indian War: The Nez Perce Story* and *The Essential West: Collected Essays*.

The Contested Plains: Indians, Goldseekers and the Rush to Colorado (1998) received five national awards, including the Francis Parkman Prize for the year's outstanding work on American history. West has twice been recognized as teacher of the year at the University of Arkansas, and in 2009 was one of three finalists for the Robert Foster Cherry Award for the outstanding classroom teacher in the nation. He lives in Fayetteville, Arkansas, with his wife, the Reverend Suzanne Stoner.

Jeannie Whayne, university professor of history at the University of Arkansas in Fayetteville, received her PhD from the University of California, San Diego, in 1989. A specialist in agricultural, Arkansas, and Southern history, she focuses her research on the lower Mississippi River Valley and the interplay of social and economic history with environmental change, agricultural development, and race relations. Her most recent book, *Delta Empire: Lee Wilson and the Transformation of Agriculture in the New South*, explored the changes in the plantation system in the twentieth-century South, concluding with some observations about the emergence of portfolio plantations in the early twenty-first century. She is now working on a book that explores Memphis as "Cotton's Metropolis," focusing on the period between 1830 and 1965. She is currently a member of the executive board of the Southern Historical Association and a distinguished lecturer with the Organization of American Historians.

Introduction and Acknowledgements

On October 10, 2015, the Arkansas Civil War Sesquicentennial Commission sponsored a seminar at the Old State House Museum in Little Rock that brought some of the state's finest historians together to explore the significance of the nation's most brutal conflict to present-day Arkansas, the final event of a commemoration that had seen more than 700 others between 2011 and 2015.

Competing Memories: The Legacy of Arkansas's Civil War collects the proceedings of that seminar. In these essays, Thomas A. DeBlack explores the post-war lives of both Union and Confederate soldiers who played prominent roles in Civil War Arkansas. Cherisse Jones-Branch delves into the lives of black Arkansans during the war and throughout Reconstruction. Jeannie Whayne discusses the many ways in which the Civil War affected the state's economic development, while Kelly Houston Jones investigates the Civil War's impact on Arkansas women and Mary Jane Warde examines the devastating effects of the Civil War on Native Americans in Arkansas and in the Indian Territory. Elliott West scrutinizes Civil War Arkansas from a continental perspective, and Carl Moneyhon considers the evolution of how we remember the Civil War.

There are many people to thank for helping bring this book to fruition. Georganne Sisco, Daniel Cockrell, and Leah Lambert of the Old State House Museum and Jamie Brandon of the Arkansas Archeological Survey provided invaluable assistance in bringing the seminar together. This book benefited greatly from the assistance of Rod Lorenzen and Ali Welky of Butler Center Books and book designer H. K. Stewart; Gail Stephens of the Old State House Museum; Bill Branch of the Delta Cultural Center; Joe Brent of Mudpuppy and Waterdog, Inc.; Michael Keckhaver of the Encyclopedia of Arkansas History & Culture; Brian Robertson of the Butler Center for Arkansas Studies; Anthony Rushing of Benton; Blake Wintory of the Lakeport Plantation; Marie Demeroukas of the Shiloh Museum of Ozark History; Barry Arthur of the *Arkansas Democrat-Gazette*; Alan Chilton and Connie Langum at Wilson's Creek National Battlefield; Jon May of the Oklahoma Historical Society; and Elizabeth Freeman of the Arkansas State Archives. Others contributed to both the seminar and the book in a variety of ways, and their assistance is greatly appreciated.

— Mark K. Christ

Chapter 1—The Arkansas Civil War Sesquicentennial Commission: Commemorating Arkansas's Civil War, 150 Years Later

By Mark K. Christ

On May 6, 1861, delegates at the secession convention meeting at what is now the Old State House Museum in Little Rock voted to leave the United States and cast their lot with the nascent Confederate States of America, leading to a long and brutal war that devastated the South and killed as many as 700,000 American soldiers. It also ultimately led to the freedom of more than 3.9 million enslaved African Americans.

Just over fifty years later, May 16–18, 1911, more than 140,000 people converged on Little Rock to attend the United Confederate Veterans Reunion, including some 12,000 men who had fought the losing battle for the South. Jim Crow laws had overturned many of the rights of African American citizens in large areas of the United States.

Another fifty years later, in 1961, the entire country began the commemoration of the centennial of the Civil War. During this period, as the civil rights movement was gaining momentum, black members of northern Civil War centennial organizations were barred from attending events in many segregated cities in the South. The memories of the battles of 1861–1865 were overshadowed by the brutal suppression of peaceful protests in the South and the presentation of new voting rights legislation.

And fifty years later, as the nation looked at the 150th anniversary of the Civil War, an African American man was serving as president of the United States and Confederate symbols were coming under increasing scrutiny as violent extremists usurped them for their own twisted causes. It was within this context that Arkansas prepared for a thoughtful, respectful commemoration of the war's sesquicentennial. The mission of the Arkansas Civil War Sesquicentennial Commission, then, would be to honor the First Arkansas Cavalry (US) and the Tenth Arkansas Cavalry (CS), and to celebrate Southern Memorial Day and Juneteenth.

As Arkansas undertook its commemorations of the 150th anniversary of the American Civil War between 2011 and 2015, the effort was led by the Arkansas Civil War Sesquicentennial Commission (ACWSC). The remembrance witnessed hundreds of events, a broad expansion of scholarship on the Civil War period, a robust historical

The Arkansas Civil War Sesquicentennial Historical Marker commemorating the Confederate capital was dedicated at Historic Washington State Park. Courtesy of Paul Oller.

The July 4, 1863, Battle of Helena was the theme of a 2013 re-enactment commemorating the 150th anniversary of the engagement. Courtesy of the Arkansas Civil War Sesquicentennial Commission.

marker program, a popular passport program that encouraged people to visit war-related sites around the state, and other activities.

Mandated members for the commission were the directors or designees of the Department of Arkansas Heritage, Department of Parks and Tourism, Arkansas State Library, Arkansas Historical Association, Old State House Museum, Arkansas History Commission (now the Arkansas State Archives), Dr. Martin Luther King Jr. Commission, and Arkansas Civil War Heritage Trails Foundation. Four others were appointed by the governor, as were two each by the speaker of the House and president pro tem of the Senate. Serving in an advisory capacity were representatives of the United Daughters of the Confederacy, Sons of Confederate Veterans, Sons of Union Veterans of the Civil War, and the superintendent of Pea Ridge National Military Park. One of these positions was difficult to fill, as it was discovered that there was not a Sons of Union Veterans camp in Arkansas, though one has since formed and is doing well in western Arkansas.

When asked what he thought the commission had done particularly well, the first thing then-director of Parks and Tourism, Richard Davies, said was, "We didn't refight the war, which was a blessing for all concerned." As Commissioner George Lankford observed, the commission "talked about the purpose of a 'celebration' of a devastating war and concluded that the major use of the Sesquicentennial would be to make it an occasion for public understanding of what really happened in the Civil War—especially things that we have not realized before, such as guerrilla warfare and the African American experience of slavery and the war." And while the commission acknowledged and honored the service and suffering of the 60,000 or so Arkansas men who fought for the Confederacy, equal attention went to the more than 13,000 Arkansans—black and white—who served in the Union army. (Of the Confederate states, only Tennessee had more native sons fight for the Union.) The commission managed to avoid internal sectarian strife despite the fact that its membership provides ample opportunities to lean pro-Blue or pro-Gray. Instead, everyone joined together to go pro-History. And while the sesquicentennial period saw rancorous arguments within the state about such things as the Confederate flag and the Martin Luther King Jr./Robert E. Lee holiday, the ACWSC remained focused on its mission to commemorate the people and events of 150 years ago, not be bogged down by current events.

The commission also commemorated the war differently than was done fifty years earlier during the centennial. Ray Granade's excellent 2014 article "Arkansas Commemorates the Civil War Centennial: An Exercise in Pragmatism" in the *Arkansas Historical Quarterly* showed that the Arkansas Civil War Centennial Commission shared *some* of the goals of the sesquicentennial commission: encouraging the study of Civil War Arkansas; spearheading the preservation of sites, documents, and artifacts; supporting local efforts to commemorate the war; and promoting heritage tourism. But much of the earlier commission's work was done with a neo-secessionist bent: Granade noted that the centen-

The Arkansas Civil War Sesquicentennial Commission awarded a grant to the Ouachita County Civil War Sesquicentennial Committee to outfit a First Kansas Colored Infantry Regiment re-enactment unit. Courtesy of Archie Lee Moore Jr.

nial commission "proposed to donate 'reliable books' on the Civil War to school and public libraries, reliability being measured by the era's consensus Civil War historiography with its pro-Confederate bias." And, incredibly, it voted to form "a Negro activities committee to show the part that Negroes played in the Confederate effort," though, Granade notes, "neither the commission's own files nor media reports indicate any success in recruiting African Americans."

***

The Arkansas Civil War Sesquicentennial Commission (ACWSC) was created in 2007 by Act 635 of the 86th General Assembly with a mandate to:

1. promote a suitable statewide observance of the sesquicentennial of the Civil War;

2. cooperate and assist national, state, and local organizations with programs and activities suitable for the sesquicentennial observance;

3. assist in ensuring that any observance of the sesquicentennial of the Civil War is inclusive and appropriately recognizes the experiences and points of view of all people affected by the Civil War; and

4. provide assistance for the development of programs, projects, and activities on the Civil War that have lasting educational value.

The ACWSC adopted the following mission statement shortly after its creation:

> *The Arkansas Civil War Sesquicentennial Commission will seek to support a statewide observance of the 150th anniversary of the American Civil War that is educational, comprehensive and inclusive; that tells the story of the Civil War in Arkansas without making judgments about the actions and motivations of the people who took part in the war; and that stresses the relevance to Arkansawyers today by promoting local observances and acknowledging the impact the Civil War had on modern Arkansas.*
>
> *The commission shall achieve this goal by:*
>
> *1) Sanctioning events around the state (re-enactments, symposia, etc.) that are appropriate observances of the sesquicentennial;*
>
> *2) Promoting historic sites around the state that are connected to the Civil War through educational efforts (brochures, websites, etc.);*
>
> *3) Promoting publications and archival collections connected to the Civil War in Arkansas and advocating donations of materials to appropriate repositories;*
>
> *4) Promoting local observances that tell the local story;*
>
> *5) Supporting efforts to teach and research Arkansas Civil War history in the state's schools and universities;*
>
> *6) Supporting efforts to preserve and interpret the state's Civil War sites and documentary heritage and artifacts; and*
>
> *7) Ensuring that the sesquicentennial commemoration includes ALL Arkansans.*

In evaluating the commission's effectiveness, we will look at each of the goals individually.

> *1) Sanctioning events around the state that are appropriate observances of the sesquicentennial.*

Early on, the commission developed a simple form that people could send to the commission that would enable the applicants to use the ACWSC logo as part of their event, as well as allow the commission to have some say in the historical standards of those events. The ACWSC sanctioned a total of 732 events attended by a total of at least 375,275 people, which shows that the 150th has been a heritage tourism boon, as trade shorthand translates 20,000 people as roughly equivalent to one million dollars. These events included 28 re-enactments, seven plays, 172 lectures, 59 living history events, 32 seminars, two teacher workshops, 97 marker dedications, and 115 exhibits. Other events that did not seek ACWSC sanction were also held between 2011 and 2015 to commemorate the Civil War.

The ACWSC also created a traveling exhibit in a partnership made up of the commission, which curated it; the Old State House Museum, which designed and built it; and the Arkansas Humanities

The Arkansas Civil War Sesquicentennial Commission's traveling exhibit was shown at dozens of locations all over Arkansas during the commemoration. Courtesy of Oxley Art.

Council, which distributed it. After its completion in June 2011, it was seen by thousands of people at dozens of venues across the state—a good way for the commission to bring Civil War Arkansas to the people.

> *2) Promoting historic sites around the state that are connected to the Civil War through educational efforts.*

Probably the most significant effort that the commission made in this regard was its Arkansas Civil War Sesquicentennial Passport program, which encouraged tourists to visit twenty-three sites around the state to have their passports stamped. Once their passports were complete, they could turn them in and receive a commemorative coin or patch. After the program kicked off in March 2011, the ACWSC distributed more than 40,000 passports. A total of 218 "Arkansas Civil

Arkansas Civil War Sesquicentennial Commission Chairman Tommy Dupree receives the first ACWSC passport stamp from MacArthur Museum of Arkansas Military History Director Stephan McAteer. The museum was one of twenty-three stamping sites for the popular program. Courtesy of the Arkansas Civil War Sesquicentennial Commission.

War Road Warriors"—including residents of Maryland, Georgia, Tennessee, Mississippi, Texas, West Virginia, Louisiana, Utah, Kansas, South Carolina, and California—completed the passport program. This program helped to promote some of Arkansas's lesser-known heritage tourism sites and to bring a greater appreciation of Arkansas history and culture to visitors. Everyone who completed the program stated how much they learned and how much they enjoyed visiting places they had never seen before, and may have never seen without the program.

The ACWSC also developed a series of sixteen audio tours of Civil War sites, by which tourists could call in on their cell phones and receive recorded messages telling the story of the site they were visiting, as well as sidebars of related historical events. Audio tour signs were displayed in Washington County (Battles of Cane Hill and Fayetteville), Nevada County (Battles of Elkin's Ferry and Prairie D'Ane), Ouachita County (Battle of Poison Spring and Fort Southerland), Cleveland County (Battle of Marks' Mills), Grant County (Battle of Jenkins' Ferry), Chicot County (Battle of Ditch Bayou), Pulaski County (Battles of Bayou Meto or Reed's Bridge and Bayou Fourche), Woodruff County (Battle of Fitzhugh's Woods), Jefferson County (Battle of Pine Bluff), Arkansas County (Battle of St. Charles), White County (Battle of Whitney's Lane), and Sebastian County (Battle of Massard Prairie).

> *3) Promoting publications and archival collections connected to the Civil War in Arkansas and advocating donations of materials to appropriate repositories.*

Scholarship on the Civil War in Arkansas was considerable during the sesquicentennial period. A bibliography compiled by Bob Razer of the Butler Center for Arkansas Studies showed that eighteen books, 148 journal and newsletter articles, and 317 Encyclopedia of Arkansas History & Culture entries on Civil War–related topics were published between 2011 and 2015.

Several archives around Arkansas sponsored exhibits or events during the commemoration, although only two reported receiving any significant donations of Civil War–related materials. Several, however, noted increased interest in Civil War materials in their collections.

4) Promoting local observances that tell the local story.

The ACWSC met this mandate through its sanctioning and grant programs, which encouraged observances of local Civil War history while helping to pay for them, and also through its historical marker program. The ACWSC awarded eighty-five grants totaling $149,913—more than a third of the funds that were received from Arkansas state government.

By far, the commission's greatest success in telling the local story was through its historical marker program. Funded by grants from the National Park Service and the Arkansas Natural and Cultural Resources Council, as well as money provided by the commission and the Arkansas Historic Preservation Program, 144 markers were approved, with at least one in each of the state's seventy-five counties. These markers were the essence of local history, from the movement of Confederate records to Rondo during the Camden Expedition to the U.S. Colored Troops serving in Helena to the skirmish in Lunenburg (a small but savage firefight in which almost all of the troops on both sides were Izard County neighbors).

5) Supporting efforts to teach and research Arkansas Civil War history in the state's schools and universities.

It is difficult to evaluate whether the sesquicentennial led to increased teaching of the Civil War in Arkansas classrooms, but a number of lesson plans and activities were developed and made available for classroom use. The ACWSC developed six educational projects for younger students and made them available through its website, along with a list of Civil War–related books that were appropriate for grades K-12. The Arkansas Historic Preservation Program and the Butler Center for Arkansas Studies at the Central Arkansas Library System in Little Rock developed Civil War lesson plans and videos.

Dr. Patrick G. Williams of the University of Arkansas reported that ten theses or dissertations on Arkansas Civil War topics were completed between 2011 and 2015, reflecting a level of interest that may or may not have been related to the sesquicentennial commemoration.

In addition, a series of 122 podcasts featuring fifty-four Civil War experts was recorded in a partnership between the ACWSC and the College of Mass Communication at the University of Arkansas at Little Rock, where David Weekley of the college staff arranged for student engineers to record the short, concise pieces about a variety of Civil War Arkansas topics. Arkansas teachers reported using the podcasts as "guest lecturers" in their classrooms.

A partnership between the ACWSC and public radio station KUAR generated 195 "Civil War Sesquicentennial Minutes" recorded between February 2011 and June 2015, providing a "real-time" narrative of the Civil War in Arkansas. These snippets were broadcast more than 4,000 times for KUAR's 62,000-plus listeners during the sesquicentennial commemoration and were also made available for broadcast on public radio stations KUAF, KASU, and KXTX.

The ACWSC used social media extensively to educate the public about the Civil War in Arkansas. More than 5,000 posts on the ACWSC Facebook page provided accounts from the *Official Records of the War of the Rebellion*, Civil War–era newspapers, and the diaries and letters of both soldiers and civilians who witnessed the Civil War in Arkansas first-hand. The ACWSC also had an active blog.

> 6) *Supporting efforts to preserve and interpret the state's Civil War sites and documentary heritage and artifacts.*

ACWSC Commissioner Richard Davies observed, "I think we added some significant support, just by our very existence if nothing else, to preservation efforts at places like Reed's Bridge, Elkin's Ferry, Jenkins' Ferry, and others." Arkansas was the scene of more than 770 engagements in which Americans fought and died, and many of these sites remain undeveloped and pristine—they would be readily recognizable to the men who saw them 150 years ago.

The signature preservation success during the sesquicentennial commemoration was an effort to acquire 448 acres of land on the Little Missouri River in Nevada County, where the April 3–4, 1864, Engagement at Elkin's Ferry was fought. The Nevada County Depot and Museum led a successful effort to raise more than $990,000 in partnership with the ACWSC, Arkansas Historic Preservation Program, Department of Arkansas Heritage, Arkansas Natural and Cultural Resources Council, Civil War Trust, Conservation Fund, American Battlefield Protection Program, National Park Service, Prescott-Nevada County Economic Charitable Foundation, Hendrix Foundation, Ross Foundation, Arkansas General Assembly, and Bank of Prescott, among others. The Civil War Trust said that this effort was one of the finest examples of local, state, and national cooperation that it had seen. The purchase was completed in December 2015.

In addition, several parcels of the August 27, 1863, Action at Bayou Meto site in Jacksonville were acquired between 2011 and 2015 through the Reed's Bridge Battlefield Preservation Society. In addition, the Civil War Trust moved toward the purchase of forty additional acres at Prairie Grove in Washington County, and a battlefield preservation plan was completed for the Friends of Jenkins' Ferry Battlefield. Although the Arkansas Civil War Sesquicentennial Commission's duties ended on December 31, 2015, efforts to preserve Arkansas's battlefields will continue.

There was success in the interpretation of Arkansas Civil War sites during the sesquicentennial, as well. The ACWSC worked closely with constituents in DeValls Bluff in Prairie County, Cane Hill in Washington County, and Reed's Bridge in Jacksonville to create groups of wayside exhibits that tell the unique stories of each of those places, and both state and national parks chose to update and revamp their interpretive materials during the sesquicentennial commemoration. The Arkansas Humanities Council was particularly helpful in contributing funds for many of these interpretive projects.

7) Ensuring that the sesquicentennial commemoration includes ALL Arkansans.

The ACWSC had a mixed record in this effort. Commissioner George Lankford noted, "We were not successful in making the sesquicentennial a widely recognized learning opportunity for African Americans. There was some participation, but it was not across the board. The Bicentennial Commission should strive to make reflection on the Civil War a useful learning experience for all Americans."

There were some shining exceptions, however. The African American community in Pine Bluff was actively involved in the efforts there to tell the whole story of the Civil War. In Helena-West Helena, Freedom Park tells the story of African Americans from slaves to contrabands to soldiers to citizens, and the ACWSC paid for several of the interpretive panels in the park. In Camden, the ACWSC worked with the Zion Hill Human Services Agency to erect a marker to the First Kansas Colored Infantry, which later led to a reconciliation ceremony attended by black, white, and Native American participants, reflecting the

The Let Freedom Ring celebration was held on April 14, 2015, to commemorate the 150th anniversary of Arkansas's passage of the 13th Amendment to the U.S. Constitution, bringing the country one step closer to abolishing slavery. Courtesy of the Arkansas Civil War Sesquicentennial Commission.

combatants at the 1864 Engagement at Poison Spring. And a grant to the Ouachita County Civil War Sesquicentennial Committee bought uniforms for a First Kansas re-enactors group, which was the first black Union re-enactment unit in the state.

The Mosaic Templars Cultural Center in Little Rock sponsored its largest ever exhibit during the closing year of the sesquicentennial, recording 20,683 visitors who saw *"Freedom! Oh, Freedom!" Arkansas's People of African Descent and the Civil War: 1861–1866* and learned about the struggle for freedom in Arkansas.

The commission's "Let Freedom Ring" event on Tuesday, April 14, 2015, saw people across the state ring bells thirteen times at 1:00 p.m. (1300 hours) to celebrate the 150th anniversary of Arkansas's passage of the 13th Amendment, which brought the country one step closer to the abolition of slavery.

A complete final report of the Arkansas Civil War Sesquicentennial Commission's activities is available at www.arkansascivilwar150.com.

Chapter 2—"What Is to Become of Us?": The Postwar Lives of Civil War Generals in Arkansas

By Thomas A. DeBlack

First, I want to apologize for doing what historians are loath to do anymore and that is to talk exclusively about dead white men. But that is who the Civil War commanders were. There was no racial or gender diversity in their ranks. Even those all-black regiments that fought for the Union were led by white men. It is, as the saying goes, what it is. I also will be bypassing some of Arkansas's most famous and accomplished generals, like Patrick Cleburne, who fought exclusively in the Western Theater east of the Mississippi River before being killed in the futile and disastrous charge at Franklin, Tennessee, on November 30, 1864. Rather, I will be looking at those generals who actually spent the majority of their wartime service in Arkansas.

I should say also that by concentrating on these men, I do not mean to imply that their post-war experiences were more important than the post-war experiences of those tens of thousands who never commanded an army, although the commanders' prominence in the war does make it a bit easier to track their careers after the war ended. And I am also aware that, like thousands of other Americans, some of these commanders never lived to see the war's end. Their lives were cut short before they had the chance to experience the comforts of peace. To some, that would have been only a fitting way for a military man to pass from the world—to be killed, as George Patton allegedly remarked, by the last bullet of the last battle of the last war.[1]

Not everyone would have agreed with Patton's assessment. No one seemed to have a better nose for sniffing out the hypocrisy and nonsense that all too often accompany accounts of war than William Tecumseh Sherman. "I think I understand what military fame is," he said. "To be killed on the field of battle and have your name misspelled in the newspapers."[2]

Still, if death in battle held little allure for those like Sherman, there were also dangers for those who survived the war. Whether their wartime service had been characterized by brilliant success or dismal failure, all of these generals had at one time been in command of large numbers of men and had been held in some esteem, if not for their abilities then at least for their rank. Many, if not most, would never enjoy that level of esteem again. And it must have been painful to reflect on those days when they had been young, powerful, and in the prime of life—and then to be constantly reminded that that prime was long past.

My title comes from the diary entry of a nineteen-year-old woman named Susan Cook, who lived on her family's plantation in Phillips County, near present-day Barton. Cook had begun to keep a diary on New Year's Day, 1864. Many of her entries for the spring of that year were filled with false rumors of Confederate success or European intervention, but by 1865 the harsh realities of impending defeat had begun to set in. Her entry for January 14, 1865, read, "This is the darkest hour our infant nation ever saw. Our armies have all been defeated and scattered, our resources nearly exhausted, our men dispirited and demoralized. My God! What is to become of us?"[3]

It was a question that tens of thousands of people, in Arkansas and elsewhere, might well have been asking, not the least of whom were those who commanded the opposing armies. No one—North or South, black or white, male or female—knew what the forthcoming years of peace would bring. I want to examine what became of the men who led the armies in Arkansas during the Civil War and then try to draw some conclusions about those experiences.

On the Union side, one of the most important commanders in Arkansas was Samuel Ryan Curtis. Curtis was born in upstate New York but grew up in Ohio. He graduated twenty-seventh (out of thirty-three) in the West Point class of 1831. After about a year in the army, he left the service and became a successful engineer. He served in the Mexican War and, upon returning to civilian life, was elected mayor of Keokuk, Iowa, and then served three terms in Congress. When the Civil War broke out, Curtis mustered the First Iowa Regiment and later was unanimously elected colonel of the Second Iowa Infantry. In early 1862, he chased Confederate forces out of Missouri and followed them into Arkansas. In March of that year, he defeated a Rebel army that outnumbered him in both men and cannon at the Battle of Pea Ridge. He was promoted to major general but failed in his attempt to capture Little Rock, instead turning east and seizing Helena in July 1862.[4]

Samuel Curtis, Courtesy of the Library of Congress.

Later in the war, his severe policies against guerrillas in Missouri and his poor relationship with his superior, John Schofield, resulted in his being relieved of command and sent to Kansas. The war found him again in 1864 when he fought against Sterling Price's army in the last great Confederate raid into Missouri. He defeated Price at the Battle of Westport and, as he had done two years previously, helped chase Price out of Missouri.[5]

After the war, Curtis was reassigned to a different kind of war, commanding the army's Department of the Northwest in the final phases of the war against Native Americans in southern Minnesota and the Dakota Territory. He negotiated a treaty with the Sioux and became a commissioner for the transcontinental railroad, which he had championed since his time in Congress before the war. Regarded by many historians of the war in the Trans-Mississippi as one of the best and most underrated generals in the Union army, Curtis did not long survive the end of hostilities. He died suddenly on December 26, 1866, at Council Bluff, Iowa, at age sixty-one and was buried in Keokuk.[6]

James Blunt, Courtesy of Wilson's Creek National Battlefield.

Another important Union commander in northwest Arkansas was James Gilpatrick Blunt. Born in Trenton, Maine, in 1826, Blunt had an unusual background for a general, having been a captain in the Merchant Marines. He later moved to Columbus, Ohio; got a medical degree from Starling Medical School; and set up practice in New Madison, Ohio. He eventually moved to Greeley, Kansas, where he became an ardent abolitionist and aided John Brown. When the war broke out, he became a cavalry commander and rose to the rank of brigadier general by April 1862. Promoted to head the Department of Kansas, Blunt defeated John Marmaduke's Confederates at the Battle of Cane Hill in November 1862 and was promoted to major general.[7]

Aggressive to the point of recklessness (a contemporary once noted that his idea of strategy was to get himself surrounded and fight his way out), Blunt decided to remain in northwest Arkansas after the battle, leaving himself dangerously isolated more than a hundred miles from his base of supply at Springfield, Missouri. Confederate general Thomas Hindman succeeded in slipping by him, but thanks to the heroic efforts of Francis Herron, Hindman was forced to stop and take a defensive position at Prairie Grove. At the battle there on December 7, 1862, Blunt rushed to the sound of the guns and arrived just in time to prevent a Confederate victory. He then hounded the Rebels as they retreated south toward the Arkansas River. In late December, his army raided Van Buren.[8]

He later defeated a combined force of Confederate Indians at Honey Springs in the Indian Territory, but a detachment under his command was nearly wiped out by Confederate guerrillas under William Quantrill near Baxter Spring, Kansas, in October 1863, and he was relieved of command. Samuel Curtis restored him to command in Kansas, and he participated in the Battle of Westport and subsequent pursuit of the retreating Rebels. Blunt was mustered out of service in July 1865.[9]

After the war ended, he resumed medical practice in Kansas and was also admitted to the bar. In 1869, he moved to Washington DC, where he became solicitor of claims. In 1873, he was charged with conspiracy to defraud the Cherokee. Though the case was eventually dropped, Blunt's reputation was severely damaged. By 1879, his behavior had become increasingly erratic, possibly as a result of his chronic syphilis. He was committed to a hospital for the mentally insane and died there in July 1881. He is buried at Fort Leavenworth, Kansas.[10]

Blunt's career was linked with that of Francis Jay Herron. A Pennsylvania native, Herron moved to Iowa in 1855, where he operated a bank with his brothers and formed an independent militia company called the Governor's Grays. Herron and his men offered their services to the Union in January 1861, four months before the hostilities commenced, but the offer was refused. When the fighting broke out in April 1861, the Grays became part of the First Iowa Infantry. Herron fought at Wilson's Creek and Pea Ridge, where he was wounded and captured.

His valor on that field earned him the Medal of Honor. Exchanged, he was promoted to brigadier general in 1862.[11]

In December of that year Herron marched a force of 6,000 men and thirty guns from Missouri to northwest Arkansas, covering 150 miles in four days, and engaged Thomas Hindman's Confederates at Prairie Grove, a remarkable feat that may have saved James Blunt from annihilation. He was again promoted, becoming, at that time, the youngest major general in the Union army. Transferred east of the Mississippi, he fought at Vicksburg and Port Hudson, and held a leadership position in the Red River campaign before bad health forced him to leave his command to recuperate. Upon his return, he served in Texas and Louisiana, and also took part in the capture of Mobile, Alabama. While in Texas, Herron worked under secret instructions to assist the Mexican nationalist Benito Juárez in his war against the French puppet emperor Maximilian. In May 1865, he negotiated the surrender of Confederate forces in the Trans-Mississippi.[12]

Frances Herron, Courtesy of the Library of Congress.

Herron resigned from the army in June 1865 and remained in Louisiana, where he did legal work and became active in Republican politics. He was appointed tax collector of New Orleans and later a U.S. marshal. In 1871, Republican Reconstruction governor Henry Warmoth appointed Herron secretary of state for Louisiana, but the two men had a falling out in 1873, and Warmoth removed Herron, charging him with corruption stemming from his time as the state's tax collector.

Herron returned to New York, where he participated in veterans' organizations and various business enterprises, but he died unemployed and impoverished in 1902. Historian Ezra Warner notes that his death certificate recorded that he died in a tenement on West 99th Street and listed his occupation as "None."[13]

Of particular significance to residents of Little Rock was James Totten. Totten was born in Pittsburgh, Pennsylvania, in 1818, but his father, Dr. William Totten, moved his family to Little Rock in 1840, where he helped select the site for the new federal arsenal. William Totten later practiced at the facility and also had a private practice in the city. James Totten graduated from the United States Military Academy in 1841 and fought against the Seminole in Florida in 1849–1850. After attaining the rank of captain in 1855, he went to "Bleeding Kansas" to try to suppress the disturbances there.[14]

James Totten, Courtesy of Wilson's Creek National Battlefield.

In November 1860, Totten and sixty-five troops of the 2nd U.S. Artillery Regiment were transferred to the previously unoccupied federal arsenal at Little Rock. Totten was a handsome man who quickly became popular in the capital city's social circles, but in February 1861, that popularity was challenged when angry secessionists from the eastern part of the state flocked to Little Rock demanding the surrender of the arsenal. Following a request from Governor Henry Rector and without instructions or reinforcements from Washington, Totten peacefully surrendered the arsenal on February 8, and he and his men boarded a steamboat for St. Louis.[15]

Totten served as chief of artillery under generals Nathaniel Lyon and John C. Fremont in Missouri, where he became widely known for the style in which he issued orders to his batteries. Punctuated with profanity, a typical order might sound like, "Forward that caisson, God d—n you, sir!" It was claimed that some soldiers would walk half a mile just to listen to Totten for five minutes.[16] Totten later served as a division commander in the Army of the Frontier (1862) and eventually commanded the artillery in the Military Division of West Mississippi. He was brevetted to the rank of brigadier general in the U.S. Army "for gallant and meritorious service in the field" and promoted to the same rank in the Missouri Militia.[17]

After the war Totten served as Inspector-General of the Military Division of the Atlantic from August 15, 1865, to August 27, 1866; of the Department of the East from August 27, 1866, to July 10, 1869; and of the Military Division of the South until April 1870. But he was dismissed from the army on July 22, 1870, for "Disobedience of Orders," "Neglect of Duty," and "Conduct to the Prejudice of Good Order and Military Discipline." In addition to his reputation for colorful language, Totten was also known to have a weakness for alcohol, and this may have contributed to his dismissal. He died in Sedalia, Missouri, on October 2, 1871, and is buried in Crown Hill Cemetery.[18]

Benjamin Mayberry Prentiss, a direct descendant of one of the settlers who came to America on the *Mayflower*, was born in Belleville, Virginia (now West Virginia), in 1819 and moved to Missouri at age seventeen. At age twenty-two, he moved to Quincy, Illinois. During the Mexican War, Prentiss raised a company of Illinois volunteers and served as its captain under General Zachary Taylor at the Battle of Buena Vista. After the war, he returned to Illinois, took up the practice of law, and became involved in the new Republican Party. He also remained active in the state militia.[19]

Prentiss is best remembered for his fierce defense of the "Hornet's Nest" at the Battle of Shiloh in April 1862 (though some recent scholarship has disputed the significance of his role) and for his defense of

Benjamin Prentiss, Courtesy of the Library of Congress.

Helena when that town was attacked by Confederate forces in July 1863. Shortly after the battle, Prentiss resigned his commission, citing personal reasons. His wife had died in 1860, leaving him with young children, and he was in ill health. He returned to Quincy to practice law.[20]

After the war, Prentiss was appointed to a number of federal positions, including pension agent under Ulysses S. Grant, land office agent under James Garfield, and Missouri postmaster under Benjamin Harrison. Despite his ill health, Prentiss survived for another thirty-six years after the war's end. He died at Bethany, Missouri, in February 1901 at the age of seventy-two.[21]

The most controversial Union officer in Arkansas was Frederick Steele. Born in New York in 1819, Steele graduated thirtieth in the West Point class of 1843, nine places behind Ulysses S. Grant. He fought at Wilson's Creek in September 1861, joined the Eighth Iowa Volunteer Infantry as a colonel, and served under Samuel Curtis in the capture of Helena. Historian Greg Urwin has noted that Steele "occasionally displayed flashes of brilliance [but] his political conservatism, fondness for fine living, and strategic limitations kept him from delivering any decisive blows against the Confederacy." In addition, during his brief stint as commander of the Army of the Southwest beginning in 1862, he reversed Samuel Curtis's policy of humane treatment of runaway slaves and "turned a blind eye to the excesses of dishonest Northern cotton traders at Helena."[22]

Steele fought at Chickasaw Bluff, Arkansas Post, and Vicksburg, and he led the Federal army that captured Little Rock in September

1863. During the Federal occupation, Little Rock experienced an economic revival, and Steele got along very well with Confederate civilians in Little Rock (the execution of convicted spy David O. Dodd notwithstanding). In fact, he got along entirely *too* well to suit many of his own soldiers, who considered him a Copperhead. Called against his will to lead the northern wing of the ill-fated Red River Expedition (known as the Camden Expedition in Arkansas), he suffered a stinging defeat and was barely able to get his depleted force back to the safety of Little Rock. When the Rebels launched another major raid into Missouri, Steele was blamed. He was relieved of command in late November 1864 and was transferred to the Department of the Gulf, where he fought in the Mobile campaign. Ironically, given his uncharitable feelings about slavery and African Americans, his best unit in that campaign was a division of black troops.[23]

Frederick Steele, Courtesy of the Butler Center for Arkansas Studies, Central Arkansas Library System, Little Rock.

After the war, Steele resumed his career in the regular army as colonel of the Twentieth U.S. Infantry. He was stationed on the West Coast and given command of the Department of the Columbia. While on leave in San Mateo, California, Steele was driving a carriage when he suffered an apoplectic fit (now called cerebral hemorrhage) and took a bad fall. He died from his injuries on January 12, 1868, and is buried in Colma, California.[24]

The Federal general who enjoyed the most illustrious career in Arkansas was Powell Clayton. Born in Pennsylvania in 1833, Clayton attended a private military academy and later studied civil engineering. In 1855, he moved to Leavenworth, Kansas, to work as a surveyor. Four years later, he was elected city engineer and surveyor for Leavenworth. Clayton was a pro-Union Democrat who voted for Stephen A. Douglas for president in 1860. At the outbreak of the Civil War, he joined the Union army and was made captain of Company E, First Kansas Infantry. He fought at Wilson's Creek and was promoted to lieutenant colonel of the Fifth Kansas Cavalry. Clayton distinguished himself at the Battle of Helena and later in repulsing the Confederate attack on Pine Bluff in October 1863. He was promoted to brigadier general a few months before the end of the war. While still in command at Pine Bluff, he purchased a cotton plantation near the town, and he married Adaline McGraw, the daughter of a steamboat captain who had served in the Confederate army, in December 1865.[25]

Powell Clayton, Courtesy of Wilson's Creek National Battlefield.

After the war, Clayton quickly became disgusted with the atrocities committed against freedmen and government officials. He switched his political allegiance to the Republican Party and helped establish the party in Arkansas. In 1868, he was elected governor and led the state through one of the most contentious periods in its history. Faced with mounting violence against Republican officials and African Americans, he actively took on the Ku Klux Klan and other terrorist groups, going so far as to declare martial law in several Arkansas counties and sending the state militia to various parts of the state to restore law and order. His tactics were largely successful, and some historians consider him the most effective of all Southern governors in suppressing Klan activity.[26]

Clayton's tenure as governor was marked by a growing division within the state's Republican Party that eventually resulted in the Brooks-Baxter War. In 1871, the state legislature elected him to the U.S. Senate, where he served until 1877, when a Democratically controlled state legislature chose a Democrat to replace him. Clayton returned to Little Rock to practice law, but in 1882 he moved to Eureka Springs, where he speculated in land and encouraged the building of a railroad to the city and the construction of the Crescent Hotel. Though he never again held elective office, he remained active in Republican politics and was the leader of the state Republican Party until his death. In 1899, President William McKinley appointed him the first American ambassador to Mexico. He resigned in 1905 and moved to Washington DC, though he remained involved in business and political affairs in Arkansas. He was a Republican national committee member from Arkansas for forty years. Clayton died in Washington DC on August 25, 1914.[27]

If the postwar careers of Union generals in Arkansas provide an interesting case study, the postwar lives of the state's Confederate generals are, if anything, more interesting. Four, however, did not survive the war. Former Texas Ranger Ben McCulloch and fellow brigadier general James McIntosh were killed at the Battle of Pea Ridge in March 1862. After failing at the Battle of Pea Ridge, their commander, Earl Van Dorn, took the bulk of Confederate forces in Arkansas east of the Mississippi River, earning him the everlasting enmity of many Arkansas Confederates. Van Dorn was a reckless, aggressive soldier, and in May 1863 his recklessness proved his undoing, though not on the field of battle. A ladies' man with a well-deserved reputation as a womanizer, Van Dorn was shot to death at his headquarters in Spring Hill, Tennessee, by a jealous husband who claimed that Van Dorn had carried on an affair with his wife.[28]

Brigadier General Lucius Marshall (Marsh) Walker was a plantation owner in St. Francis County before the war. Walker had fought in

Lucius M. Walker, Courtesy of Mudpuppy and Waterdog, Inc.

the Battle of Corinth, Mississippi, and later was part of the disastrous Confederate defeat at the Battle of Helena, Arkansas. In that battle, he incurred the enmity of his fellow brigadier general, John Sappington Marmaduke. Ill feelings between the two men escalated during the Rebels' retreat to Little Rock. On September 6, 1863, Walker and Marmaduke fought a duel at a plantation seven miles from Little Rock in which Walker was mortally wounded.[29]

Perhaps one of the least well-known and yet one of the most ubiquitous Confederate generals in Arkansas was James Fagan. Fagan was born in Clark County, Kentucky, in 1828. His family moved to Arkansas in 1838, and his father worked as a plasterer on the new state capitol until his death in 1840. Young Fagan fought in Mexico, returning after the war to run his stepfather's farm in Saline County. He was active in state politics, serving as a Whig legislator first in the House of Representatives (1852–1853) and later in the state Senate (1860–1862).[30]

With the outbreak of the war, Fagan raised a company of volunteers that eventually became part of the First Arkansas Infantry Regiment. The unit was present at the First Battle of Bull Run and fought at Shiloh. Fagan was promoted to brigadier general in September 1862 and transferred to the Trans-Mississippi for the remainder of the war. He fought at Prairie Grove, Helena, Camden, and Marks' Mills. Promoted to major general in April 1864, he took part in Sterling Price's disastrous raid into Missouri in the fall of 1864. On his return, he assumed command of the District of Arkansas and remained in that position until the surrender of Confederate forces in the Trans-Mississippi in May 1865.[31]

James Fagan, Courtesy of Wilson's Creek National Battlefield.

After the war, Fagan joined the Republican Party, and he commanded Joseph Brooks's militia in the Brooks-Baxter War in 1874. While he was on the losing side of that conflict, his Republican affiliation got him a federal appointment as a U.S. marshal in western Arkansas from President Grant, a position he held from 1875 to 1877. He later served as the land office receiver at Little Rock until 1890 when he was defeated in his campaign for state railroad commissioner. When Reconstruction ended, Fagan's association with the Republican Party cost him any chance at further elective office. He died in Little Rock in 1893 and is buried in Mount Holly Cemetery.[32]

If Fagan is often little remembered by modern students of the war, the same is not true of Sterling Price. Born in Prince Edward County, Virginia, in 1809, Price moved with his family to Missouri in 1831. He was elected to Congress from that state in 1844, commanded a regiment of Missouri troops in the Mexican War, and served as governor of Missouri from 1853 to 1857. A conditional Unionist before the war, Price cast his lot with the Confederacy after watching a detachment of Federal soldiers fire into a pro-Southern crowd. Selected as commander of the Missouri State Guard, Price not only fought in significant battles east of the Mississippi River (Iuka, Corinth), he seemed to be present at almost every major engagement in the Trans-Mississippi, including Wilson's Creek, Pea Ridge, Helena, Little Rock, Jenkins' Ferry, and

Westport. In the war's early years, Price, who was a generation older than many of the soldiers he commanded, was one of the most beloved generals—the soldiers referred to him affectionately as "Old Pap." But in late 1864, he led a disastrous raid into Missouri that failed so miserably that Price faced the possibility of a court-martial. The war ended before that action could proceed, but Price's reputation and his popularity were damaged.[33]

At the war's end, Price refused to surrender and led what was left of his army into Mexico, where he offered his services to the French puppet ruler Maximilian, who was at war with nationalists led by the deposed president Benito Juárez. Maximilian refused Price's offer of service but offered him money and land for a colony. Price helped select the site at Carlota, in the Cordova Valley about seventy miles west of Veracruz, and became the leader of the settlement. He was confident that the French would not abandon Mexico, remarking, "The Napoleon family is not in the habit of backing down in the accomplishments of its schemes." It was one in a series of bad judgments. Price's family joined him in Mexico in the spring of 1866, but shortly thereafter forces loyal to Juárez attacked Carlota and carried off thirty settlers. By summer, many colonists had left Carlota. When the French subsequently evacuated their forces from Mexico, Maximilian's government quickly collapsed, and he was captured and executed in 1867.[34]

Sterling Price, Courtesy of Wilson's Creek National Battlefield.

In the meantime, Price's health had begun to deteriorate. He started having severe intestinal problems, which grew worse in August

1866 when he contracted typhoid fever. Broke and in poor health, he returned to Missouri in January 1867, and he died of cholera (or cholera-like symptoms) on September 29, 1867. The death certificate listed the cause of death as "chronic diarrhea." Price's funeral was held on October 3, 1867, in St. Louis, at the First Methodist Episcopal Church, and the funeral procession, with his body carried by a black hearse drawn by six matching black horses, was the largest such procession that had ever taken place in St. Louis up to that point. He was buried in Bellefontaine Cemetery.[35]

As his biographer Albert Castel notes, even Price's admirers never claimed for him "a brilliant mind or genius" or "any great strategic ability" but rather noted his courage and his kindness and his benevolence toward his men. One officer who had been critical of Price's mistakes noted:

> A braver or kinder heart beat in no man's bosom; he was wise in counsel and bold in action, and never spared his own blood on any battlefield. No man had greater influence over his troops....It was impossible to find a more magnificent species of manhood in its prime than Sterling Price presented to the brave Missourians, who loved him with a fervor not less than we Virginians felt for Lee.[36]

But, Castel says, "Although Price had the ability to win the devotion of his troops, he had absolutely no talent for maintaining friendly relations with superiors and associates. Without exception he quarreled with, harbored resentments against, or was disliked, by every commanding general he served under or with."[37]

Another Confederate general whose wartime career was often linked with Price's was Joseph O. (Jo) Shelby. Born to an aristocratic family in Lexington, Kentucky, in 1830, Shelby attended Transylvania College. He moved to Missouri in 1852, and his work there as a hemp planter, rope manufacturer, and steamboat owner made him one of the richest men in the state in the antebellum years. He returned to Kentucky in 1854 to recruit a proslavery cavalry unit to fight in "Bleeding Kansas." That conflict cost Shelby most of his fortune.[38]

Joseph O. Shelby, Courtesy of Wilson's Creek National Battlefield.

At the war's outset Shelby formed a cavalry brigade that soon became known as the Iron Brigade, and he played a role in nearly every major battle in Missouri and Arkansas, including Sterling Price's raid into Missouri. At the Battle of Prairie Grove, a fellow Missourian named Frank James saved his life. (Shelby returned the favor in 1881 when his testimony helped lead to James's acquittal in a murder trial.) He was promoted to brigadier general in the spring of 1864, to rank from December 15, 1863. Sterling Price called him the best cavalry officer he had ever seen, and Union major general Alfred Pleasanton called him "the best cavalry general of the South." During the war, Shelby's exploits were chronicled and often exaggerated or even invented by his adjutant, a former newspaperman named John Edwards.[39]

Like Sterling Price, Shelby refused to surrender and led 500 of his men to Mexico, where they offered their services to Emperor Maximilian. (This episode of Shelby's life may have been the inspiration for the John Wayne movie *The Undefeated.*) When Maximilian's government collapsed, Shelby returned to Missouri, where he became a planter, built railroads, owned coal mines, and became active in Confederate veterans' affairs. He remained immensely popular in Missouri, though his support for Republican politics cost him the support of some of his former soldiers. In 1893, Shelby went to work for the federal government that he had despised and fought against when he accepted an appointment from President Grover Cleveland as a U.S. marshal for western Missouri. He served in that office until his death from pneumonia in February 1897.[40]

A much less highly acclaimed Confederate general also survived past the war's end for several years, a fact that would have surprised many of his contemporaries who remembered him largely for his chronic poor health. Theophilus Hunter Holmes was born in North Carolina in November 1804. His father, a congressman and former governor, got him an appointment to West Point (class of 1829), where he graduated forty-fourth out of a class of forty-six. Holmes fought courageously in the Mexican War, but his Civil War service was much less distinguished. One historian summed up Holmes's Civil War career, noting, "Many generals who wore the gray of the Confederacy distinguished themselves through courageous actions and daring strategic maneuvers. Theophilus Holmes was not one of them. His service to the South was filled with blunder and failed opportunities."[41]

Theophilus Holmes, Courtesy of the Library of Congress.

His old friend Jefferson Davis appointed him to the rank of brigadier general, but his mediocre record in the Eastern Theater led to his being relieved of command. Holmes wanted to retire but reluctantly accepted an assignment to command in the Trans-Mississippi in July 1862. Nearly deaf, in poor health, and prematurely old, Holmes earned the unflattering nickname of "Granny." In March 1863, Edmund Kirby Smith relieved him of command of the Trans-Mississippi and placed him in charge of the District of Arkansas. Holmes's July 4, 1863, attack on Helena was a failure. He resigned from the army in February 1864 and spent the rest of the war commanding reserves in North Carolina. Even many of Holmes's harshest critics, however, admired his personal characteristics. One newspaper editor who had been critical of him wrote, "In justice, we must add that Gen. Holmes is a man of most excellent heart, kind disposition and a gentleman in all things, and it is not his fault that he is not a general."[42]

In the postwar years, Holmes stayed out of the limelight and studiously avoided the postwar recriminations that were commonplace with many other former Confederate officers and officials. Confederate quartermaster general Lucius Northrop noted that Holmes gained some measure of solace and happiness residing with his daughter, son-in-law, and grandchildren on a farm near Fayetteville, North Carolina. Northrop also reported that, to the end of his life, Holmes revered Jefferson Davis, telling Northrop that Davis's and "not [Robert E.] Lee's name should fill the hearts of the Southern people; for he [Davis] was the embodiment of the Confederacy—pure, true, generous, and brave." Despite his poor health, Holmes lived until 1880, dying in his farmhouse on June 21, 1880, at age seventy-five.[43]

Certainly the most colorful and controversial Confederate general in Arkansas was Thomas Carmichael Hindman. Born in Knoxville, Tennessee, in 1828, Hindman moved fifteen years later to Mississippi, where his father had purchased a large cotton plantation. He studied law, fought in the Mexican War, was admitted to the bar in 1851, and served one term in Mississippi's legislature before moving to Helena in 1854. Hindman was a hot-tempered man whom one acquaintance described as having "a wonderful talent for getting into fusses" and another as seeming "perpetually anxious to have a duel." He quickly became active in Democratic politics and, with the help of the state's political dynasty known as "the Family," was elected to Congress in 1858. Hindman was a "fire eater" (a strong advocate of Southern rights) and actively urged Arkansas to secede from the Union.[44]

When the war began, he raised a regiment and became its colonel, then rose rapidly through the ranks. Hindman suffered minor wounds at the Battle of Shiloh. Shortly after that battle, he was promoted to the rank of major general and assigned to command the Trans-Mississippi. He utilized his excellent organizational ability to put together a viable fighting force with very limited resources in both men and materials. In December 1862, he led Confederate forces at the Battle of Prairie Grove. A lightning rod of controversy because of his harsh, dictatorial methods, Hindman was sent east of the Mississippi River, where he fought at the Battle of Chickamauga and in the Atlanta campaign. At Kennesaw Mountain (June 27, 1864), he was wounded and partially blinded. Shortly thereafter he left his command and joined his family in Texas, where they had fled when Federal forces occupied eastern Arkansas.[45]

Like Price and Shelby, Hindman showed an uncanny knack for choosing the wrong side in a conflict. After the war he went to Mexico and lived for a time at Price's settlement at Carlota, where he attempted to practice law and lead the life of a gentleman coffee planter. Neither enterprise prospered, and, as the Maximilian government began to collapse, he returned to Arkansas, unpardoned and disfranchised. Undeterred and with his oratorical skills undiminished, he again became active in politics, urging opposition to the new Republican government. But, unlike many former Confederates, Hindman urged his fellow conservatives to take the loyalty oath so that they could regain the right to vote. Even more significantly, he urged conservatives not only to accept African American suffrage but to openly organize black voters to support the conservative cause.[46]

Thomas C. Hindman, Courtesy of the Library of Congress.

Late on the evening of September 27, 1868, Hindman was sitting in his living room at his Helena residence when one or more assailants fired at him through the parlor window. Hindman was mortally wounded and died early the next morning. No one was ever arrested for the murder, but, given Hindman's propensity for making enemies, the list of possible suspects would have been a long one.[47]

If Hindman was the most controversial Confederate general in Arkansas, a close second might go to John Sappington Marmaduke. Marmaduke, a native of Missouri, was the fourth of ten children born to a politically prominent family. His father was elected lieutenant governor and became governor briefly upon the elected governor's death. One of the best-educated men on either side in the Civil War, young Marmaduke attended both Harvard and Yale before accepting an appointment to West Point (class of 1857), where he graduated thirtieth in a class of thirty-eight. After graduation he served under Albert Sidney Johnston in the "Mormon War" (1857–1858) and was on duty in New Mexico in 1861 when the Civil War began. He returned home on leave, resigned his commission, and became a colonel in the pro-Confederate state militia and later a lieutenant in the regular Confederate army.[48]

He rose to the rank of colonel by the end of 1861 and was wounded at the Battle of Shiloh. In October 1862, he was promoted to brigadier general and assigned to Arkansas. Marmaduke fought at the battles of Prairie Grove and Helena, and took part in several raids into Missouri and in the unsuccessful defense of Little Rock. It was there on September 6, 1863, that he fought his infamous duel with Lucius Marshall (Marsh) Walker. Avoiding court-martial due to the dire necessity of Confederate fortunes, Marmaduke led an unsuccessful attack on Pine Bluff in October 1863, helped turn back Frederick Steele's army in the Red River campaign, and was captured in Price's last great raid into Missouri in late 1864. Marmaduke was imprisoned at Fort Warren, Massachusetts, until the summer of 1865. While in captivity, he was promoted to major general, becoming the last major general appointed in the armies of the Confederacy.[49]

After the war, Marmaduke traveled for a while in Europe before settling in St. Louis. He worked for a time in the insurance business but gave up the profession because he "did not believe its principles in accord with the strictest code of honesty."[50] In 1869, he founded the Southern Historical Society and edited the *St. Louis Journal of Agriculture*. He later served as secretary of the State Agricultural Board, was appointed to the state's first railroad commission, and lost a bid for Democratic nomination for governor in 1880 to former Union general Thomas Crittenden. In 1884, he ran for the office again and was elected, becoming the first ex-Confederate to be elected to a major political office in Missouri. He successfully settled railroad strikes in 1885 and 1886 by overseeing a fair negotiation between workers and management and ultimately signed into law legislation to regulate the railroads. He was actively involved in securing adequate funding for the state's public schools and developed a reputation for incorruptibility. In 1887, while still in office, he contracted pneumonia (his biographer claimed that this was because of damage done to his lungs by the ill treatment he received at Fort Warren as a prisoner of war) and died in Jefferson City, Missouri, on December 28, 1887. He never married and was buried by the state in Woodlawn Cemetery in Jefferson City. His grave shaft reads "He was Fearless and Incorruptible."[51]

John S. Marmaduke, Courtesy of Wilson's Creek National Battlefield.

Former Confederate general Thomas Churchill also entered politics after the war. The Kentucky-born Churchill had studied law at Transylvania University in Lexington and enlisted for service in the Mexican War. On its way to Mexico, his unit stopped in Little Rock, where he was entertained in the house of Judge Benjamin Johnson.

There, he met Ann Sevier, daughter of Ambrose Sevier, one of the state's first U.S. senators and the leader of Arkansas's Democratic political dynasty. After the Mexican War, Churchill settled in Little Rock, and he and Ann were married on July 31, 1849. In 1857, President James Buchanan appointed him postmaster at Little Rock.[52]

Thomas Churchill. Courtesy of the Old State House Museum.

At the beginning of the Civil War, Churchill raised a regiment of cavalry, fought at Wilson's Creek, and was promoted to brigadier general in March 1862. That same month, he took part in the Battle of Pea Ridge. In late 1862, he was given command at Arkansas Post and charged with protecting the river approach to Little Rock. His command was overrun by Federal forces in January 1863, and he was captured, spending three months as a prisoner of war at Camp Chase, Ohio, before being exchanged. He returned to duty and fought against Federal forces in both Louisiana and Arkansas in the Red River Campaign. In March 1865, he was promoted to major general but surrendered with Confederate forces in the Trans-Mississippi in May.[53]

Churchill returned to his farm near Little Rock, became a member of the United Confederate Veterans, and took an active role in political affairs. Though a Democrat, Churchill actively supported Elisha Baxter in the Brooks-Baxter War and raised troops for his militia. When the Democratic Party regained control of state government, he was elected state treasurer in 1874 and again in 1876 and 1878, and then was easily elected governor in 1880. As governor, he secured a 1 mill tax to fund an appropriation for the establishment of care for the mentally ill and an appropriation of $10,000 to establish Branch Normal College at Pine Bluff (today's University of Arkansas at Pine Bluff). Churchill also established a medical department at Arkansas Industrial University (today's University of Arkansas) and a state board of health, and he supported a resolution stating that Arkansas should be pronounced in three syllables with the final "s" silent, the a in each syllable with the Italian sound, and an accent on the first and last syllables.[54]

After Churchill's inauguration as governor, allegations surfaced of financial malfeasance while he was state treasurer. After a subsequent legislative investigation, Churchill paid the state almost $24,000 but did not admit guilt. The accusations nonetheless tarnished his reputation. He retired as governor in 1883 after only one term and devoted his attention to farming.

Churchill died in Little Rock in 1905, shortly after his eighty-first birthday.[55] He had dictated the terms of his funeral to a friend. "Should I die I wish to be buried in a plain coffin not to cost over twenty-five dollars....We are spending too much money on funerals and I hope my example may be followed by others—However, I want to be buried with military honor—I have served in the United States Army as a First Lieutenant in the Mexican War, As maj. Gen in the State troops and a Maj. gen in the Confederate Army." He was buried in Mount Holly Cemetery in Little Rock in his Confederate uniform. In summing up Churchill's military career, fellow Confederate general Richard Taylor wrote that he was "a worthy, gallant gentleman...but not fortunate in war."[56]

One of the most accomplished men to serve as a Confederate general in Arkansas also had one of the most disappointing wartime careers. Albert Pike was born in Boston, Massachusetts, on December 29, 1809. His received an education that provided him with a background in classical and contemporary literature and in Hebrew, Latin, and Greek. He passed the examination required for entry into Harvard when he was sixteen but was unable to pay the tuition. He took work as a schoolteacher and in 1831 came to Fort Smith, where he briefly worked again as a teacher. Pike was a skilled writer of both poetry and prose, and his letters to Little Rock's leading Whig newspaper, the *Arkansas Advocate*, caught the attention of the paper's owner, who subsequently asked Pike to come to Little Rock to serve as the paper's editor. Pike accepted the invitation, and he had become the *Advocate*'s sole owner by 1835.[57]

Albert Pike, Courtesy of the Arkansas State Archives.

While editing the newspaper, he studied law, and within less than two years had passed the Arkansas bar exam. He then sold the newspaper and developed a profitable legal practice. His clients included many of the so-called civilized tribes in the Indian Territory, and Pike learned several native languages while working as their attorney. He served in the Mexican War, fought a bloodless duel with a fellow Arkansas officer whom Pike had sharply criticized in the *Arkansas Gazette*, and returned to Little Rock to practice law. In 1850, he became a Mason and rose rapidly through the ranks of the organization, becoming grand commander of the Supreme Council, Southern Jurisdiction of the United States, in 1859, a position he held until his death. A strong supporter of states' rights, he left the Whig Party over what he considered its lukewarm defense of the rights of Southern slave owners and in 1856 joined the short-lived Know-Nothing Party. Finding that party also too timid in its defense of the pro-slavery position, he joined other Southern delegates in walking out of the party's national convention.[58]

When the war broke out, Pike's knowledge of the Native American tribes led the Confederate War Department to appoint him a brigadier general in the Confederate army and assign him to the Indian Territory. There, he negotiated treaties between the various tribes and the Confederacy and raised troops to defend against a Federal invasion. Pike believed that these Indian troops should be used only to defend the Indian Territory, but in the spring of 1862 Earl Van Dorn ordered Pike to lead his Indian soldiers into northwest Arkansas to meet an army of Federal troops threatening to enter the state.[59]

Pike reluctantly obeyed the order, and his troops took part in the Battle of Pea Ridge on March 7–8, 1862. Some of his Indian troops scalped and mutilated several Union soldiers and killed others as they lay wounded. Pike had witnessed the killing of one wounded Union soldier but did not learn of the other atrocities until after he had returned to the Indian Territory. He sent a note to the Federal commander expressing his horror at the actions, and he ordered his Indian troops to refrain from such actions in the future, but the damage was done. Pike's reputation was permanently tarnished.[60]

After the battle, Pike continued to quarrel with his superiors over Confederate policy in the Indian Territory. When the commander of Confederate forces in Arkansas, Thomas Hindman, tried to extend his authority over the Indian Territory, Pike strenuously objected. When the Confederate government in Richmond sided with Hindman, Pike resigned on July 12, 1862, and effectively sat out the rest of the war.[61]

After the war, Pike led a peripatetic existence, living for brief periods New York City and Canada. After receiving amnesty from President Andrew Johnson in late August 1865, he returned for a time to Arkansas and resumed the practice of law, but in 1867 he moved to Memphis and, in 1870, to Washington DC, where he edited a Democratic newspaper and practiced law. In 1880, he ended his law practice. He devoted much of the remainder of his life to the Masons, rewriting the rituals of the Scottish Rite Masons and even exploring the relationship between Indian spiritualism and Masonry. Pike died at the Scottish Rite Temple in Washington DC on April 2, 1891. Ten years later, the Masons erected a statue to him in

Washington, making him the only former Confederate general to have a statue in the nation's capital.[62]

What conclusions can we draw from the postwar lives of these men? Some, like Francis Herron, who performed with great distinction in the war, were never able to translate that wartime ability into civilian life. Others, like Powell Clayton, demonstrated the same leadership abilities in peacetime that had served them so well during the war. Some, like Totten, were done in by character flaws. Some, like Theophilus Holmes, faded into obscurity, while others, like Clayton, Marmaduke, and Churchill, became actively involved in postwar politics—all three became governors in the postwar period. In short, it is difficult if not impossible to draw any hard and fast conclusions from the postwar careers of these men. Wartime accomplishment appears not to be a guarantor of success in peacetime; wartime mediocrity or worse, no predictor of peacetime failure.

Perhaps the saddest case of all concerns a man who was intimately involved in the wartime fate of Arkansas, though he never spent much time in the state. Edmund Kirby Smith rose from a mediocre student at West Point to command of the Southwestern Army and the entire vast and sprawling territory known as the Trans-Mississippi. After the fall of Vicksburg, Smith enjoyed such a great degree of autonomy in both military and civilian affairs that the Trans-Mississippi was often referred to as "Kirby Smithdom." After the war, how-

Edmund Kirby Smith, Courtesy of the Library of Congress.

ever, this man who had once held such great power suffered through several failed business ventures and eventually was forced to seek employment in the academic world. From 1870 to 1875, he served as president of the University of Nashville, then spent the final eighteen years of his life as a professor of mathematics at the University of the South in Sewanee, Tennessee.[63]

Sic transit Gloria. Amen.

Chapter 3—"How Free Is Free?": A Historiographical Review of African American History in Post-Civil War and Reconstruction Arkansas

By Cherisse Jones-Branch

African Americans crafted a rich and varied history in Arkansas after the Civil War and Reconstruction. As Arkansas ends its statewide commemoration of the 150th anniversary of the Civil War, an occasion that involved black Arkansans' contributions, it seems a good time to reflect on the scholarship regarding African American history in Arkansas—most especially during and after Reconstruction until just after the turn of the twentieth century. This latter period is particularly important because the events that occurred therein shaped how African Americans navigated a new world and a new reality as freed people in a state that, like most of the South and indeed the nation, desperately and often violently imposed its own version (and limitations) of freedom upon them.

Slavery existed in Arkansas before it became a state in 1836. By 1860, the slave population statewide had reached 111,115.[1] Slavery was a very important institution in Arkansas, particularly in the southeastern part of the state, although slave experiences in Arkansas and

By 1860, Arkansas's population of slaves rose to 111,115, including these African Americans picking cotton near Helena before the Civil War. Courtesy of the Permanent Collection of the Historic Arkansas Museum, Little Rock.

throughout the South varied from place to place. More than a few sources speak to these topics. Orville Taylor's seminal work *Negro Slavery in Arkansas* is perhaps the earliest study to address bondsmen in the twenty-fifth state to join the Union. Further, and perhaps more importantly, an explication of formerly enslaved African Americans' experiences is found in George Lankford's *Bearing Witness: Memories of Arkansas Slavery: Narratives from the 1930s WPA Collections*. Slave narratives are also available in *Born in Slavery: Slave Narratives from the Federal Writers' Project, 1936–1938*, available online at the Library of Congress at www.loc.gov. More recent scholarship, like Kelly Houston Jones's 2012 *Arkansas Historical Quarterly* article, "'A Rough, Saucy Set of Hands to Manage': Slave Resistance in Arkansas," analyzes how enslaved African Americans understood and undermined their oppression specifically in Arkansas. Yet another example of Jones's scholarship, "Bondswomen's Work on the Cotton Frontier: Wagram Plantation, Arkansas," provides a rarely seen analysis of gender and slavery by productively complicating enslaved black women's experiences on an absentee-owned farm in Chicot County. In particular Jones speaks to how women understood and employed gender and spatial politics in a space run by white men without the presence of a "white domestic sphere."[2]

Additional scholarship addresses African American experiences in Arkansas during the Civil War as they sought opportunities for freedom. Although Abraham Lincoln's Emancipation Proclamation freed blacks in 1863, it liberated only those in states that were in rebellion against the United States. African Americans in Arkansas were emancipated, for example, but slaves in Missouri, Kentucky, West Virginia, Maryland, or Delaware were not. But black people did not wait until the passage of this document to embrace opportunities to procure their freedom. They empowered and liberated themselves by escaping from bondage in Arkansas and throughout the South and flocking to nearby Union troops.

Blacks served in the U.S. Army after the passage of the Emancipation Proclamation and as a result of General Order Number 143, issued by the War Department in May 1863, authorizing the formation of the United States Colored Troops. Many are familiar with the Fifty-fourth Massachusetts Regiment, most often because they have seen *Glory*, the 1989 movie starring Denzel Washington and Morgan Freeman, but African American troops also fought in battles throughout Arkansas during the Civil War. In 1863, black companies that formed in Helena, Arkansas, became part of the First Arkansas Volunteer Infantry Regiment of African Descent. More information on African Americans in Civil War Arkansas can be found in Mark Christ's *"All Cut to Pieces and Gone to Hell": The Civil War, Race Relations, and the Battle of Poison Spring*, Brian K. Robertson's "'Will They Fight? Ask the Enemy': United States Colored Troops at Big Creek, Arkansas, July 26, 1864," and David Walls's "Marching Song of the First Arkansas Colored Regiment: A Contested Attribution," in the Autumn and Winter 2007 issues of the *Arkansas Historical Quarterly*. Another useful resource to illuminate African Americans' participation in the Civil War is James M. McPherson's 2003 study *The Negro's Civil War: How American Blacks Felt and Acted During the War for the Union*.[3]

The primary objective of this piece, however, is to explicate how African Americans understood their freedom and crafted their lives following the Civil War and during and after Reconstruction. Carl H. Moneyhon's study "Race and the Struggle for Freedom: African American Arkansans after Emancipation," addresses the reality that black people were "free, but exactly what freedom signified was unclear."[4] With the passage of the Thirteenth Amendment, African Americans sought to make sense of their new lives as free people. Unfortunately, many blacks did not live long enough to enjoy their freedom or any of the meanings with which it was infused. Some African Americans emerged from slavery sick from disease, malnutrition, and mistreatment. Two monographs published in 2012, Jim Downs's *Sick From Freedom: African-American Illness and Suffering during the Civil War and Reconstruction* and Gretchen Long's *Doctoring Freedom: The Politics of African American Medical Care in Slavery and Emancipation*, analyze how black people's physical well-being, or the lack thereof, as they emerged from slavery often compromised their newly gained status as free people and as American citizens. In particular, Downs points out how women and children, now free people, were often left vulnerable to sickness, disease, and exposure during and after the Civil War. Although his work focuses generally on black illness and suffering throughout the South, in one example he notes how in contraband/resettlement camps in Helena, the bodies of emancipated blacks were "placed in the same carts with carcasses of mules and horses to be buried in the same pit," thus attesting to the suffering that freedom brought African Americans in its wake. Downs further elucidates how the circumstances that caused thousands of people to congregate in limited and unsanitary spaces following the Civil War led to the outbreak of such illnesses as smallpox, pellagra, yellow fever, cholera, and pneumonia, which often resulted in death.

Much of the medical assistance that emancipated African Americans received after the war came from the Freedmen's Bureau.

Established in 1865, the Freedmen's Bureau—known officially as the Bureau of Refugees, Freedmen and Abandoned Lands—was designed to help free blacks "adjust to the social, economic, legal, educational, political, and medical challenges that emancipation posed."[5] The Freedmen's Bureau, unbeknownst to many, had a Land, Educational, Legal, and Medical Division. The Medical Division was especially important because the federal government understood and assessed emancipated black bodies in terms of their labor power. According to one source, thousands of freedmen's graves could be found in Little Rock by 1866. African Americans were felled by smallpox in Camden and DeValls Bluff, where they had taken refuge. Any available drinking water was contaminated by raw sewage, and thousands died from cholera.[6] Dead or sick bodies could not be productive laborers, so the federal government, through the Medical Division of the Freedmen's Bureau, was deeply interested in ensuring that healthy black people became laborers rather than dependents.

An African American settlement called "Blissville" was established immediately after the Civil War near what is now the Old State House Museum, as shown in this A. R. Waud drawing. Courtesy of the Permanent Collection of the Historic Arkansas Museum, Little Rock.

Freedom meant very little to African Americans without an accompanying access to education. In Arkansas, the Freedmen's Bureau partially funded what later became known as Southland College in Phillips County. This institution, established by Indiana Quakers Alida and Calvin Clark in 1864, began as an orphanage for destitute children and a boarding school before becoming a teachers' college that trained African American educators until it closed in 1925. The most recent works to analyze the founding and operation of Southland College are Thomas Kennedy's "Another Kind of Emigrant: Quakers in the Arkansas Delta, 1864–1925" in the summer 1996 issue of the *Arkansas Historical Quarterly*, and his 2009 monograph *A History of Southland College: The Society of Friends and Black Education in Arkansas*. Another institution established to educate African Americans was Branch Normal College in Pine Bluff (later it became Arkansas AM&N, which then became the University of Arkansas at Pine Bluff), founded as a land-grant institution in 1875.

Religion also sustained African Americans through this period as they turned to black churches for sanctuary during these dangerous years. Within predominantly African American churches, black people wielded an autonomy often denied them outside of those spaces. Randy Finley has argued that black churches were further testing grounds where "all of the critical questions of the day about politics, economics, education, social standing, gender were debated and answers were formulated."[7] They were spaces where black Arkansans created and shaped their own identities free from the gaze of the outside white world. Much of this process was facilitated by black educational institutions with religious underpinnings. Walden Seminary, for instance, was a Methodist school founded in Little Rock in 1877 and renamed Philander Smith College in 1882; Baptist Institute, which was renamed Arkansas Baptist College in 1885, is another example. African Methodist Episcopal (AME) church funds created Bethel College in 1886, which was renamed Shorter College in 1892 in honor of AME Bishop James A. Shorter (the school was moved to Arkadelphia in 1891

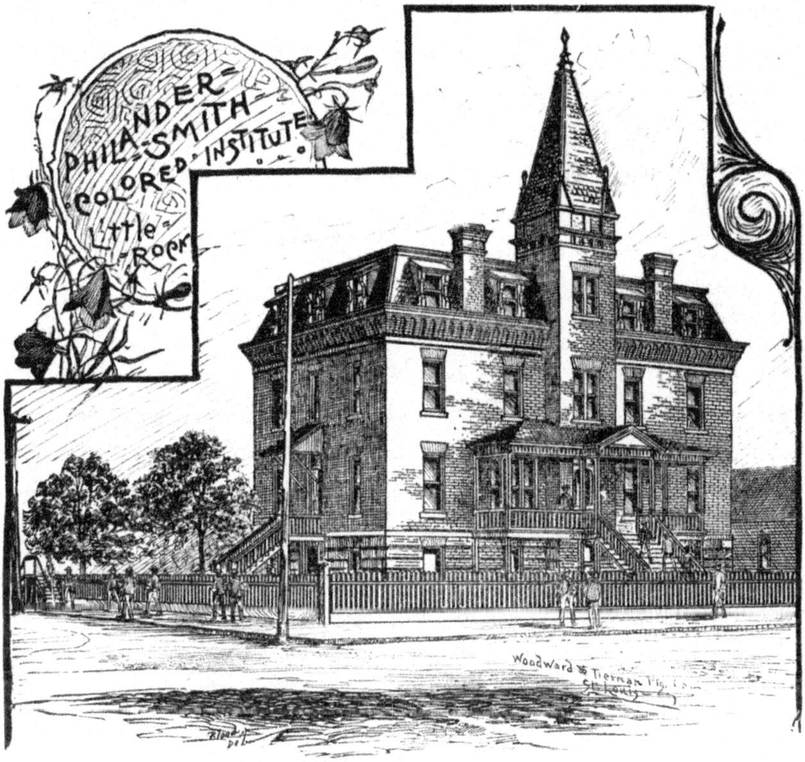

Walden Seminary, a Methodist school for black students, opened in Little Rock in 1877 and was renamed Philander Smith College five years later. The institution still serves a largely African American student body. Courtesy of the Arkansas State Archives.

and then to North Little Rock in 1897, where it remains today).[8] Like Southland College, though not funded by the Freedmen's Bureau, these institutions educated and cultivated Arkansas's black teachers and community leaders.[9]

African Americans further looked to the Freedmen's Bureau to legalize their marriages. The Freedmen's Bureau Online: Records of the Bureau of Refugees, Freedmen and Abandoned Lands, which can be found at www.freedmensbureau.com, contains lists of African Americans who married in Fort Smith, one of the Freedmen's Bureau's subordinate offices, from 1865 to 1867. The Freedmen's Bureau's records are currently being digitized as part of the collaborative efforts of FamilySearch International and the National Archives and Records Administration (NARA), the Smithsonian National Museum of African American History and Culture, the AfroAmerican Historical and Genealogical Society (AAHGS), and the California African American Museum. This will further provide a wealth of much needed information about the contours of black lives after the Civil War.

At least one work speaks directly of black Arkansans' experiences with the Freedmen's Bureau. Randy Finley's *From Slavery to Uncertain Freedom: The Freedmen's Bureau in Arkansas, 1865–1869* examines African Americans' battles to make real the meanings and promise of freedom. At every step, they challenged stereotypes about black inferiority and pathology by creating economic, social, educational, and political institutions to support and sustain their communities.[10] This task proved difficult, as African Americans faced not only planters and former owners who refused to accept slavery's end and blacks' freedom, but also Freedmen's Bureau agents who often, according to Finley, "perceived themselves as surrogate planters and white patriarchs taking care of infantile Sambos."[11] Unfortunately, Freedmen's Bureau scholars have paid scant attention to the gender dynamics at play between agents and freedmen in the post–Civil War years. Freedmen's Bureau agents expected African Americans to replicate the patriarchal model imposed upon white women, whereby it was assumed that black men would be the head of their households. Finley briefly addresses this by arguing that black women pushed back against patriarchal gender norms, understanding and constructing their freedom on their own terms and rejecting the patriarchal norms projected onto them by Freedmen's Bureau agents and black men. Finley highlights at least one example in Helena, where a freedwoman received permission from the Freedmen's Bureau to remain with her crop rather than move with her husband. Black women also refused to accept physical and sexual abuse by white and black men, and turned to the bureau for assistance. In some instances, black women wrested freedom for themselves from abusive circumstances by separating from and divorcing their husbands. They further understood themselves as acting on behalf of all African Americans and inserted themselves into political spaces and arguments, asserting their political efficacy even if they could not actually cast a ballot.[12] As a case in point, Finley noted that black women made up the majority of those who attended an 1867 Arkansas constitutional convention rally.[13]

Self-determined agency best describes the actions African Americans employed to create lives for themselves as free people. Although legalizing marriages was important because it was a right that had been denied them during slavery, locating lost loved ones was perhaps equally important. Well into the late nineteenth century, African Americans sought family members who had been wrested from them. Heather Andrea Williams has written about this in *Help Me to Find My People: The African American Search for Family Lost in Slavery*. She analyzes black newspapers containing advertisements paid for by people searching for relatives from whom they had been separated for decades. Williams demonstrates African Americans' painful losses during slavery to be sure, but she also underscores their resilience as they invested "emotional capital" in creating new families while simultaneously searching for those they had lost.[14] As she argues most eloquently, "losing a family member did not necessarily mean that people came to see family bonds as insignificant."[15] Locating family members often proved difficult. Freed people had scant information and were forced to rely upon their fragmented memories to advertise information about their loved ones in an array of African American, Republican, and church newspapers. While Williams does not mention many Arkansas examples, her analysis is instructive about the ways in which newspapers can be read to understand the emotional labor African Americans spent to find relatives. The website "Lost Friends in Slavery," http://www.hnoc.org/database/lost-friends/browse.php, includes numerous newspaper ads placed in the *Southwestern Christian Advocate*, published in New Orleans by the Methodist Episcopal Church between

1873 and 1929, from African Americans trying to locate relatives who had been enslaved in Arkansas.[16]

Even after slavery had been abolished in the United States, African Americans in Arkansas—like blacks elsewhere in the South—found their freedom severely circumscribed. They were free, but many white southerners refused to accept that they were entitled to the full benefits of American citizenship. For black Arkansans, attaining equality and citizenship was an uphill battle that was fraught with disappointment and danger, particularly after former Confederates regained control in the state. "Black Codes" instituted in 1866, for example, granted African Americans certain rights that had eluded them as slaves, such as the right to marry and hold property. However, these codes also prohibited them from voting or holding public office. Congress, having grown impatient with southern whites' recalcitrance, issued the Reconstruction Acts of 1867, which gave African American men access to the political arena. Eight black men attended and participated in Arkansas's constitutional convention in 1868.[17] All of these men were literate, and their total property holdings averaged about five hundred dollars. Of the eight, two were formerly enslaved and five were of mixed racial ancestry.[18] Two African Americans obtained cabinet-level positions. Oberlin College graduate Joseph Carter Corbin was Arkansas's superintendent of public instruction from 1873 to 1875; and Washington DC native William H. Grey, representing Phillips County, was the commissioner of immigration and state lands. Twenty black men served in Arkansas's General Assembly and held offices in predominantly African American counties in the Arkansas Delta. One example was James Mason, an educated man of mixed racial ancestry who was elected to the General Assembly in 1868. He was later appointed county judge in Chicot County.[19] More recent scholarship on African Americans' political efficacy includes Helen Hoguet's 2004 University of Wisconsin master's thesis, "Protecting the Perfect Africa: The Politics of Race and Property in Post-Reconstruction Arkansas," and Chris W. Branham's "'The Africans Have Taken Arkansas': Political Activities of African

Americans in the Reconstruction Legislature" in the autumn 2014 issue of the *Arkansas Historical Review*.[20]

Although Democrats regained control of the state government as a result of the 1874 Brooks-Baxter War,[21] African Americans continued to enjoy limited political involvement in Arkansas for more than two decades after Reconstruction's end. John William Graves's scholarship speaks to black Arkansans' political activism during and after Reconstruction and asserts that it continued with white Arkansans' support. Indeed, white politicians often brokered political deals with African Americans, particularly those who resided in the Arkansas Delta, through an arrangement known as the "fusion principle." This entailed a pre-voting meeting during which black Republicans and conservative white Democrats "allotted each other places on the ballot." A fusion ticket was then presented at the election. According to Graves, this system continued well after Arkansas's Reconstruction period ended, with African Americans holding county offices and seats in the state legislature until 1894.

William H. Grey, a native of Washington DC, served in the 1868 constitutional convention, in the Arkansas General Assembly, and as commissioner of immigration and state lands after settling in Helena. Courtesy of the Arkansas State Archives.

Graves also unearths black lives in Arkansas's urban spaces and analyzes how African Americans' geographic location often determined what was possible and what was not in the post–Civil War and Reconstruction years. In Little Rock in the 1890s, African Americans and whites were integrated and interacted with each other to an extent that would be unimaginable in later years. For instance, Graves wrote about northern visitors who witnessed black doctors, lawyers, and businessmen with white clients. Public facilities were also integrated, as in the case of Little Rock's West End Park. That is not to say, however, that segregationist policies were not constructed during this period. Graves notes that the Capital Theatre followed a "curious half-way segregation policy" by reserving a section of the theater for whites only but allowed the races to commingle freely in the balcony.[22] It was further unclear what policy dictated African Americans' access to dining and drinking facilities at the time.

African Americans' entry into Little Rock's public and private spaces was at least legally supported by a civil rights bill passed in Arkansas's last Reconstruction legislature in 1873 providing for equal service to all in public accommodations regardless of race. It further provided for equal educational facilities for black and white children. This civil rights law remained on the books until it was repealed in 1907. As Graves astutely notes, the very enactment of such a law suggests that African Americans often had to contend with discriminatory practices. In the 1890s, it was not unusual to encounter references to "Negro" restaurants, saloons, and hotels in the newspapers.[23] While this can certainly be read as a means to segregate and marginalize African Americans, it is also sound evidence of their business acumen during these years. This and African Americans' relative mobility and success in urban Arkansas spaces were a double-edged sword.

What then were the circumstances that led to African Americans' increased subordination and marginalization in Arkansas's public and private spaces? According to Graves, it was an agrarian revolt coupled with Democratic politicians' willingness to distract poor white farmers from their economic concerns and court their votes by appealing to their demands to "keep the Negro in his place." By 1890, the Democratic

Party called for railroad car segregation. In 1891, the General Assembly enacted the Separate Coach Law.[24]

Scholar Fon Louise Gordon has also written about black Arkansans' experiences in the post-Reconstruction years. In her 1995 work *Caste and Class: The Black Experience in Arkansas, 1880–1920*, she, like Graves, notes that this was the period during which Jim Crow laws crystallized, putting limits on black lives and aspirations. Yet, Gordon provides a nuanced analysis of African American voices to show how they understood and reacted to their experiences during these years. Her examination of black Arkansans' lives in the post–Civil War years is more than a story of their victimization, real though it was. Rather, it is a chronicle of African Americans' triumphs despite and perhaps because of the limitations they increasingly endured. Gordon describes Arkansas's black middle class, for example, as "rich and economically varied." That is, they became ministers, landowning farmers, and teachers, doctors, lawyers, editors, and publishers, as well as businessmen and post office and railroad employees. The black middle class's economic position was important because it was a testament to what was possible for African Americans in the decades immediately following slavery's end. It, however, was also a testament to the very real choices black people were forced to make in response to increased discrimination and political and social marginalization.[25] Gordon posits that, despite racial discrimination, or more likely because of it, middle-class black Arkansans set the bar high for African Americans. Informed by what historian Evelyn Brooks Higginbotham termed the "politics of respectability," middle-class blacks often embraced Booker T. Washington's conciliatory purview, which included "inculcating assimilationist values of self-improvement, piety, thrift, industry, and hard work."[26] This sentiment was deliberately radiated downward to the African American masses, particularly uneducated, non-landowning blacks in the Arkansas Delta whose lives were unfairly regulated and circumscribed by agricultural labor and the social, educational, and political control of local whites, landowning or not.[27]

African Americans did not passively accept Arkansas's deteriorating conditions, marginalization, or a second- or third-class status in the late nineteenth century, instead protesting racial discrimination and segregation, up to a point. Some middle-class blacks engaged in "conservative protest," which reduced the risk of violence to themselves, their families, and their community. Gordon argues that, by the 1880s, African American leaders had largely abandoned their open struggle for civil rights.[28] Yet when the Arkansas General Assembly passed the Separate Coach Law in 1891, Little Rock's black middle class protested and issued resolutions condemning the legislation at a meeting at First Missionary Baptist Church. This protest, unfortunately, was short lived, as were African Americans' boycotts in Little Rock, Pine Bluff, and Hot Springs when the Streetcar Segregation Act was passed in 1903.[29]

The ephemeral nature of African Americans' rights in Arkansas quite likely intensified the need to maximize economic opportunities within their own communities. Gordon suggests that some attempted to soften the blow of racial segregation by directing blacks to patronize African American or Jewish establishments, where their dignity would not be assailed. Yet middle-class blacks were not always particularly concerned about protecting the dignity of their poor and rural counterparts whose alleged failures were often blamed for the racial injustice meted upon all African Americans.[30]

As conditions worsened in the late nineteenth century, some blacks began to look to other locales for safety and opportunity. Mobility was a means of resistance and agency for African Americans following the Civil War, and many blacks from other parts of the South regarded Arkansas as a "promised land" of sorts because of its relatively tolerant racial climate and enticing economic opportunities. Planters and political officials welcomed African American laborers and sharecroppers from Louisiana and Mississippi, parts of which bordered Arkansas, and from South Carolina. Between 1870 and 1890, Arkansas's black population almost tripled.[31] Story Matkin-Rawn's 2013 article "The Great Negro State of the Country: Arkansas's

Reconstruction and the Other Great Migration" also addresses this and asserts that, between the end of the Civil War and World War I, more than 200,000 African Americans migrated to the state and, in fact, "black migration consistently outpaced white migration." Furthermore, African Americans were neither necessarily "coerced or deceived" into moving to Arkansas. Rather, they made careful decisions about migrating that were informed by communal, familial, political, and economic connections, aspirations, and concerns. They assessed opportunities as well as risks as they contemplated relocating their entire families and lives to Arkansas.[32] The threat of violence was ever present in Arkansas, and indeed throughout the South and the nation. Yet, according to Matkin-Rawn, African American migration crested between 1873 and 1874 at the very same time that racial and politically motivated violence intensified. Despite this, however, Matkin-Rawn argues that the availability of inexpensive land, better wages, and state suppression of Ku Klux Klan violence underscored African Americans' desire to seek their fortunes in the western South.[33]

Some African Americans also employed mobility as a form of agency and activism by leaving the United States altogether. During the late nineteenth century, more African Americans left Arkansas for the Republic of Liberia, West Africa, than those in any other state. Historian Kenneth C. Barnes chronicles their experience in his monograph *Journey of Hope: The Back-to-Africa Movement in Arkansas in the Late 1800s*. In one poignant example from 1892, as a Dutch steamer was sailing into the New York Harbor laden with European immigrants, it passed another ship, the *Liberia*, which was headed to West Africa. Most of its passengers were African Americans from Morrilton, Arkansas.[34]

While Arkansas was a land of many political and economic opportunities for a number of African Americans in the late nineteenth century, social and political marginalization and racial violence convinced many of them that their fortunes were not to be found in the South or in the United States. For many African Americans, according to Barnes, Liberia was a place of wonder, a refuge, and "an ancestral land that helped define a national identity," particularly as the limited protections of Reconstruction ended.[35] African Americans surely imaged Africa as a balm for the many physical, psychological, and emotional wounds they had suffered in the land of their birth. It was perhaps an oasis for many rural blacks who were unable to avail themselves of their urban counterparts' more fruitful, though troubled, circumstances in Little Rock. Barnes chronicles the exodus to Liberia and the forces that encouraged serious letters and inquiries to the American Colonization Society, an organization founded in 1816 to assist two groups generally in opposition—southern white slave owners and antislavery factions—of the threat from and to a free black population.[36] By the late 1890s, however, when it became patently clear that many black Arkansans could not afford to immigrate to Liberia, they began moving to the Indian Territory (present-day Oklahoma), which, as Barnes notes, did not yet have Jim Crow laws.[37]

The Horsa *prepares to depart for Liberia with around 200 passengers, half of them from Jefferson County, Arkansas, in March 1895.* Harper's Weekly *image courtesy of the Encyclopedia of Arkansas History & Culture.*

Black lives in Arkansas in the decades following the Civil War were most often supported by the activism of African American women. While there is scant mention of them in most of the scholarship on black Arkansans, their ways of being, understanding, and contending with critical moments of change are noteworthy. Much emphasis has been placed on African American men's political, economic, and educational leadership in Arkansas, but black women's experiences can be unearthed by mining the hidden spaces where their activism occurred.[38] As mentioned earlier, black women could not cast a ballot in late nineteenth-century Arkansas, but this did not mean that they were not politically involved or responsive. Indeed, their political acumen was most often cultivated through their membership in black women's organizations. At least one source—Jeannie M. Whayne, Thomas A. DeBlack, George Sabo III, and Morris S. Arnold's *Arkansas: A Narrative History*—attests to this. Like white women, black women who were excluded from the political process exerted their influence through their membership in fraternal order auxiliaries. For example, when the Mosaic Templars of America was established in Arkansas in 1883, black women joined the "lady chambers...under the special watch-care and guardianship of the Grand Mosaic Master," an organization through which they certainly must have wielded some influence.[39] Although this is not mentioned in most scholarship on Arkansas in the late nineteenth century, black women also joined the Royal Grand Chapter of the Order of the Eastern Star, Prince Hall Affiliated, which was established in 1885.[40]

Black Arkansas women further embraced the activism of the 1890s women's club movement by forming and joining organizations to address their communities' political, educational, and health concerns. As noted in *Arkansas: A Narrative History*, black women, who were excluded from white women's clubs, established the National Association of Colored Women (NACW) in 1896. The first black women's club in Arkansas was established in Little Rock in 1897. In 1905, middle-class, educated black Arkansas women founded the Arkansas Association of Colored Women (AACW) as an affiliate of the NACW. The AACW adopted the national organization's motto, "Lifting As We Climb," and held its first annual convention in Hot

Springs in 1908. Known today as the Arkansas Association of Women, Youth, and Young Adults Clubs, Inc., it remains dedicated to effecting change in the state's black communities.[41]

Access to and support for education remained one of the most consistent concerns among African Americans, and perhaps black women in particular, in the decades following the Civil War. Although educational institutions had been aided by the Freedmen's Bureau, as in the case of Southland College in Phillips County, African Americans mounted their own initiatives to ensure educational access for their communities. As historian C. Calvin Smith has argued, many blacks emerged from slavery understanding that education was a fundamental element in their success in the post–Civil War years. During Reconstruction, when the Arkansas legislature authorized white-only public schools, African Americans reacted by raising funds to operate free schools for blacks. In 1868, the Arkansas legislature adopted a new state constitution that provided free, albeit segregated, education both for its black and white citizens.[42] This same year, Charlotte Andrews Stephens, a charter member of the NACW, was the first African American teacher hired in Pulaski County.[43] Unfortunately, following African Americans' disfranchisement in the 1890s, funding for Arkansas's black public schools decreased precipitously. Black Arkansans then were forced to look to such philanthropic organizations as the John F. Slater Fund, the General Education Board, the Anna T. Jeanes Fund, and the Julius Rosenwald Fund, which were established in 1882, 1902, 1908, and 1912, respectively.[44]

The Anna T. Jeanes and Julius Rosenwald Funds in particular buttressed black educational efforts in Arkansas. The Anna T. Jeanes Fund, also known as the "Negro Rural School Fund," employed what were known as Jeanes Supervising Teachers, who were funded by an endowment from a foundation created by Pennsylvania Quaker Anna T. Jeanes to support rural black education in cooperation with white state and county school officials who selected them to work under their supervision. The Jeanes Supervising Teachers program lasted in Arkansas until 1950.[45]

The Julius Rosenwald Fund contributed to black education in Arkansas by helping African Americans build Rosenwald Schools. Established in rural communities, these schools helped African Americans access equal educational opportunities throughout the South. Its partnership with local southern black communities, which were responsible for raising a portion of the necessary monies, provided funds to construct rural schools. Between 1912 and 1930, as Smith has noted, Rosenwald funded the construction of more than 320 rural black schools in Arkansas.[46] It also provided grants and fellowships for black teachers to further their educational and career goals.[47]

Charlotte Stephens, a charter member of the first federated black women's club in Arkansas, became the first African American teacher hired in Pulaski County; she taught for seventy years. Courtesy of the Archives and Special Collections, Torreyson Library, University of Central Arkansas.

While black Arkansans' political and educational achievements were notable in the last years of the nineteenth century, these achievements were accompanied by the ever present threat of racial violence. Because some African Americans had been successful in and/or had supported the Republican Party, they suffered repercussions from angry whites. Black men had served as militiamen during Reconstruction and had been involved in the Brooks-

Baxter War in 1874. At a time when the nation, not just the South, was still reeling from the chaos and instability wrought by the Civil War, black social, economic, and political attainments placed them directly in the line of white violence from the late nineteenth century well into the next.

Racial violence in post–Civil War Arkansas was, for African Americans, a fact of life and a reason for extreme caution as they created and navigated the boundaries of their lives. African American and mainstream newspapers are replete with stories about the horrors meted upon black bodies in the late nineteenth and twentieth centuries. This was particularly true in rural areas where white landowners sought to render African Americans politically and economically impotent and force them to undertake agricultural labor. Racial violence was also the means most often employed by whites to assert their claims to superiority over African Americans. Although most rural dwellers were pathetically poor, regardless of race, in the years following the Civil War, poor whites did not, as Carl Moneyhon has astutely argued, imagine themselves anyone's inferior, least of all African Americans'.[48] Even relatively prosperous African Americans, such as St. Francis County's Scott Bond and Little Rock attorney Scipio Africanus Jones, understood the importance of navigating difficult and potentially dangerous circumstances by accommodating and working within the constraints of the racial status quo.[49] This did not mean, however, that Arkansas blacks as a whole

Julius Rosenwald, the president of Sears Roebuck and Company, helped fund hundreds of schools for African American students throughout the South through the Julius Rosenwald Fund. Courtesy of the Library of Congress.

accepted their marginalization. Black agricultural workers often resisted unfair treatment through their mobility or through destruction of landowners' property. That is, they revealed their discontent by wielding the limited power they possessed. Unfortunately, this display of agency precipitated racial violence. According to Moneyhon, between 1882 and 1903, at least 139 black lives were extinguished by white violence.[50]

Black leaders in Arkansas opposed racial terrorism in their communities, and their concerns about racial violence and cries for support pervaded African American local and religious newspapers in both the South and the North. Arkansas lynching reports, for instance, were recorded in Philadelphia's *Christian Recorder*, established in 1852 as the newspaper of the African Methodist Episcopal Church. In an 1892 report in the paper, a black preacher recounted, "There is much uneasiness and unrest all over this State among our people, owing to the fact that the people (our race variety) all over the State are being lynched upon the slightest provocation; some being strung up to telegraph poles, others burnt at the stake and still others being shot like dogs. In the last 30 days there have been not less than eight colored persons lynched in this State. At Texarkana a few days ago, a man was burnt at the stake." African American religious leaders further met in Little Rock to draft a letter of protest to be sent to Arkansas's governor.[51]

Scores of lynchings and acts of racial violence occurred after this period and are explored in such studies as Vincent Vinikas's "Specters in the Past: The Saint Charles, Arkansas, Lynching of 1904 and the Limits of Historical Inquiry," in the August 1999 issue of the *Journal of Southern History*.[52] Richard Buckelew's 1999 University of Arkansas dissertation, "Racial Violence in Arkansas: Lynchings and Mob Rule, 1860–1930," also fleshes out the meanings of systematic racial terrorism in ways that continue to illuminate understandings of the precariousness of black lives following the Civil War.

More recent studies unpack how racial violence was employed to erase the African American presence from the landscapes of Arkansas cities and towns in the late nineteenth and early twentieth century.

Racial violence was often conflated with labor violence. The presence of African Americans, to whites, meant economic competition. Kimberly Harper's 2010 study *White Man's Heaven: The Lynching and Expulsion of Blacks in the Southern Ozarks, 1894–1904* illuminates the racial and economic challenges African Americans endured in turn-of-the-century Arkansas and Missouri.[53] Scholar Guy Lancaster, however, focuses exclusively on the state of Arkansas beginning with his 2010 encyclopedia entry, "The Bonanza Race War of 1904," an incident that occurred after coal mine owners "employed" convict lease labor and imported African Americans to break strikes at the Kansas and Texas Coal Company in Sebastian County. The riot erupted in Bonanza, a coal-mining city in Sebastian County. In the aftermath, African Americans retreated from the city.[54] Racial cleansing was part of the matrix of racial expulsions that shaped the contours of African American lives throughout Arkansas before World War I. Lancaster has written extensively[55] on this topic, but he expertly detailed accounts of racial atrocities all over Arkansas in his 2014 monograph *Racial Cleansing in Arkansas: 1883–1924, Politics, Land, Labor, and Criminality* and adeptly analyzes the complex and nuanced web of racial conditions that circumscribed black Arkansans' freedom in the late nineteenth and early twentieth century.[56]

Between the end of the Civil War through the post-Reconstruction years, African Americans wrestled with the meanings of freedom within their communities and with those outsiders who attempted to define it for them. For formerly enslaved black people in Arkansas and their progeny, freedom meant reifying and reestablishing family bonds. Their analysis of freedom directed their desire to access educational, economic, and political opportunities not only for themselves but also for their communities. Unfortunately, these initiatives often resulted in increased political and economic marginalization, social erasure, and exposure to racial violence, as many white Arkansans refused to understand and accept African Americans as free people entitled to the rights and benefits due to all American citizens.

Little Rock attorney Scipio Africanus Jones was a prominent leader of Arkansas's black community in the late nineteenth and early twentieth centuries. Courtesy of the Butler Center for Arkansas Studies, Central Arkansas Library System, Little Rock.

Black people in Arkansas and throughout the South were forced back into near servitude by southern whites wielding violence while standing on the scaffolding of state and local power. Freedom for many African Americans, even after legal emancipation, seemed elusive. Yet many wrested concessions from a hostile racial environment, as is evidenced by black people who engaged in institution building, and political and economic efficacy, beyond the nineteenth century and into the twentieth and twenty-first. At every possible juncture African Americans challenged the limitations of the ever present query "How free is free?" by deploying their determination, diligence, and dedication to make real the promise of freedom in post–Civil War and Reconstruction Arkansas.

Chapter 4—The Civil War's Impact on the Arkansas Economy

By Jeannie Whayne

According to historian Morton Sosna, World War II brought far more change to the South than did the Civil War. Sosna is correct, but his explanation is incomplete. He effectively compares the absence of meaningful change after the Civil War to the significant economic transformation that took place after World War II. What he overlooks is that the "cotton empire" was in full vigor in 1860 and enveloped southern planters into a complex global network. By 1940, however, the modern global economic complex was shifting to other commodities that would soon eclipse the one created by cotton.

According to Sven Beckert, the Civil War reflected the tensions arising from the creation of a new phenomenon in world history: the emergence of modern industrial capitalism based on cotton production, trade, textile manufacturing, and distribution. Beginning in the 1780s, cotton united various players in sometimes profoundly unequal roles, with the industrial capitalists of Manchester and Liverpool assuming the part of a many-headed emperor. The various other characters included slaves in the fields of the Americas, planters who exploited land and labor, ginners who made cotton ready for the market, factors brokering the cotton through the financiers who sold it to textile mill owners, ship captains and seamen who transported the ginned cotton, and cotton textile mill workers who labored in horrific conditions in the world's first factories. The industry also included similar actors after the product left the factory floor in the form of cotton fabric or yarn, including the shippers who transported the finished product to almost all corners of the globe. The profound dissatisfaction of slaves exposed the weakest link in this web of relationships and led to massive emancipations in the Americas in the nineteenth century. The American Civil War was but one of a series of struggles that challenged but failed to unravel the cotton empire.

On the ground in places such as antebellum Arkansas, however, it was the plantation system with its peculiar way of organizing land, labor, and capital that constituted the most obvious manifestation of the cotton empire.[1] Its survival reflected the power of the cotton empire and the complicity of elites across the North/South divide to maintain a wealth-making industry. Even as the plantation system's persistence ensured the South's—and Arkansas's—continuing participation in the worldwide cotton enterprise, it also inhibited other forms of economic development.[2] It concentrated wealth in the hands of men who were either somewhat indifferent or downright hostile to other enterprises. The emergence of "another kind of slavery" to replace that peculiar institution fashioned the yoke of poverty on African American freed people, played a role in establishing a new caste system that stimulated the rise of a virulent racism, and created an antediluvian political economy.

While the plantation system adapted and re-invented itself after the Civil War, it transformed even more significantly in the twentieth century. But certain key features of its operational model remained in place even after cotton was no longer essential to the cotton empire in the post–World War II period. Almost all available resources resided in the hands of a few individuals who owned vast acreage dedicated to the production of certain commodity crops; they fed a world demand for those crops that reaped significant profits for them while most of the population within plantation areas suffered from poverty, poor health, and a lack of access to adequate educational facilities; and they were able to enlist the power of the state and local officials to serve their interests. Throughout its history and in virtually every location in the world where the plantation exists or has existed, other forms of economic development are anemic or non-existent.[3] As Caribbean economist George Beckford has argued, "Plantation economy never gets beyond the stage of underdevelopment. For within the system itself there are structural factors which impede further economic progress for plantation society as a whole."[4]

The survival of plantation agriculture and the imposition of laws that were designed to undermine black freedom stand as among the most negative legacies arising out of the failure of Reconstruction. The attention scholars have devoted to the issue and their ongoing efforts to understand its implications continue to enliven historical debates. Some of the most provocative recent work on the topic places it into the context of global capitalism, examines the role of colonial powers and nations in erecting structures to maintain it, or probes its renewed appearance in the twenty-first century in the guise of agribusiness. Sven Beckert's *Empire of Cotton* stands as one of the most noteworthy works of this new generation of scholarship and demonstrates that it is no wonder that Arkansas planters, like those elsewhere, remained devoted to cotton even as their world and their labor system were crumbling around them during and immediately following the Civil War. Cotton was deeply enmeshed in the world capitalist system that emerged in the nineteenth century, and there was a certainty to it that both transfixed and beckoned men who sought to restore their fortunes.[5]

Post–Civil War cotton planters resumed playing their assigned role in the global cotton complex, in part because the networks that had been established in the antebellum period, although strained to the breaking point, had never been fully severed. They also remembered fondly the high prices and accumulation of fortunes in the 1850s. In fact, in the decade before the Civil War, much of Arkansas was experiencing a period of prosperity after having faced some daunting challenges in the early antebellum era. Although the collapse of the state banks in the 1840s continued to tarnish the state's financial reputation, between 1850 and 1860, corn production doubled, the value of livestock nearly tripled, and the cash value of farms increased by more than six times, from $15,265,245 to $91,649,773. The driving force in the prosperity of the 1850s, however, was cotton production, which likely accounts largely for the increase in the value of farms. Cotton production in the state rose from 65,344 bales in 1850 to 367,393 in 1860.[6] The value of the 1860 cotton crop was probably between seventeen and eighteen million dollars.[7] However, the state remained overwhelmingly focused on agricultural production; the value of manufactured items for the state stood at only a relatively minor three million dollars.[8]

As historian C. Fred Williams has argued, the upland areas of the state dominated in both settlement and agricultural production in the early antebellum era but were toppled from that position once the plantation system in Arkansas expanded in the 1840s and, particularly, in the 1850s. The land in the mountains was largely unsuitable for large-scale row crop cultivation, and there was no great river like the Mississippi easily accessible to transport a sizeable harvest to market. As a result "most farming was done on hillsides," and though upland farmers might devote a few acres to cash crops like cotton, they focused more on the cultivation of corn, cereal grains, potatoes, and, occasionally, a little tobacco.[9] They also raised livestock and customarily ranged them widely on unfenced land not their own. Farmers in Washington County, for example, transported any excess production over rough mountain roads, south toward Fort Smith or north toward Kansas City. Although historian Steven Hahn has characterized such areas as only nominally connected to the market and more oriented toward subsistence and bartering, it is clear that commercial agriculture of a sort was underwriting the growth of towns and small-scale operations such as gristmills. A small number of slave holders began plantation agriculture in the few suitable areas in the upland, and as historian Ted Smith argues regarding their operations in Washington County, they "farmed the best land along rivers and opened up some of its earliest business establishments." However, planter operations in northwestern Arkansas were unimpressive in comparison to what was taking shape elsewhere in the state.[10]

A review of conditions in two very different counties on opposite corners of the state in 1860 illustrates the distinctions between the two regions. Washington County was the most populous place in northwestern Arkansas in the early antebellum period; Chicot County in southeastern Arkansas developed later but soon surpassed its counterpart on the other side of the state. Washington County was engaged in a productive model that pre-dated the emergence of the cotton/industrial complex, one in which farmers co-existed with small planters. Together they grew wheat and some corn for the market but harvested only 15 bales in cotton in 1860. Some of that cotton might have been marketed, but most of it was likely processed the time-honored way: women working home-owned spinning wheels. According to Smith's analysis, planters represented only three percent of the free population but "often produced or manufactured 40 to 50 percent of the county's goods."[11] Even though, as Smith argues, the larger slave owners reached Washington County early and captured the land most suitable for row crop cultivation, they shared power with non-slaveholders, and little evidence of social tensions exists.[12] Together with smaller slave owners, the planters numbered a total of 298 slave holders, keeping 1,493 people in bondage; this amounts to about five slaves per person. Although the planters among them would have used slaves to till their fields, even they would have employed some of them in household work or, given that a few of the planters also operated mills, their slaves likely carried on tasks unrelated to farming.[13]

In the other corner of the state, a very different relationship to the cotton economy and slavery developed. In Chicot County, 225 slaveholders held 7,112 African Americans in bondage, averaging more than 30 slaves per owner. The average does not tell the full story, however. Elijah Worthington owned 543 slaves, making him one of the largest slave owners in the South, and, like neighboring planters, he was devoted to the production of cotton for export to a global market.[14] This devotion to cotton was unwavering, moreover, as the planters in cotton-growing areas of eastern Arkansas enjoyed great prosperity, particularly in the 1850s when sky-rocketing prices for the staple stimulated a robust expansion of the plantation system. While only 15 bales of cotton were harvested in Washington County in 1860, Chicot County cotton production amounted to 40,948 bales, an increase of more than fourfold from the 1850 figure of 8,450 bales.[15] Chicot County planters had clearly become a link in the chain of the global cotton economy.

Lycurgus Johnson owned a large plantation in Chicot County, Arkansas, at the start of the Civil War. The pragmatic Johnson, an avowed supporter of the Confederacy, would be trading cotton through Federal forces by 1864. Courtesy of Annie Paden.

The Civil War undermined and then destroyed slavery, but it also challenged cotton producers, which ultimately weakened their loyalty to the Confederacy. The horror and destruction brought by the war, however, was felt throughout the state regardless of affiliation to the cotton empire. Although two significant battles were fought in northwestern Arkansas, most of the fighting elsewhere was on a small scale.

The greatest havoc was created by a relentless guerrilla war. Historian William Shea argues that the "fabric of society unraveled" by the second year of the war, saying, "In Arkansas, state, county, and local governments ceased to function as judges, sheriffs, constables, clerks, and other office-holders fled or failed to carry out their duties. Taxes went uncollected, lawsuits went unheard, and complaints went unanswered."[16] Criminals were released from jails because there was no one to guard them, or they went unprosecuted because the courts were closed. Lawlessness prevailed unchecked, and civilians fled in such numbers that some counties became virtually depopulated. Escaped or unprosecuted criminals formed guerrilla bands to take advantage of the chaos, and they were able to plunder, murder, and rape with little fear of punishment.

Both armies employed "irregulars," guerrillas by another name, who worked in conjunction with military operations and often proved difficult to control or rely upon to function in tandem with army objectives. Even these sanctioned guerrillas sometimes treated civilians roughly, perhaps acting on old grudges or simply taking advantage of the general disorder to plunder and seize supplies. The presence of the Confederate or Union army was often more welcome than not, as it represented at least some semblance of law and order. But civilians often suffered at their hands too, as they were required to open their smokehouses and surrender their horses and other supplies to support the officers and men.[17] Given the state of unrest and lawlessness in Arkansas, many found it impossible to carry on farming operations. Guerrillas or armies had seized livestock, looted smokehouses, and burned down homes and barns. Some civilians lost everything. With the virtual depopulation of entire mountain counties on the northern border, no one was left to plant and harvest crops. Most able-bodied men had joined one army or the other, and their wives and children fled the area once guerrilla warfare made life intolerable.

Fayetteville, the seat of local government for Washington County, was in the unenviable position of enduring occupation by both the Confederate and Union armies, and the destruction of its flour mill upon the departure of Confederate forces illustrates the implications of the kind of damage that armies could inflict. Although General Benjamin McCulloch, who would fight and die at Pea Ridge in March 1862, declared that "as for Arkansas, every man who is a patriot and sound southern man will be the first to put the torch to his own grain or mill rather than have them left to aid the enemy," events in Fayetteville suggest that some were not nearly as willing as McCulloch suggested. When the Confederates evacuated Fayetteville, they were leaving it open to Union troops to capture, and they meant to leave nothing of significant value for them to exploit. Before they departed, the Confederates burned the flour mill, which was the "only steam mill in that part of the country." Its owners had implored the commander to allow them to "remove the machinery sufficient to insure it against use as a mill" but to no avail.[18] The burning of such structures was devastating, as they served a number of purposes beyond what their name alone suggests. Michael A. Hughes explains that they "did more than just grind the corn, wheat, and rye of homes, farms, and distilleries. Area mills not only sawed timber but ran planes and lathes which converted wood into furniture and farm implements." The mills of northwestern Arkansas also "carded wool, ginned cotton, and wove cloth for the two states [Arkansas and Missouri] and the Indian Territory."[19] While the loss endured by the owners of Fayetteville's flour mill was severe, the disruption to agriculture in the countryside became so serious that people could no longer grow grain to bring to a mill, even if one had remained standing.

In part to address the very real possibility of civilian starvation, Colonel Marcus LaRue Harrison, a native of northwestern Arkansas and a Union officer, concocted a plan to create post colonies in northwestern Arkansas in the fall of 1864. As historian Rebecca Howard points out, they were also called "military farm colonies," and were intended not only to provide safety for civilians in the path of guerrilla warfare but also to enable them to grow crops to feed themselves.[20] Initially, Harrison had been equally inspired by the idea that by gathering Unionist families together in colonies, he could "create an information and security network of loyal unionists," but the safety of the colonies attracted the families of Confederates as well. Clearly, the situation had become desperate in Washington County.

Col. Marcus LaRue Harrison established a series of military farm colonies in northwestern Arkansas to allow Unionist farmers to grow crops while resisting guerrillas terrorizing the region. Courtesy of the Shiloh Museum of Ozark History/Washington County Historical Society Collection (P-1628).

The planters in Chicot County did not face quite the dire circumstances endured by the people of northwestern Arkansas, but they suffered severe reversals. Their first significant challenge arose because of Confederate policies. Just a year after the war began, the Confederate command ordered the army to put to the torch all cotton within reach of the Mississippi River. The order was given in late April 1862 after most of the previous year's crop had been marketed—if planters had been able to transport it past the Union blockade—and what remained was stockpiled and stood to bring great profits to planters the next year when prices rose dramatically.

Practicing what has come to be called "cotton diplomacy," Confederate officials were attempting to create a shortage of cotton in an effort to convince the British to recognize the Confederacy as a separate nation. In the years immediately preceding the war, however, the British had watched events transpiring in the United States with growing concern and had built up a surplus in their warehouses, hoping to prevent a disaster in their own economy should war interfere. Not all planters embraced the Confederacy's program of burning cotton in the early years, but many planters accepted the rationale. They did not know that the war would last four years and that, during that time, England would develop a thriving cotton production system in its colony of India. This would have severe long-term consequences for the cotton economy of the American South, but in 1862 planters were too preoccupied with the business at hand to foresee the transformation of the global cotton economy that was taking shape.[21]

Arkansas planters felt the full meaning of the Confederate government's cotton diplomacy in late April 1862. On April 29, just six weeks before Memphis, Tennessee, was captured by the Federals, Captain O. P. Lyles of the Sixth Battalion Arkansas Cavalry (CSA) left the city with enough men and officers to accomplish the orders he had been given: "burn and destroy all cotton within reach of the Mississippi River." Traveling on four steamships, they scoured the riverbanks ten miles inland on either side, looking for stockpiled cotton. He reached Lake Providence, just a few miles south of Chicot County, Arkansas, where he "was reliably informed that all the cotton between there and Vicksburg had already been destroyed by provost-marshals appointed for that purpose." He claimed that it had been "wholly unnecessary to use force." Although "there were but few planters or persons willing to apply the torch themselves to their own cotton," some were willing enough to have Lyles's men do it for them.[22] Lyles was likely exaggerating the willingness of planters to so mildly concede, as the price of cotton was rising dramatically as the Union blockade of the coast became more effective and the Confederacy's policy of creating a shortage began to have an effect, though not the one the Confederate commanders had in mind when they began ordering the destruction of cotton. The British remained unaffiliated, though they were sympathetic

Confederate authorities ordered Arkansas troops to "burn and destroy all cotton within reach of the Mississippi River" in late April 1862. Courtesy of the historical image collection by Bildagentur-online/Alamy.

to the South, but those able to produce and market cotton were enjoying a new bonanza. Prices rose from as little as 10 cents a pound early in the war to $1.89 per pound by 1863. Lyles claimed that his men had destroyed 13,612 bales, which at 400 pounds per bale would have equaled 5,444,800 pounds. At $1.89 per pound, that would have amounted to a fortune: $10,290,672 in 1862 or, correcting for inflation, $245,016,000 in 2015 dollars.[23]

Federal forces also burned cotton, but planters in Chicot County and elsewhere along the Mississippi River faced military actions that disrupted operations even further. A major objective of Union strategy was to secure the Mississippi for the Union and to isolate the segment of the Confederacy lying west of it. By late 1862, they had all but accomplished that task except for the capture of Vicksburg, Mississippi. That city, located on a bluff with a commanding view of the river and firmly in Confederate hands, had almost impregnable defenses and stymied every Union effort to capture it. Chicot County served as one of the important staging grounds in the campaign against the Confederates at Vicksburg, but guerrilla activities there served as a serious obstacle to Union objectives. A series of treacherous "bends, bars, and snags in the river" at the Greenville Bends in southern Chicot County required river traffic to slow considerably, making it more vulnerable to sniping from the many Confederate guerrillas who could conceal themselves in the dense swamps and forests alongside the river. When the last offensive against the city of Vicksburg was under way, Union officials "ordered the levees to be cut which flooded the fields," intending to eliminate the guerrilla threat at the Greenville Bends, but the destruction was devastating to Chicot County planters.[24]

The capture of Vicksburg secured the Union's hold over the Mississippi River, and planters hoping to produce a crop learned to make peace with that. With Confederate authorities too distant to prevent trade with the enemy, planters marketed their cotton in the best way open to them. General Edmund Kirby Smith (CSA) complained that he found it nearly impossible to enforce a Confederate government order to prevent cotton and other agricultural products from being sold to Union quartermasters. According to historian Thomas DeBlack, Lycurgus Johnson, a prosperous plantation owner and avowed Confederate supporter, exchanged 12,000 pounds of cotton through the Federals in March 1864.[25] He was not the only one. Historian Daniel Sutherland suggests that planters in Arkansas and elsewhere were willing to engage in trade with the Union because they had grown weary of Confederate policies that included the destruction of supplies, including cotton, that might fall into the hands of the enemy. Some went so far as to disavow the Confederacy entirely, but most, like Johnson, at least professed loyalty to the South while engaging in activities that might suggest otherwise.[26]

While planters might be willing to trade with the enemy, they engaged in a fierce struggle to keep their slaves out of Union hands. Slaves keenly understood that a victory by the North would translate into freedom, something many of them intended to embrace without hesitation. Planters, however, were at least as aware of the very real possibility of losing not only their labor but also losing their own investment in human property. Early in the war, planters east of the Mississippi River—from as far away as Virginia—began moving their slaves to Arkansas to prevent their escape. By mid-1862, however, planters along the Mississippi River, such as Elijah Worthington of Chicot County, transported their slaves to Texas where they owned or leased land.[27] Others attempted to conceal their slaves in nearby swamps and forests until the immediate danger passed. Slaves were often intimately familiar with these marginal spaces on the edges of plantations, but these spaces had a different meaning to them. Before the war, it was in these peripheral areas where slaves enjoyed a measure of relief from the oversight of their masters, but it was also where they

Though slave owners desperately tried to hold on to their slaves by moving them to Texas or hiding them in swamps and forests when Federal troops were near, thousands fled and sought freedom within Union lines, such as the men, women, and children at this refugee camp at Helena. Courtesy of the Nebraska State Historical Society.

hunted, fished, and gathered in order to diversify their diets. In some cases, they were able to sell those and other forest products to accumulate cash to purchase other small necessities. The forced movement to the margins probably presented no great hardship to slaves, but most slaves understood the significance of the removal and resented the implications. According to historian Kelly Houston Jones, who recounts the experience of slave Solomon Lambert, "slaves who complied with their concealment did so out of fear" of their master's wrath, but others reported the location of concealed slaves to Union officials.[28]

Whether they escaped from their masters' attempts to conceal them or left the plantations of their own volition, slaves typically headed for Union lines to embrace liberty when that army drew near. This occurred wherever the Union army appeared and was devastating to plantation operations. It was likely the most serious blow that cotton growers faced during and after the war. The labor shortage introduced by the departure of slaves greatly reduced the amount of cotton that could be grown and harvested. At the same time, the appearance of self-freed slaves at army encampments presented Union officials with a quandary. The necessity to provide for them often overwhelmed available supplies, and able-bodied self-freed men were soon building fortifications or performing other services. The numbers of slaves reaching the safety of Union lines, however, quickly outran the ability of the army to handle them.

The problem became acute in Helena, for example, which Union troops captured in 1862. From the moment Union troops took possession, self-freed men, women, and children flocked to Helena, and Union officers grappled with how to provide for them. In 1863 President Lincoln called for leasing plantations to loyal men—usually northerners—and procedures were developed to implement the president's plan and place freedmen to work on "abandoned" plantations. As historian Carl Moneyhon suggests, records are not sufficient to establish the number of freedmen employed on leased plantations in Arkansas, but at least 3,561 were at work on plantations in the summer of 1864. This was meant to be an experiment in free labor, but in fact there was far too little oversight by the army. Even on plantations leased by northerners with free labor sentiments, insufficient observation prevailed, a crucial omission, as northerners—who were unfamiliar with cotton cultivation—often hired experienced overseers who employed traditional gang labor (something that was too great a reminder of slavery to many freedmen) and were unafraid of using the customary means of coercion. Regardless of the organizational structure or methods they used, the lessees were rarely interfered with.[29]

Freedmen work the fields in a leased plantation near Helena. Courtesy of the Nebraska State Historical Society.

However much their freedom was circumscribed, freed people's self-emancipation severely interrupted plantation operations, and it turned out to be permanent. Even as late as 1864, many southerners held out hopes that if they could not win the war, they could negotiate a settlement that would leave their slaves in their hands or have their slaves returned to them if they had already departed. No such negotiated settlement took place, and as Beckert's work suggests, there were powerful players in the cotton empire who worked against the desire of freedmen for economic independence. New York financiers who played a crucial role in the financing of the cotton crop wielded greater influence than the four million freed people could muster. Once the war ended and as the old radical Republicans in Congress died off or became absorbed in other concerns, freed people had little representation at the national level. The failure of the federal government to confiscate and redistribute the plantations of disloyal southerners was never very likely given the desire for the restoration of the cotton plantation system. The end result of the survival of the plantation economy in the South, including in Arkansas, was disastrous for the freed people.[30]

There was a moment during Reconstruction when a different outcome seemed imaginable. President Andrew Johnson's mild Reconstruction had returned the former Confederates to power, and their treatment of freed people was one of the reasons the Republicans in Congress seized control of the Reconstruction process in 1867. By that time, the possibility of confiscation and redistribution of plantation lands was no longer on the table, but the political participation of newly freed men was a prime objective of Republican efforts. After all, they understood that only by enfranchising African American men would they have any hope of establishing a viable Republican Party in the South. The white Republicans in Arkansas, made up mostly of newcomers to the state, spoke to African American political rights, but only some of them were fully committed to it, particularly when it became clear that true freedom of movement for African Americans undermined plantation agriculture.

Meanwhile, the Republicans pursued a new relationship between the state government and its people, a radical concept for its time. They raised taxes, heavily promoted railroad development, created a statewide educational system meant to reach all children, and founded a state university which, under the Morrill Land Grant Act, was intended to bring scientific ideas to agriculture. Although many former Confederates and Democrats participated in the frenzy of railroad building after the war, some were hostile to the creation of a university, few were enthusiastic about education for the masses, and none welcomed the taxes imposed to fund such improvements. In fact, the vision of the Reconstructors was blurred by conflicts within their own ranks and ultimately undermined by the determined opposition of the former Confederates.[31]

The return of former Confederates to power in 1874 was the harbinger of disaster for African American freed people. Once the Democrats seized power, they took steps to fashion a "smaller" state government, but they created problems that challenged their own interests. The 1874 constitution, in part as a response to the power wielded by Reconstruction governor Powell Clayton, limited the authority of the governor by placing power in the hands of county judges and local authorities. But this worked against the Redeemers in black-majority counties where local officials struggled with an unprecedented challenge from newly enfranchised African Americans. The 1874 constitution also limited the taxing and spending power of the state government in a manner that made it difficult to underwrite economic development and to fund a school system that might have produced a better-educated population capable of greater productive capacity.

Though Redeemers invested in certain infrastructure enterprises when it served their purposes—such as the expansion of the railroad system and the construction of levees—they had less success, and perhaps less interest in, developing an adequate manufacturing sector. Meanwhile, Redeemer legislatures supported lien laws that worked to the advantage of planters in the plantation areas; in the hill counties, they gave merchants greater power to foreclose on small farmers trying to recover from the calamity caused by the war. Although most mountain farmers were only nominally connected to the market in the antebellum era, they needed to produce cash crops in order to rebuild their farms, fences, barns, and homes once the war was over. Because the economy in the late nineteenth century endured two long recessions that hit farmers particularly hard, they found themselves competing in the marketplace at the worst possible time.

The 1874 constitution provided former Confederates with everything they thought they wanted, but conflict in black-majority counties presented an unexpected challenge. The former Confederates were determined to subjugate the freed people and understood what their enfranchisement would mean to them politically. However, the hostility of whites and their willingness to carry those sentiments into action complicated the effective functioning of plantation agriculture. Even after the national Republican Party—and many in the state Republican Party—had forsaken the cause of African American political and economic liberty, blacks pursued their own version of the meaning of emancipation: they wanted full citizenship and the right to assume control over their economic futures. With power vested at the local level after the 1874 constitution, they were able to do so in counties with large black populations well into the 1880s. In response, white Democrats frequently resorted to violence. Although quashing black political participation was crucial to controlling their economic behavior, using violence to accomplish that task sometimes resulted in the opposite of what planters desired. With plantation lands expanding rapidly in the late nineteenth century, the need for labor was greater than ever, and only substantial black migration from southern states east of the Mississippi filled the need.

In a provocative essay analyzing the movement of freed people to Arkansas after the Civil War, historian Story Matkin-Rawn challenges the assumptions of other historians who have underestimated the extent of African American migration in the late nineteenth century while ignoring entirely their migration to Arkansas. Citing Bureau of the Census figures, Matkin-Rawn points out that "between the end of the Civil War and World War I, Arkansas attracted more African-American migrants than any other state, well over 200,000."[32] African Americans chose Arkansas over other destinations in part because of energetic labor agents eager to satisfy the needs of planters. As Matkin-Rawn asserts, even an agent of the Freedmen's Bureau in Georgia urged the freed people there to forsake that state's low wages for the promise of better opportunities in Arkansas. Land was plentiful and cheap in Arkansas, and a surprisingly large percentage of African Americans were able to secure landownership, at least for a time.[33] Not every African American who migrated to Arkansas was so lucky. Some purchased a ticket to paradise only to land in a situation similar to the one they had left in Georgia or elsewhere: working on a plantation for men who were determined to maintain what Douglas Blackmon has called "slavery by another name." Nevertheless, whether land owner or landless laborer, they contributed to the ability of blacks in some locales to secure election to political office. In Crittenden County, for example, the African American population increased from 2,575 in 1870 (67%) to 11,890 in 1890 (85%), and blacks continued to vote well into the 1880s. African American elected officials served in important elective positions until they were forcibly removed by extra-legal means from their offices in 1888.[34]

The creation of a labor system approximating that of slavery preoccupied planters but occurred unevenly and was ultimately incomplete. Although it is not inaccurate to refer to sharecropping as another kind of slavery, it was not the same thing. Although Congress would turn its back on African American political and economic freedoms in the 1870s, the Thirteenth Amendment made it impossible for planters to ignore that the peculiar institution no longer had legal sanction. African Americans would not let them forget that fact even when others chose to turn away. However, by the late 1860s and early 1870s, the sharecropping system emerged as a compromise between planters who held the land and freedmen who had little but their labor to offer in the marketplace. Attempts to forge a wage-labor system, which dated back to the Civil War when the army leased abandoned plantations to "loyal" planters and northern men who came south with profit in mind, foundered on the severe lack of available cash to pay wages in the post-war period. But the planters' possession of the land gave them a distinct advantage. The federal government's unwillingness to confiscate the plantations of former Confederates and redistribute the acreage to freedmen left the latter at a tragic disadvantage in the economic system emerging in the post-war period.[35]

Between 1868 and 1893 the state legislature passed a series of laws that established an onerous burden on sharecroppers and, taken together, tied them almost irrevocably to the planters for whom they worked and to the cotton empire. The state gave sanction to the crop lien in 1868, which allowed planters to require that sharecroppers sign legal documents pledging to grow cotton; in 1883, the state revised mortgage laws so that failure to pay debts could be prosecuted as a criminal offense; and in 1885, the state established that, if a sharecropper took an advance from a planter, his crop was subject to forfeiture to the planter. In 1893, the final nail in the coffin was two acts of the legislature that prohibited "tenants and sharecroppers from disposing of personal property they had mortgaged to their landlords." The cycle of debt the sharecropper endured was further cemented when planters began to open "commissaries" and required their sharecroppers to purchase supplies there at exorbitant interest rates. Typically the sharecroppers had already signed crop liens pledging to grow cotton. Thus the commissary system and the crop lien, accurately viewed by historians as means of compelling the freedmen's labor, were necessary to the functioning of the cotton economy.[36]

Workers in the sharecropping system were often mired in a cycle of debt to planters who controlled almost every aspect of their financial lives. Courtesy of the Delta Cultural Center.

However much the workings of the cotton empire favored the planter over the sharecropper, they also had the effect of ensnaring the planter in his own trap. A key feature of the system was the financing of the crop. As historian Harold Woodman has noted, cotton factors in southern cities played a crucial role in financing the cotton crop prior to the Civil War and largely regained that position in the postwar years. They served as the middlemen between planters and the cotton textile industry and, essentially, marketed the crop for the planter. They also provided a number of other services. For example, they typically operated as a kind of banker, using funds in a given planter's account to pay for goods that could not be found in the countryside given the absence of a furnishing merchant system. The cotton factor also advanced sums in the form of crop loans to planters and compelled them to sign contracts that required them to grow cotton and market it through them. This pernicious financing arrangement enmeshed all parties—factor, planter, and sharecropper in the production of cotton and created a rigidity that defied free-market ideology. None of the parties involved could seriously consider moving into another crop or another enterprise altogether.[37]

An early Reconstruction struggle between planters and merchants largely explains the emergence of plantation commissaries. The state legislature gave sanction to the crop lien in 1868, thus binding black laborers to the planters/landowners for whom they worked, but soon the planters were engaged in a financial and legal battle with merchants. The struggle between the two arose even as the new labor system—sharecropping—was taking shape. Sharecroppers were signing crop liens with planters, but they were also securing credit accounts with local merchants. Legal battles began to surface over which creditor was to be paid first when the crop was harvested. Legislators representing plantation owners were able to secure passage of a law in 1875 establishing the primacy of the planters' lien.[38] Planters had already begun to open commissaries as one way around the legal dispute, but they would find that running a mercantile establishment had its own perils. As historian C. Vann Woodward observed, they became entangled in yet another web of debt, this time with wholesale suppliers of the goods they sold to their sharecroppers. "The prices and interest rates were exorbitant, but so were the risks the merchant took. Nor did he pocket the take of his till. He in turn paid outrageous interest to factors, which paid their tributes to the ultimate lords of credit. The merchant was only a bucket on an endless chain by which the agricultural well of a tributary region was drained of its flow." Whether planter or merchant or combination thereof, they were merely a part of a larger web of debt, playing a crucial but relatively minor role in global capitalism. In this context, the cotton planters and Woodward's "lords of credit" to whom they were obligated might be better understood as in service to the empire of cotton, the basis upon which the capitalist system was built in the nineteenth century.[39]

Because of the importance of the agricultural sector in states such as Arkansas, the system also had the effect of undermining alternative economic undertakings even outside the plantation districts, which, as Beckford indicates, experienced underdevelopment. In Arkansas and the rest of the South, planters wielded sufficient statewide political influence to shape policy-making through their association with state legislators and governors. The only appreciable manufacturing sector developing in the late nineteenth century often worked to the advantage of planters. The state's wealth of forests, which had first appeared as a hindrance to farmers and planters alike, began to attract the attention of northern investors who typically practiced a "cut and run" business model. It was extractive industry at its worst, as a wealth of forest reserves was exploited and the only manufacturing that developed involved sawmilling. The milled lumber was transported to North Carolina or northward, where it underwrote the manufacturing economies in those locations. Although a few homegrown lumber barons arose in Arkansas, most hailed from the North, and they did not fulfill Henry Grady's dreams of creating a New South by using northern capital to fund industrial development. Instead of investing in southern

The delta region's abundant forests, boasting mammoth trees like this one (left) near Elaine, Arkansas, were exploited by lumber barons who would cut the trees, mill them at places like the Howe Lumber Company at Wabash (below), and transport the lumber out of state. Courtesy of the Delta Cultural Center.

manufacturing in a meaningful way, the northern lumber barons exported the profits back to their own regions.[40] They cut trees in the areas they purchased or leased, paid low wages to workers who cut the timber or manned the sawmills, and then moved on when they had exhausted the supply, leaving behind tracts of cut-over land that appealed only to the most far-sighted of individuals. They might temporarily build up a community or create a sawmill town, but it was what came next that decided whether the town lived or died. That "next" something was always plantation agriculture, particularly if the investors were timbering in the Arkansas delta, which held some of the richest land remaining in America at the time.[41]

Even though planters continued to exercise considerable influence in the state legislature, they had to make way for new players, including representatives from farming interests in other areas of the state and, particularly, as Moneyhon stresses, an "entrepreneurial class of bankers, brokers, and retailers in Little Rock."[42] As the lien law passed in 1875 suggests, the planters retained the advantage. Even when planters grew more and more restive as crop prices declined steadily in the late nineteenth century, their devotion to the Democratic Party remained steady, and this linked them inextricably to their economic competitors in Little Rock. Woodward has pointed out that the union of planter and merchant interests into the commissary system on plantations served as one link across the divide of the struggle over the primacy of the landlord lien, but nothing did more to unite Democrats in Arkansas than the emergence of a farmers' organization that launched a third-party movement challenging Democratic control.[43]

A broad spectrum of farmers across the state supported the various farmers' organizations that formed in the 1870s and 1880s. A look at the situations in Chicot County and Washington County in this period sheds light on the problems confronting planters and farmers in the two regions. Washington County had undergone tremendous change in the years since the Civil War, some of which worked to the advantage of agricultural producers. The penetration of railroads into the region in the 1880s gave producers better access to the market, and cooperation with the land grant university established in 1872 in Fayetteville provided them ready access to expert advice. By the end of the century, the county became known for the high-quality apples produced in its many orchards. Wheat and corn production increased to 417,100 and 1,899,550 bushels, respectively. As a result of this intensification of farming activity, the acres devoted to farming increased from 130,874 to 489,711 in 1900. The total value of farm property rose from $2,818,871 to $6,317,410. These are impressive figures, but they were accompanied by some unfortunate ramifications. Not only did the railroad bring better access to the market, it also provided Washington County citizens with the opportunity to purchase items they had previously either done without or made for themselves. This new reliance on store-bought merchandise increased the costs of running a household and, ultimately, operating a farm. Farmers were purchasing more and better equipment as they modernized and, likely because of access to the state's agricultural college, they were the first in the state to experiment more widely with the use of fertilizers.

Perhaps one of the most important difficulties involved farm indebtedness. Before the Civil War, the county's farmers had produced some crops for the market, but most of them had only a peripheral connection to it. Given the destruction that took place during the war, they borrowed money to rebuild their homes, farms, and out-buildings and became more fully engaged in the market in order to secure the cash to pay their creditors. After the panic of 1873, which turned into a long period of decline with only brief moments of recovery, many farmers found it impossible to meet their obligations and lost their farms as a result. Farm tenancy went from a negligible amount in 1860 to 23 percent in 1900. To add insult to injury, the legislature modified the state's mortgage laws to the disadvantage of both tenants and small farm owners. As Moneyhon puts it, "New legislation made a mortgagee's failure to carry out a contract a criminal offense and the basis for forfeiting all property."[44]

Although only 300 miles separated Washington County from Chicot County in southeastern Arkansas, the differences between them had never been more glaring. The tenancy rate was 78.1% in 1900, three times what it was in Washington County. The attachment of Chicot County planters to the empire of cotton had made many of them wealthy in the early years and continued to enrich a new generation, but declining soil fertility combined with the reluctance to embrace fertilizers reduced the bales per acre they could harvest considerably. Counties along the Mississippi River also faced problems that mountain counties did not have to endure. Even in the best of times, the river could deliver unwelcome gifts in the form of floods that could rupture levees and flood farmlands. The existence of impenetrable swamps in the lowlands of the county rendered the area a dangerous malarial zone and limited the amount of land that could be easily turned to cultivation.

In the post-war period, adjusting to the realities of free labor was complicated by the emergence of a powerful political challenge mounted by the son of a plantation owner in Chicot County. Little is known about James Mason's mother, a slave woman whose name has been lost to history, but his father was Elijah Worthington. Mason had secured election to the state legislature and later served as the county judge, but even his death in 1874 and the end of Reconstruction did not extinguish black activism in Chicot County.

The fate that befell one of the four plantations owned by Elijah Worthington, the largest planter in Arkansas in 1860, demonstrates the difficulties planters faced in rebuilding after the war. His 3,000-acre Sunnyside plantation was the jewel of his four plantations, and in 1860 it produced 1,700 bales of cotton worth approximately $68,000 at the going rate of 10 cents per pound. Together with the cotton harvested on his three other plantations, he was producing nearly 10 percent of the 40,000 bales of cotton grown in Chicot County. The war brought disaster to him, one from which he would never recover. He took a number of his slaves to Texas, where he ran a plantation during the war, but he returned to Chicot County in 1865 in ill health and a "virtual invalid" to find that his land had been classified as "abandoned" and in the hands of the Freedmen's Bureau. Much of it had been traversed by armies or flooded out by breaks in the levees, and some of it had gone uncultivated for years and become overgrown with weeds. He secured the return of his land but almost immediately sold Sunnyside in an effort to recover his losses. The price of cotton briefly rose sharply but then plummeted; it rarely provided a sufficient return on investment during the late nineteenth century. Sunnyside passed through several hands—including those of the nephew of the seventh vice president of the United States, John C. Calhoun—until finally coming into the possession of New York financier Austin Corbin in 1886.

Corbin would discover that, for himself and other planters in Chicot County, securing sufficient labor would present daunting challenges. He employed the sharecropping system, but keeping labor in place proved difficult. Chafing under the burden of the crop lien and debts to the commissary, many African Americans departed for Kansas or Liberia. In 1895, Corbin resorted to importing Italian labor, but he left it to local managers to run the plantation, and the Italians proved no more willing to accept their overbearing supervision than did African Americans. The experiment failed and many of those immigrants left the swampy, disease-ridden delta for northwestern Arkansas, landing in Washington County in 1897. The departure of the Italian immigrants signaled the attractions of the northwestern Arkansas region but also the disadvantages they faced working as landless laborers within a plantation complex. The 1883 law that made it a criminal offense to default on a debt worked against the interests of small landowners and white tenants in the mountains, but it fell more heavily on African Americans, especially after the imposition of disfranchisement and segregation statutes.

Some white and African American farmers were sufficiently frustrated by the mid-1880s to move a step toward recognizing their common interests. Founded in Prairie County in 1882, the Agricultural Wheel was initially an all-white organization that focused on economic solutions and attempted to influence the Democratic Party to address their concerns: the differential rates charged in southern states to transport goods to market by railroad; generous land grants to railroad speculators and the tendency of those speculators, whether the railroad was built or not, to hold on to those lands; the need for more equitable means of financing the crop; and, ultimately, the demand for a cooperative marketing system that would empower producers to demand a higher price for their crops. All of these concerns challenged the economic links forged by the global cotton economy: infrastructure improvements to move crops to market, the financial structure designed to facilitate the movement of profits ever upward on the chain, and a marketing system that served the purposes of the cotton empire. Even the national depressions that persisted, almost without interruption, for the last three decades of the nineteenth century were manifestations of the global economy.[45]

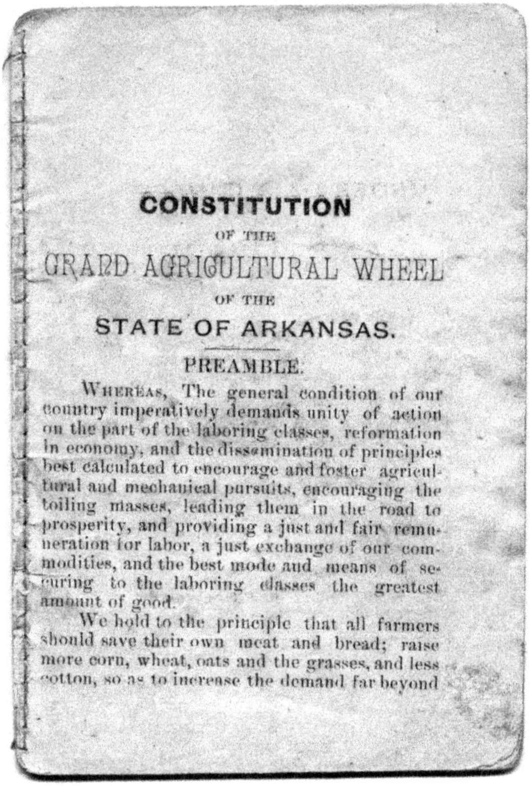

CONSTITUTION

OF THE

GRAND AGRICULTURAL WHEEL

OF THE

STATE OF ARKANSAS.

PREAMBLE.

WHEREAS, The general condition of our country imperatively demands unity of action on the part of the laboring classes, reformation in economy, and the dissemination of principles best calculated to encourage and foster agricultural and mechanical pursuits, encouraging the toiling masses, leading them in the road to prosperity, and providing a just and fair remuneration for labor, a just exchange of our commodities, and the best mode and means of securing to the laboring classes the greatest amount of good.

We hold to the principle that all farmers should save their own meat and bread; raise more corn, wheat, oats and the grasses, and less cotton, so as to increase the demand far beyond

The Agricultural Wheel was formed in 1882 in Prairie County to represent interests of Arkansas farmers and to try to influence government policy in their favor. Courtesy of the Museum of American History, Cabot Public Schools.

Made up principally of white small and middling farmers, the Wheel eventually included an allied but separate black organization. The Wheel demanded a state government willing to represent its interests, thus it was asking for a more activist state, something repudiated by the 1874 constitution. When Democrats failed to address these demands, the Wheelers formed an uneasy alliance with the Union Labor Party and nearly won the 1888 election. They lost through fraud, violence, and intimidation perpetrated by Democratic supporters, but the alliance with the Union Labor Party undermined the Agricultural Wheel from within. Some prominent Wheelers burned their membership cards after the state convention in response to association with the Union Labor Party, particularly when opponents alleged a connection between the Wheel and the Republican Party, a connection made more plausible by the Republican Party's decision to support the Wheel candidate rather than mount its own gubernatorial candidate.[46]

Although the Arkansas Democratic Party prevailed over the Wheelers in 1888, it could not rest easy until it took steps to eliminate the threat of the disgruntled farmers in a formal way. Democrats focused their efforts on African American voters and devised an effective strategy for separating them from the franchise. Other southern states were following a similar process, reflecting the fact that African Americans all over the South had shown themselves remarkably resilient in the face of the determination of white Democrats to either minimize or control their voting behavior. The process of disfranchisement was remarkably similar across the South although it took slightly different forms and occurred unevenly. It began in Mississippi in 1889 and reached Arkansas in 1891 when the Arkansas legislature passed a bill that effectively eliminated illiterates from voting. The act instituted the "Australian" or secret ballot and disallowed the use of pre-marked ballots, something illiterate voters of both races had relied upon previously. Upon implementation of the act, illiterates were required to have an election official mark their ballot for them, a process that was both humiliating and risky. Few African American voters by this point would have trusted a white Democrat to carry out that duty honestly, and although a member of the opposing party (presumably Republican) was supposed to be present at each polling place, this requirement was rarely observed. The next year, the legislature passed a poll tax measure that further limited the ability of African American—and poor white—voters to exercise the ballot. The third and final practice that eliminated African Americans specifically from the political process was the implementation of the White Primary in 1906. Although it was not an act of the legislature but a ruling of the Democratic Party, it served the purpose of excluding African Americans from voting in the only election that counted: the primary election in which a white Democrat representing the interests of whites would be selected to run against the Republican Party in the fall election. By the early twentieth century, no Republican stood a chance of securing election to local, state, or national office in Arkansas or any other southern state.[47]

At the same time that Arkansas and other southern states were passing disfranchisement measures, they were also implementing segregation statutes that sought to prevent African Americans from having access to public facilities enjoyed without restriction by whites. Arkansas's segregation statute—a separate coach law—dates to 1891 and was intended to inhibit black agency. Although African Americans continued to resist the power of state and local officials whenever and wherever they could, the legislation served the purposes of the plantation system because it theoretically rendered African Americans unable to exercise either political or economic freedom. In creating a permanent underclass of poorly paid workers, it fulfilled George Beckford's criteria of the plantation economy. It was accomplished by using the power of the state to support the production of a commodity crop for a world market, and it guaranteed underdevelopment within plantation areas by creating structural barriers to advancement.

In using racist rhetoric to justify and implement these measures, however, it also created an even more volatile and hostile reaction against African Americans by whites. The lynching of African

Americans reached epic levels in the 1890s and, together with the inexorable poverty that prevailed in the plantation areas, led to the Great Migration of African Americans from the South—and Arkansas—to the North. This was hardly the outcome southern planters wanted or expected. Although planters hoped to accomplish through disfranchisement and segregation what decades of struggle against a resistant black population had failed to do, they were to discover that their measures only drove black labor away. Those who remained there during the Jim Crow era were far less quiescent than early historians realized, but they organized through their churches and fraternal organizations. They developed a set of political skills that would serve them well in the post–World War II era civil rights movement, a movement forged in southern cities by refugees from the revolution taking place in the no-longer-quite-so-cotton-dominated countryside.[48]

In the antebellum era, Arkansas planters became entangled in a global cotton economy over which they had little meaningful influence. The plantation system was the means they used to fulfill their part in the cotton empire, and it facilitated the production of cotton even as it consigned the region to underdevelopment and poverty. Planters, however, had maneuvered themselves into the deadly embrace of an empire that would modernize in the second half of the twentieth century and turn to other suitors. After the British Empire crumbled in the wake of nationalist movements in its colonies in the post–World War II era, the center of cotton manufacturing began to shift. At the same time, because of the rise of scientific agriculture in Arkansas and elsewhere in the American South, planters there turned to other crops and eventually transformed into agri-businessmen more familiar with corporate boardrooms than rural landscapes. Meanwhile the British merchants gave way to a new group of entrepreneurs. As Sven Beckert puts it, "The empire of cotton saw the emergence of a new breed of merchant…immense corporations that source their branded goods globally to sell them to consumers worldwide." A different infrastructure exists to support the marketing of Arkansas's current agricultural products—soybeans, rice, chickens—but it is not the old alternative practiced by antebellum era northwestern Arkansas farmers. Rather, it is the model that the cotton empire forged of globally connected players assuming the role assigned to them by the new masters of worldwide capitalist agriculture.

Chapter 5—Women after the War: Profiles of Change and Continuity

By Kelly Houston Jones

Women across the state must have breathed a sigh of relief when the Civil War ended. White, black, young, old, poor, wealthy, slave, free, Union, and Confederate, they had spent years navigating the conflict, weighing their options, and often stepping into empowering yet dangerous roles. They had also spent years saying goodbye—often forever—to the men in their lives. Women who had supported the Union may have felt satisfaction and relief that their bet paid off. Women who backed the Confederacy, though they may have lamented its failure, surely welcomed the end of the devastation that had arrived early in wartime Arkansas. Women's lives in Arkansas changed a great deal in the decades following the war as populations grew, modes of transportation and communication improved, and women took on a more public role in society. In terms of race and class, however, much remained the same.[1]

Slavery had been the underlying cause of the war, and it served as a foundation of the Confederacy.[2] Women from both sides of that institution—women masters and women slaves—built new lives when the Civil War ended the system that had long ordered their labor and society. Nearly 55,000 African American women and girls had been held under slavery in Arkansas in 1860.[3] Their freedom from bondage constituted the most significant transformation wrought by the Civil War upon the history of women in Arkansas. Freedom opened new opportunities to women who had been held as chattel and required women of the slaveholding class to reorder their lifestyle on free labor. Arkansas's daughters would be neither bondswomen nor mistresses.

Sources related to the white and black Bullocks of southern Arkansas reveal the complicated legacy left by slavery among women who had been masters and slaves. Eliza, former nurse to Harriet Bailey Bullock Daniel, wrote from Witherspoon, Arkansas, to her former young mistress in North Carolina on March 19, 1917. Their correspondence shows that a power differential continued to frame interaction between the women. Eliza began her first letter with an affectionate "My Dear Miss Harriet" followed by several lines catching up, explaining where she lives and saying that she is doing well. Then Eliza got to the point of her letter, asking, "Miss Harriet I wish you would please tell me my age." Enslaved people had been prohibited from learning to read or write, meaning that if any records of slaves' births and deaths were recorded, whites kept them. Eliza no longer knew anyone who remembered when she was born, and she probably hoped that by getting in touch with the white Bullocks, she might get access to information they may have kept. Eliza explained that only three of the former slaves were still living that she knew of, and that she had written to Harriet's sister first but learned later that she had passed away. Although Eliza was older than Harriet, she saw Harriet as her link to information. Eliza speculated about her age: "I will be so glad to hear from you. I feel young & am very little gray & everybody says I look young & I sure take the very best care of myself now. I wish you would please write to me." Clearly, Eliza was eager to hear an estimate of her age. She signed the letter with deference: "Your Old Slave Gal, Eliza."[4]

According to her next letter, Eliza received a response from Harriet that displayed more nostalgia for the old days than it provided information applicable to Eliza's question. It seems that either Harriet did not provide a guess at Eliza's age, or at least not a satisfactory one, because Eliza got to the point more quickly in her following letter, writing,

> Yours 25th rec'd & I sure was glad to hear from you & to know you are well & so pleasantly situated and where you say ["]I just cried["] I had to stop and have a cry too & in reading a letter from you makes me feel just like I was in our old home. Silla was older than Line & I came next to Line now about how old would that make me?[5]

The rest of the letter provided more information about the fates of former Bullock slaves, and Eliza reminisced about such moments from the past as Harriet's antics as a child and the death of a beloved pet. And although Eliza claimed that connecting with the former young mistress after all those years was as emotional for her as it was for Harriet, she clearly did not write simply to relive old times. It bothered her that she still did not know her age. Freedom had not changed everything.[6]

White women felt the blow of losing their domestic labor force more acutely in their everyday observations than they did the absence of the field laborers who had created the wealth that supported their lifestyles. White women, some of whom had enjoyed the uncompensated labor of black women for generations, reacted with sincere surprise when their cooks and maids fled during the war. They were dismayed to have to adjust to either paying for that work or doing it themselves. It is true that many African American women stayed on at places where they had been slaves and continued to work in that same type of domestic labor as freedwomen, but white women remained frustrated that they no longer had an *imprisoned* staff on the place. White slaveholding women reluctantly let go of slavery even if they had affection for bondswomen. Becky Franks of Drew County, for example, cried when she had to recognize the freedom of Addie Haynes, but she sent Addie and her children with some dried meat when they departed anyway.[7]

Harriet Bailey Bullock had gone away to school by the time the slaves had left her family's Dallas County plantation. When she returned, however, she experienced firsthand the frustrations of coping with the new responsibility of household chores. She remembered decades later:

> Cooking, washing, housecleaning and attending to the milk were not easy for us girls. Sister Nannie bought a washing machine, but after her first attempt at laundry she stayed in bed a week. Being unaccustomed to hard work, we did not know how to go about it. This made us irritable and fussy...

She went on in her memoirs, published in the 1990s by the University of Arkansas Press, to recall how the lack of slave labor in the house truly disoriented herself and her sisters—women who had been raised under completely different rules. Growing up, Harriet and her sisters "had never been required to wash our own faces," much less perform the laborious chores of washing clothes and cleaning house.

Following the Civil War, the relationships of Arkansas women, black and white, changed forever. This image shows enslaved women near a Helena mansion before the war. Courtesy of the Permanent Collection of the Historic Arkansas Museum, Little Rock.

She wrote, "Pa had tried to prepare us for it, but such a change as was produced by freeing of the slaves had to be worked out by actual necessity."[8] It did not sink in easily.

Widowed women planters in charge of their family economy likely worried more about how the loss of slavery affected the bottom line of their operations than about who would wash the clothes. Amanda Trulock, a Connecticut woman who had married a southern planter and moved to Jefferson County before the war, had been running her own plantation as a widow long before the conflict began. Although Trulock had not grown up being served by enslaved people as had the Bullock girls near Tulip, she had wholeheartedly embraced her role as mistress of a plantation for years, and she was frustrated that slaves took advantage of the chance to flee. Before the war was over, Trulock complained that all the slaves on her place had been "taken" from her, except a woman named America and her children. Her choice of the word "taken" seems to reveal her inability to comprehend their flight as a choice. Reuben, the enslaved overseer in whom Trulock had placed so much trust in the efficient management of the farm for years, also left to find work elsewhere. Trulock scoffed at what she perceived as Reuben's infidelity in moving on.[9]

Women who had been in the slaveholding class tried to salvage their operations as best they could. Nancy Bean, the widow of wealthy Washington County planter Mark Bean, returned to the family land in northwestern Arkansas after the war where she was joined by her son, who had fought for the Confederacy.[10] Martha Bradley looked to recover her finances after the devastating blow dealt by the war. Bradley had been a slaveholding widow in Des Arc. She declared her unwavering loyalty to the Union in her claim to the federal government after the war to recover damages by and loss of her property to Union troops. According to her story, and the testimony given by former slaves of the area, the Bradley place had been closely watched during the war by Confederates who feared Mrs. Bradley would head to Federal lines with her slaves. One slave witness claimed that although a Confederate officer had threatened Bradley's life, she remained steadfast. Sylvester Caldwell, who had been a slave of a neighbor, testified that he knew Mrs. Bradley to be a Unionist and had joined her in that support. He explained:

> Our fences joined. I was well acquainted with her. I knew her sentiments about the Union for she told me she proposed to be a Union woman. She said to me, "Sylvester people that is Union is far better than secessionists" and I said "Miss Martha those that are Union is on the right side and they ought to stand fast."

Caldwell said these conversations took place early in the war, when the fighting was still far away.[11]

Whether or not Martha Bradley had truly remained the patriot she claimed to be throughout the war, it is significant that in her postwar life, she had managed to round up testimony in her favor by slaves she had owned as well as from those in the surrounding area. Whether she was being truthful or not, Bradley was surely enterprising. She did what she could to regain financial losses from the war. Much of her claim related to the amount of wood that had been cut from her farm, value that could not be replaced by a few years of sapling growth. She knew her land and its value well, and was determined in the postwar years to continue taking care of herself.[12]

Some slaveholding women tried to hold on to slavery as long as they could. Sometimes it took the intervention of family to help workers feel safe enough to get away from their former mistresses. Sallie Crane, who was owned by the Bishop family in Hempstead County, said that her mistress, Polly Bishop, refused to let her go. "My brothers would see me and tell me to run away and come on home and they would protect me, but I was afraid to try it. Finally Miss Polly found that she couldn't keep me any longer and she come and told me I was free."[13] When Elizabeth Hulsie became free, she knew how much her mistress had relied upon her labor, and, feeling sorry for her, got permission from Union officers to leave their camp and spend a day washing and working to catch "Mother Hulsie" up on chores so she could begin living without servants. Elizabeth "did all the washing, every rag that she could find," and when she left, her former mistress wringed her hands and cried.[14]

For African American women in Arkansas, freedom was a godsend accompanied by challenges. The Freedmen's Bureau, a federal agency associated with the Union army, assisted African American families in registering their marriages, securing and enforcing work contracts, and supporting schools. In southwestern Arkansas, an African American teen girl had performed domestic work for the family of a farmer named Washington Miller for the year of 1866 but had not been paid in January 1867. Her father, Billy Piggees, pled her case at the Freedmen's Bureau office in Paraclifta to the local superintendent there. After a public shootout between the farmer (aided by a friend) and seven Union infantrymen, it was Mrs. Miller, the farmer's wife, who paid the back pay of twenty-four dollars for the girl's work the next morning. The Union

The Leake-Ingham Building in Camden served as offices for the Freedmen's Bureau after the Civil War, providing a place where newly emancipated African Americans could go to register marriages, secure work contracts, and seek assistance. Courtesy of the Arkansas Historic Preservation Program.

army had enforced, despite Miller's declarations that the young woman's work was worthless, the fact that a black teen's labor should and would be paid. Reconstruction promised women freedom in their labor, equality in their citizenship, and the franchise to their black men via the Thirteenth, Fourteenth, and Fifteenth Amendments. However, black women had to make hard choices in the decades after the war, as a return to power on the part of white Democrats would mean the rolling back of these freedoms and the rise of sharecropping as the dominant agricultural labor arrangement.[15]

One woman who had survived slavery and war, Rachel (like Eliza above, formerly a slave at the Bullock plantation) had settled into freedom in Ecore Fabre Township in Ouachita County. She was forty years old in 1870, worked as a seamstress, and lived with the family of Sheridan (a painter born in Tennessee) and Sarah Peters (born in North Carolina). How did Rachel come to live with this younger couple? It is probable that Rachel had connections with them by blood or friendship from before the war, as the Bullock family, for whom Rachel had labored, had ties in both states before migrating to Arkansas. Rachel's husband may have died during the war. Freedwomen who were single probably saw the convenience of this kind of pooling of resources to make ends meet (as did poor white women). Elsewhere in the same township that year, one household sheltered three African American families—the Whitfields, Chanleys, and Thompsons.[16]

Some freedwomen focused on working in their own homes, rather than in the fields, to avoid the disruptions that their home and family lives had been subject to under slavery. Some historians have posited that black families did the best they could to model their home life after Victorian values—women busy caring for families and keeping up the economy of the home rather than working in the fields.[17] However, most recent works point out that African American women did not seek to "play the lady." They were faced with such struggles economically—much like their poor white counterparts—that they started out to the fields with energy fueled by their desire to work alongside their men to provide as much for their families as possible. The destruction of slavery allowed black women to make new meaning out of their work outside the home.[18]

An investigation of black households throughout Rachel's township in 1870 offers some glimpse at the work lives of African American women (most of whom would have been former slaves) in Arkansas after the war and suggests the frequency with which families chose to have women working outside the home in farming or other jobs. In the Warren family, for example, all of the family members, including five females (ranging in age from nine years old to thirty-five), were recorded by the census taker as working on a farm, except little Maggie, who was only five years old. Next door lived two more women (also Warrens, perhaps related), sixty-year-old Mary and sixteen-year-old Catherine, who worked on a farm as well. Down the road, Rebecca Robertson labored on a farm while her husband worked as a blacksmith. Twenty-three-year-old Margaret Smith and her husband were both listed in the census as day laborers, and seventy-five-year-old Tamar Young worked in gardens while her husband farmed. Young girls and elderly women alike employed themselves in farming and other labor outside their homes in order to make ends meet.[19]

Farm work and outside labor were not the only types of work that women performed to get by after freedom, however. Washing and cooking for whites provided a steady stream of employment for some. In one household of Ecore Fabre Township in 1870, a single mother made her way via domestic work. Louisa Threadgill (forty years old) was a cook, while Feriba Threadgill (sixteen), probably her daughter, worked as a domestic. Young Cora, at seven years old (probably also a daughter of Louisa's), was the youngest in the house, but she also had to work. She too was listed by the census taker as a domestic worker.[20]

In a nearby household, however, the family economy looked a bit different than those described above. John Lillie was a minister owning $500 of real estate and $250 of personal possessions. The census taker did not record an occupation for fifty-five-year-old Caroline

Lillie, John's wife. Their son, Ransom Lillie, at twenty-five years old, was listed as working on a farm (possibly theirs), while Marandy, eighteen, was without an occupation. The four boys in the household, ranging from ten to seventeen years old (Abe, Albert, Robert, and Cicero), all worked in farming, while Fannie, seven, and Ned, five, did not work. Farm labor was indeed important to their family economy if they chose to have ten-year-old Abe contribute to that work, but seemingly not important enough to have the women at the task. Surely eighteen-year-old Marandy was physically capable of more than a ten-year-old boy in farming, but she either did not do that work or her family chose not to offer that as her occupation. The Lillie family had either decided that Caroline and her daughter Marandy would not perform farm work or that they would not indicate that the women performed farm work to the census taker. Either case seems to indicate a preference of keeping the Lillie women from performing manual labor outside the house. Perhaps John Lillie's status as a property-holding minister influenced the family to keep up a household work arrangement that looked more middle-class.[21]

By 1880, however, the family's economic status became more precarious. Marandy was no longer living with her parents, having likely gotten married since the previous census. Catherine was described as "keeping house," while her husband was not identified as a minister, as he had been in the previous census, but as a laborer. Indeed, his sons Albert and Abram (Abe) were laborers as well. And, significantly, Catherine and John's daughter Fannie, now seventeen years old, was also recorded as a laborer although her sister had not been recorded as having done that kind of work when she was a teen during the last census. It seems that somehow the Lillie family had lost some of the economic security that had allowed them to be more selective in who went out to the fields in previous years (and had even perhaps lost land ownership).[22] The important takeaway, then, from the story of the Lillies and other black families described above, is that African American families made their own choices about work after the war as best they could in an economy that was still largely tied to the exploitation of their labor. Those choices might fit only for a time as families reassessed their situations. Black women might work in or out of the home as their families' needs required.

Like that of African American women who scraped together a living, the economic security of poor white women was precarious after the war. White women of humble backgrounds in Arkansas were surely glad to have their sons, brothers, and husbands back home—or what was left of it—when the fighting ended, whichever side of the conflict they were on. For example, the guerrilla war of northwestern Arkansas had been especially hard on women, and by late 1864, "only those too poor to leave, especially dogged, or under the explicit protection of the Union army remained." Many women fled to safer places to farm while the war raged.[23]

Many of Arkansas's white families of lesser means lived in rural areas and worked in agriculture. Most Arkansas women were farm women before the war, and that remained the case for decades after the war. But by the 1870s, most Arkansas farms were commercial and not simply subsistence. Commercial farming in Arkansas continued to focus on cotton—the crop that had ruled the South for decades and would continue to for decades more. Farm families outside of the cotton regions focused on corn and cattle, and they undertook more diversified pursuits as time went on. Like African Americans, poorer white families scraped a hard living out of the least desirable land and could find themselves indebted to their wealthier neighbors. The end of the war did not bring greater prosperity to poor white women, and their families did not have the social capital to recover from the devastation in the way that their wealthier counterparts did.[24] As farm sizes in Arkansas shrank, farm families struggled to get by. Poor whites increasingly became part of the tenant farming system, and the state's laws changed to provide as little recourse as possible to farm families who owed debts to landholders. Women faced malnutrition and disease across the state for decades after the war.[25]

Some white women remained in rural areas in the years following the war while others moved to town. A return to Ecore Fabre Township in 1860 and 1870 may shed some light on the movement of some of Arkansas's white women of wealthy and humble backgrounds. Of twenty-four adult white women (single women, wives, and widows, many of whom had children) traced from that township in 1860, less than half certainly resided in the same area by 1870. The war seemed to affect the households of Elizabeth and Margaret Leggett, perhaps sisters-in-law, who lived in different places before the war. By 1870, however, they had combined their households in Ouachita County. Margaret and her husband, Christopher, who worked as a policeman, had two young daughters. Elizabeth, at forty-nine years old, was not listed as having an occupation, while Margaret and Louiza (perhaps a sister of Elizabeth) were described as keeping house. A young stage driver named M. D. Howard, perhaps another relative, resided with the Leggetts in 1870. In the Adams household, Elizabeth and John had lived with their adult daughter Martha (thirty-one years old) and other children. Ten years later, John and Elizabeth were either back in Ecore Fabre or had never left. Martha still lived with her parents, as did thirty-year-old J. D. and sixteen-year-old Franklin. Martha's sister Savannah, however, may have married, and two of her brothers may have moved or perished during the war.[26]

Some women's families made the move to more urban places after the war. Rebecca Ward lived alone with her children in 1860, but in 1870 resided in a hotel in El Dorado, Union County, where her son John worked as a printer and her daughter Kate attended school. Her other son, Lafayette, who would have been around twenty years old, was not listed with the family in 1870. He may have died or moved away. Sophia Chambliss had lived with her husband, a farmer named W. W. Chambliss, with their children in Ecore Fabre before the war. By the census of 1870, however, the family had moved to Camden. They continued farming, and their son John was old enough to contribute to the family economy as a wood hauler.[27] The Green family made a similar choice. Elizabeth and her husband, James, who was a grocery merchant, had resided in Ecore Fabre before the war, but by 1870 they were living in Camden, where James kept his same occupation and their son C. J. made money as a dray master. Elizabeth had by then given birth to a total of eight children (including a pair of twins) and although she was probably very busy caring for them, she did have some help at home in the form of a young white cook named Lou Wages.[28]

Women of means who stayed (or returned) were often less well off than they had been before the war. Amannual Word, her husband, and their five children sat at the top of the farming class in 1860 with $2,880 in real estate and $27,225 in personal estate. By 1870, however, her husband, who would have been fifty-five years old, and daughter Bernice, who would have been less than twelve years old, seem to have died. A new addition to the family, Octavia, was present. Word's worth in 1870 was estimated at $35,000 in real estate but only $700 in personal property. Her young son Thomas worked as a ferryman to help the family income. The wealthy Bragg (including Martha and Florence) and Yarbrough women also came out of the war fairly well-to-do, if not as wealthy as they had been before.[29]

Some of the turn-of-the-century developments did reach rural women, and those with some means were in the best position to enjoy it. The expansion of the postal service allowed women in Arkansas to feel more connected than ever to their family members who did not live close by. Antebellum Arkansas had been populated by white families moving westward, and those ties to places such as Virginia, North Carolina, and Tennessee would have still been strong in the years after the war. Parcel service also changed rural women's consumption. Women with a little money to spend now had the opportunity to order new products via mail-order catalogs. For access to some of these products, however, rural women would need to travel to nearby towns, which grew quickly in post-war Arkansas.[30]

In fact, one of the most important aspects of the aftermath of the war in Arkansas was urbanization. There were no truly urban areas in Arkansas before the war. Little Rock was home to only 3,727 people in

1860. The war and the economic growth and expansion of railroads that followed it pumped more people into Little Rock than had ever lived there before. By 1870, more than 12,000 people resided in Little Rock, and the population rose to about 38,000 by the census enumeration of 1900. Fayetteville had been home to fewer than 1,000 people in 1860. After shrinking, the population grew to 4,000 by 1900. Nearly 1,400 people resided in Pine Bluff just before the war, and more than 11,000 lived there by 1900.[31] As Arkansas's town life grew after the war, elite rural women also urbanized as wealthy landed families increasingly made the choice to live away from the land they owned. Women in more urban areas of Arkansas were able to engage in more social activity and find out more news about current events than their counterparts in the countryside.[32]

Carrie Breysacher (née Pynchon) of Little Rock provides a profile of Arkansas upper-to-middle-class urban life after the war. She came to Little Rock from Alabama as the bride of Doctor Augustus Louis Breysacher in the mid-1870s, after Augustus had spent a few years practicing in Pine Bluff. In 1880, Augustus and Carrie lived on East 6th Street, in Little Rock's first ward. By then, Carrie had three children: Hattie P., Augustus, and Mable. The Breysachers were situated comfortably in the city's professional class. Carrie and her husband were served by a black woman named Harriet Higgins and a black man named Charles Grisom, both of whom lived with them. Carrie's socioeconomic status was shared by her neighbors, who also employed black women as domestic servants. Thirty-seven-year-old Elissie Brown worked for William and Elvira Adams. Louisa Walker, a nineteen-year-old single woman, served the Gordon family. And the married eighteen-year-old Lizzie Hubert served the Bryants.[33]

A taste of the material lives of Carrie, her family, and her social circle survives in her recipe book. Carrie recorded recipes of a wide range of dishes, many of which reveal an emphasis on entertaining guests, including coconut cake and instructions for three different types of tea cakes. Carrie compiled recipes from her family and friends.

Recipes for corn bread (calling for "a piece of lard the size of a hen's egg") and pound cake came from Sallie Jordan, who was a forty-six-year-old widow who lived with her daughter and son-in-law, Ida and B. C. Brown (a lawyer), on western Scott Street. Like the Breysachers', the Brown household was supported by a servant (named Mary Rucker). Instructions for citron preserves (including steps for a red variation requiring the use of cochineal) may have been offered by T. Brandon (wife of W. M. Brandon, a "commercial agent") who lived on Center Street. Some of the names of recipe contributors are of women as far away as Nashville, Tennessee (as indicated by Carrie's notes), while others have surnames that exist in both Pulaski County and Jefferson County census records from 1880, and so might have been shared from either place. The Breysachers and their circle entertained each other with rich treats that at times might have been prepared by black cooks in Little Rock.[34]

Women in Arkansas's towns and cities after the war often looked beyond their kitchens and parlors, however. Urbanization facilitated Arkansas women's participation in what historians call the Progressive Era—a chapter of history bursting with reforms that ranged from sanitation and labor laws to the prohibition of alcohol. Like women elsewhere across the country, Arkansas's progressive women, often middle and upper class, used their critical mass in Arkansas's more populated areas to organize for the improvement of Arkansas society. They formed organizations to work on a wide array of issues. The Arkansas Federation of Women's Clubs (AFWC) entered the General Federation of Women's Clubs in spring 1897. The meeting organized to get this branch of the national federation off the ground in Arkansas was held in Little Rock, and included attendance of women from towns such as Helena, Pine Bluff, and Van Buren.

At the heart of these women's interests was education. One of their most energetic efforts was the establishment of libraries. They worked to encourage libraries in family homes, traveling libraries for the use of children in rural areas, and the establishment of large urban

In the Progressive Era, Arkansas women banded together to make improvements in Arkansas society in groups such as the Arkansas Federation of Women's Clubs, pictured here at its eighth annual convention in Eureka Springs, on April 26, 1905. Courtesy of the Arkansas State Archives.

libraries supported by the state and counties. Evidence that these women of Arkansas's Progressive Era believed in the value of government to create positive change in society is seen in their successes, including acts of the state legislature that allowed cities to tax for the support of libraries. In fact, it was the AFWC that originally agitated for the preservation of the Old State House in 1904, where the final seminar of the Arkansas Civil War Sesquicentennial Commission was held in 2015. They distributed photos and other images of the building for sale to raise funds for the preservation effort, although the fruits of their labor were not realized right away.[35]

As reform movements matured and progressed, it seemed natural for women who sought to improve society, in whatever reforms they pursued, to also work to empower themselves to directly participate in the system of electing their state and community leaders. The women's suffrage movement in Arkansas blossomed after 1914. The Political Equality League had been established in Little Rock in 1911 and took a few years to pick up steam across the state, but it came to include several branches. Many women saw the franchise as the direct ticket to enacting reform.[36]

The club movement was also influenced by women seeking to make sense of the meaning of the Civil War and Arkansas's role in the Confederacy. White women had founded the Fayetteville chapter of the Southern Memorial Association in 1872 to reinter Confederate dead in one centrally located cemetery and afterward held annual decorations to carve out time to remember the loss of their Confederate relatives and friends. The first chapter of the United Daughters of the Confederacy (UDC) in Arkansas was officially created in spring 1896. UDC women dedicated their efforts to constructing and restoring monuments across the state that memorialized Confederate soldiers. UDC members also crafted a memory of the war that softened the role of slavery and emphasized the valor of Confederate men. Even in Unionist areas of the Ozarks, this so-called "lost cause" version of the conflict won over public memory of the war.[37]

In many ways, African American women in urban areas of Arkansas quickly saw that modernity and "progress" in the minds of whites resulted in segregation for blacks. Increased access to railroads—the very symbol of modern life for Americans at the time—was soiled for black Arkansans by the General Assembly's 1891 separate coach law that required blacks and whites to be separated on railcars.[38] And white women reformers often snubbed their African American counterparts in Arkansas towns. For example, white women banded together and agreed to limit black women's involvement in the Woman's Christian Temperance Union (WCTU), which worked more like "missionary paternalism than organization building" in its involvement of African Americans in the temperance crusade. Not until 1916 did black WCTU chapters surface in the organization's documents, and these were from more rural areas in eastern Arkansas, not from Little Rock or Pine Bluff—two important centers of reform with a significant black population. The black chapters of the organization that existed in Arkansas seem to have disappeared in the 1920s. Black women did not take equal part in some of the perks that might have come with urbanization after the Civil War in Arkansas.[39]

Where change occurred in post–Civil War Arkansas, it related to increasing urbanization. While most women had lived in rural areas for much of Arkansas's history, the years after the war brought many to the state's towns and to the capital city looking for opportunity in employment and in their social lives. That urbanization facilitated social and political change. For example, the organizing ability of white middle- and upper-class women was supported by town life. However, Arkansas's early segregation laws came from that very same historical process of urbanization. Segregation worked to enforce continuity in race relations, in which African Americans were relegated to an under class. In rural areas, change occurred as women had greater access to information and goods, but many aspects of their farm labor and exploitation by landed elites remained the same.

Ultimately, the most significant factor determining what a woman's life in Arkansas was like after the war, was what her life was like before the war. That is not to say that women's lives did not change due to the war. Freedom, urbanization, and the reforms of the late nineteenth and early twentieth centuries brought change to Arkansas women. But the ways in which women's lives were affected by these developments depended heavily on their circumstances before the war began. A woman's prewar status and condition set her trajectory for the end of the nineteenth century and into the twentieth century. Women in poverty and those of color continued to face familiar disadvantages.

Chapter 6—"Scattered Like Leaves": The Impact of the Civil War on the People in the Indian Territory

By Mary Jane Warde

In the May 1, 1878, issue of the *Indian Journal* newspaper published in the Muscogee (Creek) Nation, a writer who knew the Indian Territory's people and their recent past stated:

> The war to preserve the union of States surged over the boundaries of the Indian Territory and swept the Indians from their homes, scattered them like leaves from the forest to the ends of the earth. The third year of the war found the land here but only because it was immovable.[1]

A study of the period from 1861 to 1865 demonstrates that the events and conditions of the Civil War in the Indian Territory, so often overlooked in scholarly and popular works on that national crisis, were truly devastating to its people and their property. Moreover, the consequences of the war in the territory extended far beyond its boundaries.

In the mid-nineteenth century, the Indian Territory—most of today's state of Oklahoma minus the Panhandle, northeastern corner, and southwestern corner—belonged to the Cherokees, Chickasaws, Choctaws, Muscogees (Creeks), and Seminoles. These were often called the "Five Civilized Tribes."[2] There were small reservations in the northeastern corner, and people of several tribes lived, camped, hunted, farmed, and traded on the five nations' frontier of settlement.

The story of how those nations were pulled into the Civil War between the northern and southern states has most often been told in the tribes' individual histories.[3] To summarize, beginning in early spring 1861, neighboring Texas and Arkansas, looking to their own interests, pressured their Indian neighbors to become Confederate allies. Meanwhile, the federal government failed to communicate with the Indian nations as the crisis intensified. It also withheld the treaty-guaranteed annual payments to the Five Civilized Tribes for their old eastern homelands; federal officials said that this was to prevent them from falling into the hands of "armed rebels and banditti."[4] In May 1861, the federal government further violated the removal treaties by abandoning the three forts that protected their western frontiers from intruders and Plains Indian raiders. The Indian nations concluded that the federal government was leaving them to fend for themselves. Meanwhile, Confederate envoys Albert

Betsy Love Colbert was the wife of Holmes Colbert, who was among the signers of the Chickasaw treaty with the Confederate States of America. Salley Carr Collection, Courtesy of the Oklahoma Historical Society, #2385.

Pike of Arkansas and Ben McCulloch of Texas visited the Indian nations and frontier tribes to solicit their friendship and support. So, by July 1861, when Union and Confederate guns opened fire along Bull Run near Manassas, Virginia, in the first major battle of the Civil War, the Choctaw and Chickasaw nations had declared their independence from the United States and formed an alliance with the Confederacy. By late summer, the Seminole, Cherokee, and Muscogee nations had also signed Confederate treaties.[5]

Debates over that decision reignited some bitter, decades-long internal conflicts. In the Seminole Nation, dissention flared that summer between Chief John Jumper, who was influenced by Albert Pike, and John Chupco, his political rival and a recent convert of abolitionist missionary John R. Ramsey. Principal Chief John Ross was able to hold the Cherokee Nation together into the fall. However, tension intensified between adherents of his old nemesis Stand Watie, who was pro-Confederate, and "Pin Indians," traditionalists influenced by abolitionist Baptist missionaries Evan and John B. Jones. In the Muscogee Nation, Opothle Yahola, who was a longtime enemy of the McIntosh faction that now supported a Confederate alliance, held firmly to neutrality and his nation's treaties with the United States. Unable to win over the Muscogee national council, he left it to meet with the frontier tribes. The council then signed a Confederate alliance.[6]

The summer months also saw the beginning of mass migration within the Indian Territory. The creation of Confederate-allied military units in each nation testified to the seriousness of recent events and suggested worse to come. In those early days of the Civil War, there was time to make plans, decide what property to take, and travel at a comfortable pace. White residents—missionaries, teachers, merchants, millers, doctors, and federal officials—began leaving for "the States," sometimes under threat.

That first wave of refugees included Dr. Ward Howard Bailey, who had practiced medicine in North Fork Town and raised his family there. Now he took them to Fort Smith, Arkansas, his wife's hometown, and went on alone to his native New York. Likewise, Presbyterian missionaries Dr. William S. Robertson and wife Ann Eliza Worcester Robertson left their work at Tullahassee Mission in the Muscogee Nation. As a child, Ann Eliza had come with the Cherokees over the Trail of Tears. The territory was her home, but they now packed their children and some valued belongings into a wagon and drove toward safety in the States. A retired teacher came with them to teach the children. They left behind Ann Eliza's sister Hannah, who was the wife of Abijah Hicks, a Cherokee and their guide out of the territory.[7]

Joseph M. Perryman fought for the Confederacy in Company H of the First Creek Mounted Volunteers and would later serve as principal chief of the Muscogee tribe. William Sapulpa Collection, Courtesy of the Oklahoma Historical Society, #692.

Some Indians, too, prudently gathered their families, livestock, slaves, and movable property and set out for somewhere they hoped would be safer. Often that was the Red River Valley in the far-southern Choctaw and Chickasaw nations and northern Texas. George W. Stidham, a well-to-do Muscogee rancher, merchant, and council member, moved thirty of his most valuable slaves to a farm in eastern Texas. Among them was Tom, a blacksmith on Stidham's ranch near Honey Springs. Tom's family circle was broken, as his wife, Flora, teenaged son, twin daughters, and young son Jim were left behind.[8] According to Jim Spaniard, then a young boy, the Muscogees of Tulmochussie Town loaded their belongings on sleds and pack horses and set off south together. They crossed the Red River near the mouth of the Washita River and resettled in North Texas. There they resumed their communal way of life, Jim said, "dancing, hunting, eating, and multiplying." He explained, "We had taken our council fire so that we established it at the place of our camp. Just to forget our troubles and weariness, we began to hold our tribal dances and other forms of tribal customs."[9]

That summer a large number of Indians who shared the views of Opothle Yahola also abandoned their homes and camped near his ranch on the Deep Fork River. Many were conservative Muscogees from the Upper Creek tribal towns who favored neutrality over the new Confederate treaty, but some who wanted no part of a "white man's war" were from other Indian nations. Others were free blacks who lived among the Muscogees and Seminoles or runaway slaves seeking the freedom Opothle Yahola offered them, even though they knew his reputation as a slave owner. While trusted envoys took a letter from him to President Lincoln, his followers—including twenty-seven Muscogee tribal towns—became so numerous they could not all camp together. They divided into sub-camps then and used runners to maintain contact. The flight of so many Muscogees, Seminoles, slaves, and freedmen from their homes, farms, stores, and blacksmith shops left the western part of the Muscogee Nation and much of the Seminole Nation nearly deserted. Malucy Bear, a young Muscogee girl at the time, remembered how the crops ready for harvest were left standing in the fields. Lonely dogs howled and milk cows lowed around abandoned homes.[10]

The gathering of so many dissidents alarmed the pro-Confederate Indian nations that at first distanced themselves from what they saw as primarily a Muscogee quarrel. However, concern grew that the dissidents might link up with Union forces in Missouri and sweep down on the Arkansas River Valley, putting others at risk, too.[11] In October, a force of pro-Confederate Indians led by former Indian agent Colonel Douglas H. Cooper and troops from Texas approached Opothle Yahola's camps. Alarmed, the Indian and black dissidents began moving northward toward the western Cherokee Nation. On November 19 near the junction of the Cimarron and Arkansas rivers and again on December 9 at Chusto-Talasah (Bird Creek) west and northwest, respectively, of today's

Tulsa, Oklahoma, the first battles of the Civil War in the Indian Territory took place.[12] In each case, Opothle Yahola's war chiefs sent the noncombatants ahead toward safety, while Seminole, Yuchi, Muscogee, and Kickapoo warriors, freedmen, and runaway slaves stayed behind to block pursuit. They succeeded twice against Choctaw, Muscogee, and Cherokee troops as well as the Texans. However, each victory cost the dissidents ammunition, supplies, and time as winter approached. Christmas Day saw Opothle Yahola's followers still some forty miles away from the Kansas border across what one Cherokee pursuer called "the roughest country I ever saw."[13]

Douglas Cooper led Confederate troops in pursuit of Opothle Yahola's refugee Indians as they sought safety in Kansas, bringing them to battle at Achustenalah. Courtesy of the Library of Congress.

By then, Indian Territory troops and their horses needed time to recover from weeks of pursuit, but fresh Texas troops were able to stay close on their trail. Once more, at Achustenalah—just west of today's Skiatook, Oklahoma—the noncombatants followed orders to go ahead some three miles and shelter in a small valley, while their fighting men blocked pursuit by taking stations on a steep, rocky, timbered hillside and along its crest. Time and supplies, though, had run out for Opothle Yahola's followers. Their ammunition was quickly used up as Texans commanded by Colonel James McIntosh charged up the rugged hillside and drove them from the rocky top. The black and Indian warriors who survived collected their families and ran for the Kansas state line as a fierce winter storm closed in.[14]

Those later called the "Loyal" Indians passed down accounts of the immediate aftermath of their defeat at Achustenalah. A Seminole survivor said later, "We were whipped and our people cut to pieces badly....Our men were killed and women and children were not spared. Those that escaped death did not escape without some wound being inflicted on them and all our horses and provisions were captured."[15] Likewise, Phoebe McIntosh Banks, a Muscogee freedman infant at the time, related her family's account of fleeing from the battle area:

> Dead all over the hills when we get away; some of the Negroes shot and wounded so bad the blood run down the saddle skirts, and some fall off their horses miles from the battle ground, and lay still on the ground. Daddy and Uncle Jacob [Perryman] keep our family together somehow and head across the line into Kansas.[16]

To make matters worse, as the survivors struggled to reach the Kansas line, the threatening winter storm swept over them. James Scott, a Muscogee boy then nine or ten years old, recalled, "[W]e were often without food....We fled and left our wagons with much needed provisions, clothing, and other necessities....Many of our friends, [and] loved ones perished from sickness, and we all suffered from the cold."[17]

As the survivors struggled across the Kansas state line in December 1861 and January 1862, Indian Office personnel, who oversaw several Indian reservations in the state, were stunned. They had not expected the exodus of Indian refugees from the territory and were unprepared to deal with a horde of sick, starving, impoverished people. The problem quickly overwhelmed them, and this was only the first wave of refugees fleeing the Indian Territory. Eventually refugee camps would extend along the southern Kansas border from the Neosho River to the Arkansas River.[18]

In spite of the Confederate victory at Achustenalah, Indian refugees continued to make their way north hoping to escape trouble. The Confederate allies turned some back, but they could not seal a border that stretched from Arkansas and Missouri to the High Plains. Among those who left the territory in early 1862 was the family of Thomas Wildcat Alford, part of the Absentee Shawnee community driven out of Texas in 1859 and living on the Muscogee Nation's western frontier. They hoped to stay out of the war, but a party of Muscogee and Confederate soldiers came to demand that their community move farther east. Once the strangers left, the Shawnees got away in small groups by pretending to go west to hunt bison on the plains. That meant Thomas's family left behind their house, farming equipment, that year's crops, hogs, cattle, and most of his mother's herd of fifty horses. With other "hunters," they slowly made their way to Kansas, joining other Shawnees at Belmont, which became a focal point for Indian Territory refugees.[19]

The Caddo tribe was divided in its loyalties as the Civil War began. Showetat, or Caddo George Washington, chose to stay in the Leased Lands west of the Chickasaw Nation and would lead the Confederate Caddo Frontier Guard. Oklahoma Historical Society Collection, Courtesy of the Oklahoma Historical Society, #3983.

The Caddo tribe, also recently driven out of Texas, was likewise divided over whether to support the Confederate-allied Indian nations or to remain loyal to the United States. Showetat, or Caddo George Washington, chief of the White Bead Band, refused to leave his new lands in the Leased District west of the Chickasaw Nation. He signed a Confederate treaty and headed the Caddo Frontier Guard.[20] However, Caddos were involved in the October 1862 massacre of the Tonkawa Indians at Wichita Agency near Anadarko. Perhaps that was why in

January 1863, twenty-six Caddos, Ionies, Shawnees, and Comanches from the Leased District approached Indian Agent S. G. Colley at Fort Larned, Kansas. Although they had been surviving by hunting buffalo, they told him, they were farmers as well as hunters and asked permission to settle near the fort for the time being. Colley granted their request and arranged for them to receive provisions and clothing.[21]

By this time the war was having a strong, often immediate impact of the lives of many Indian Territory people. In the pre-war years some Cherokees had settled in the Cherokee Neutral Lands, the rectangular area set aside for the Cherokee Nation and today in the southeastern corner of Kansas. Among those who farmed there in the Neosho River Valley near the town of Chetopa was George Washington Walker, or Tahlakitehi, a survivor of the Cherokee Trail of Tears, and his wife Rachel. At the outbreak of the war, George Walker and his neighbors sided with Stand Watie in supporting the Confederacy. They formed a home guard unit that Watie quickly incorporated into the First Cherokee Regiment he had created over opposition from John Ross. Walker's unit was ordered south into the Cherokee Nation proper to guard its border with Kansas. Watie's raids in the Neutral Lands and on Humboldt, Kansas, a Unionist stronghold, brought federal retaliation. Walker escaped the first round-up of pro-Confederate Cherokees, but in 1863 another punitive federal raid saw most of them arrested and their property destroyed. Civilians, including Rachel Walker and her four children, were forcibly removed to Fort Scott, Kansas, for the duration of the war. Homeless and with his family out of reach, Walker rode with Watie for the rest of the war.[22]

In the Cherokee Nation, the exodus of Opothle Yahola's dissidents further increased hostility between the Ross and Watie factions. Many Cherokee troops sent to Chusto-Talasah to disperse them were conservative Pins. Opposed to fighting like-minded men, they deserted the night before the battle, and some even crossed the lines to join the dissidents. For the time being, Principal Chief John Ross managed to control affairs in his nation and keep peace with Stand Watie. In the Kansas refugee camps, though, displaced Indians, freedmen, and former slaves provided a large pool of men willing and able to fight for their home country. The First, Second, and Third Indian Home Guard units were created in 1862, as was the First Kansas Colored Volunteer Infantry. In late spring 1862, the Union "Indian Expedition" marched from Kansas down the Texas Road into the Cherokee Nation and occupied Tahlequah, its capital. A new wave of frightened pro-Confederate Cherokees and Muscogees left their homes and standing crops that summer for the relative safety of the Red River Valley. For a brief time, though, there was open rejoicing among pro-Union Cherokees, who had carefully kept their views quiet until then. However, the Indian Expedition faltered and collapsed because of poor planning and even worse leadership. It soon withdrew to Kansas, taking with it Principal Chief John Ross as a compliant captive. Slaves who had been told they were now free trailed the retreating expedition. Some carried property that members of the expedition had encouraged them to loot from their former owners. Still unsure about their new status, however, they feared being recaptured before they could reach safety in

Stand Watie led Confederate troops in the fratricidal war in the Indian Territory and, on June 23, 1865, became the last Confederate general to surrender, ending the Civil War. Courtesy of Wilson's Creek National Battlefield.

Kansas. However, pro-Union Cherokees who were left behind were in a worse position. They had been exposed during the brief occupation and were now vulnerable to reprisal from pro-Confederates such as Stand Watie.[23]

Violence flourished in the Cherokee Nation between the pro-Union Pins and pro-Confederates, and ordinary people were not exempt from it. On July 4, 1862, Abijah Hicks, a Cherokee, was killed by Pin Indians on his way to Van Buren, Arkansas, to buy stock for his store. He was the husband of Hannah Worcester Hicks, who was the daughter of white missionaries, and they had five young children. Hannah's neighbor Stephen Foreman, a close associate of Stand Watie, found the murder of this "inoffensive man" inexplicable—except that violence had become the norm in the Cherokee Nation.[24] Later Hannah learned that Abijah's killers had shot him because they mistook him for someone else.[25]

This was only one disaster the war brought to her door. Hannah discovered in September that the Park Hill Mission Press had been vandalized and the equipment demolished. It had been founded by her father, missionary Samuel Austin Worcester, and Hannah had learned the printer's trade working there. The press had produced some 14 million pages in the Cherokee, Choctaw, Muscogee, and English languages. Worse was to come to her family. On November 17 raiders stripped her home and family of almost everything of value. Hannah wrote in her diary:

> Today we have had experience in being robbed. As soon as it was light they came and began: They took many valuable things and overhauled every closet, trunk, box and drawer they could find. The most valuable things are gone for good and all. So many things the robbers took that I would regret so much if I felt that the loss of anything short of life itself, was worth regretting now. They took about three barrels of sugar, *all* [her emphasis] my blankets, most of my quilts, sheets, pillow cases, towels, table cloths, my teaspoons, all but one, and oh, that large pretty white bed spread that Mrs. Ross had given me; so many little things that I most highly prized; ribbons, sewing

> silk, pins, needles, thread, buttons, boxes of letters, my mantilla, calicoes, woolen stuffs, white cloth I was saving to make up, part of my underclothes and stockings, with the childrens [*sic*] new shoes, their little shawls, &c.; from Mother they took some blankets, one shawl, her shears, mine also, her best shoes and all, some other things, the linen sheet and table cloth of my mother's weaving. If the officers had not made them return some things, I and my children would have been left utterly destitute, for they bundled up all our clothing of every kind; (my knives, forks and large spoons were returned) they opened and overhauled the letter box which was under my bed, took some letters and some little things of Mrs. Vann's that I had put in to save. They tore the trimming off Susie's bonnet, broke open a chest which was locked, and took what they pleased. They drove off nearly all our cattle, but most of them got away and came back.[26]

Hannah Hicks did not identify and perhaps never knew the men who took so much from her home and family. Later, though, she mentioned that troops commanded by Confederate brigadier general John Sappington Marmaduke emptied her corncrib of the wheat and grain she had hauled herself and stored there.[27]

The presence of Confederate troops in the Indian Territory became common even as Indian troops were pulled into the conflict in neighboring Missouri and Arkansas. The Confederate treaties the Indian nations had signed in 1861 stipulated that Indian troops would not be used outside the Indian Territory without the consent of their governments. However, the Battle of Pea Ridge in March 1862 saw that requirement ignored as the Confederate commanders sent word that they were needed on the Arkansas battlefield. Watie's Cherokee troops arrived in time to fight, and Muscogee troops protected the Confederate withdrawal afterward. Thereafter, the Confederate-allied Indians were frequently in action in Missouri and Arkansas, while there were usually Confederate troops from those states and Texas in the Indian Territory. Union Cherokees and Muscogees qualified as the enemy, and those Indians' belongings, crops, and livestock were appropriated with little repercussion. Complicating the issue was the problem of communication if soldiers and civilians did not speak the same language.

Robert M. Jones, with the largest slave holdings in the Indian Territory, supported secession. A Choctaw, he is pictured here with his wife, Susan Colbert Jones. Robert L. Williams Collection, Courtesy of the Oklahoma Historical Society, #11397

Likewise, federal troops sometimes took what they wanted and destroyed the rest. Cherokees Sarah Hudson and Thomas Joshua Buffington Hudson were living near today's Fairland, Oklahoma, when federal troops with the Indian Expedition came to their prosperous farm. Their daughter Mary E. Hudson James, then a child, recalled,

> The first raid through here the Federals took all of our stock, except one gray horse. They killed mother's chickens and turkeys... between three and four hundred. They raided our smoke house and took our bacon and meat and set the cans of lard out in the yard and greased their guns with the lard and destroyed what was not used.

> Stand Watie, our friend, came up through the country and left with us a horse....Father hitched this horse with our gray one to a hack and loaded his wife and children into this with what few things we could carry.[28]

As the war dragged on, Confederate-allied Indian troops were just as likely to take, or "yamp," whatever they needed or wanted. They were at the extreme end of a supply line that stretched far eastward. The infrequent shipments of uniforms, weaponry, medicines, and other military paraphernalia sent their way had usually been pilfered or redirected before reaching them. Consequently, a Confederate-allied Indian soldier rarely had a uniform and made do with civilian clothes and a Confederate hat that he decorated according to his personal taste. The war often took Indian soldiers and their allies from Texas and Arkansas past abandoned Indian houses, barns, and crops. They were rarely paid, and when they were hungry and cold, they took what they needed.[29]

The Civil War in the Indian Territory took an ominous turn for Confederate-allied Indians in April 1863. Federal troops again marched southward from Kansas along the Texas Road intent on reoccupying Fort Gibson near today's Muskogee, Oklahoma. Fort Gibson had been constructed in 1824 at the Three Forks—the junction of the Arkansas, Grand, and Verdigris Rivers. While it was strategically placed near the Muscogee and Cherokee national boundaries, its unhealthful location earned it the title, "charnal [*sic*] house of the Army"[30] for the high number of deaths among soldiers stationed there. Even rebuilding it farther uphill from the Arkansas River did not bring much improvement. In 1857 the fort was abandoned and its campus and remaining buildings returned to the Cherokee Nation. In 1861 Confederate troops reoccupied it. According to Rochell (Rachel) Allred Ward, then a slave about fourteen years old, some Cherokees sent slaves like her to Fort Gibson for safe-keeping. She recalled,

> The negroes piled in there from everywhere, and I mean there was lots of them, too. Cooking in the open, sleeping most anywhere, mak-

> ing shelter places out of cloth scraps and brush, digging caves along the river bank to live in. There was no way to keep the place clean for there was too many folks living all in one place, and if you walk around in the nighttime most likely you stumble over some negro rolled up in a dirty blanket and sleeping under a bush.[31]

Then in early 1863 Major General James G. Blunt, commander of the Union Army of the Frontier, planned an invasion of the Cherokee Nation to retake Fort Gibson as the first step in bringing the Indian Territory back under federal control. By then the new Indian Home Guard regiments in Kansas were eager to get back to their own country and settle scores with the pro-Confederate factions. At the same time, federal Indian Office officials were still dealing with the influx of Indian refugees. By January 1862 there were about 4,500 Indian refugees in Kansas—3,168 Muscogees with fifty-three slaves and thirty-eight freedmen, 777 Seminoles, 136 Quapaws, fifty-nine Cherokees, and thirty-one Chickasaws, as well as some Indians from other tribes.[32]

Jacob W. Bartles served in the Sixth Kansas Cavalry in the Trans-Mississippi and, as an intermarried Delaware, would later found the Oklahoma towns of Dewey and Bartlesville. Joe Bartles Collection, Courtesy of the Oklahoma Historical Society, #1254.

Dealing with the refugees was a major headache for federal officials in Kansas. Since no one had expected the arrival of Opothle Yahola's people in late December 1861, there had been little or no food, clothing, or housing available. That first winter they lived in whatever shelters they could contrive, and many died from cold, hunger, injury, or disease. Indian Office personnel responsible for the Indian reservations that lined the eastern Kansas border had settled them on currently vacant lands assigned to the New York Indians. It was an unsatisfactory temporary solution and more reason to get the refugees home as quickly as possible. Meanwhile, the Indian Office bureaucracy in Kansas engaged in administrative warfare with its U.S. Army counterpart. As winter approached in 1862, Blunt moved the Cherokee refugees to Neosho, Missouri, to occupy homes vacated by the town's Confederate supporters. Superintendent W. G. Coffin of the Office of Indian Affairs for the Southern Superintendency was shocked that they were being sent to Neosho, which he viewed as "one of the worst, if not the very worst, secession strongholds in Missouri."[33] However, their Neosho quarters were at least an improvement over the make-shift shelters in which they had endured the previous winter.

By spring 1863, federal officials in Kansas were as eager to get the Union Indians back into the Indian Territory as the Indians were to go home. The timing was critical. The returning column could not set off before the grass grew enough to feed the livestock. Nor could it leave so late that the Indian farmers would lack a long enough growing season to produce the crops needed to feed themselves. They set off in early April in a mile-long train of wagons loaded with seed for corn and vegetables along with the tools and supplies needed for farming. They drove back along the Texas Road through the Indian Territory and arrived at Park Hill in the Cherokee Nation on April 9. From there the returned refugees scattered to their old homes in the Cherokee and Muscogee nations, while the soldiers refurbished Fort Gibson.[34]

For a while things remained relatively quiet in the Three Rivers area, with people going about their normal business. Some local men came in to Fort Gibson to enlist in the Indian Home Guard. Rumor had it that the military there was handing out rations to Indian women and children, which drew some hungry Cherokee families closer. Random violence and raiding in the Cherokee Nation caused still more Union sympathizers to congregate near the fort.[35]

Meanwhile, that April, Union colonel William A. Phillips twice led raids from Fort Gibson through the Webber's Falls area near the Arkansas River, where there was a community of well-to-do pro-Confederate Cherokee planters.[36] Among the homes the Union raids destroyed was that of the John Salaule Vann family. Vann's step-daughter Ella Coodey, then sixteen, was home alone with her younger siblings the first time Phillips's men came. They looted the Vanns' fourteen-room home, destroyed what they could not carry, and took all the food in the house while Ella stood by helplessly with the terrified younger children. That night after her mother came home, the soldiers returned with Colonel Phillips. Ella recalled, "They went through the house with an axe and broke every mirror and marble slab on the furniture." When her mother protested, Phillips replied, "Madam, it's entirely too fine." He ordered the house burned, and his men kindled a fire in every room. The family saved little except some mattresses and quilts, which they moved into an empty slave cabin. A few days later another raid destroyed Webber's Falls, and its inhabitants left for safety in Texas. Ella said later, "We did not have much to move after being robbed and burned out."[37]

The Union occupation of Fort Gibson that April signaled a new stage for the Civil War in the Indian Territory and heightened concern about the future among its people, whatever their politics. Stephen Foreman, a Cherokee Presbyterian minister who had been his nation's first superintendent of education and later served in other high offices in the Cherokee government, was a close associate of Stand Watie. That had probably been the reason Pin Indians came looking for him in late 1862. Foreman escaped then by hiding in his cornfield and in Hannah Hicks's attic. Convinced the Cherokee Nation was becoming too dangerous for Watie supporters, he moved his motherless children over into the Muscogee Nation and settled into George W. Stidham's abandoned house near North Fork Town. The Foremans were looking forward to spring planting when the Union troops re-occupied Fort Gibson across the Arkansas River.[38]

Their arrival signaled the start of another year of warfare after winter's inactivity. On July 16 pro-Confederate spies and observers on the heights opposite Fort Gibson reported activity as Blunt began ferrying troops over to the west side of the Arkansas River. His objective was the Confederate depot at Honey Springs just south of Elk Creek, a night's march along the Texas Road from Fort Gibson. Confederate-allied Indians and Texans commanded by Brigadier General Douglas H. Cooper were unable to stop the advance of the Union troops—white, black, and Indian—across Elk Creek and on to Honey Springs on July 17. The victorious Union soldiers destroyed the supplies the Confederate allies had deposited there and then returned to Fort Gibson, taking slaves from local farms and ranches with them.[39]

The Union victory at Honey Springs had a major impact on Indian Territory civilians as it set off what they later called "the stampede." Pro-Confederate Muscogees and white people who lived among them feared what might happen in the aftermath should federal troops push on into their country. Most agreed with Stephen Foreman, who concluded, "All things considered, I think we had better go to Texas as soon as we can."[40]

Panicked civilians collected their families and essential belongings and fled south down the Texas Road toward the Canadian River, which was the Choctaw Nation's northern boundary. Lucinda Davis, then the teenaged slave of Muscogee farmer Tuskaya Hiniha, remembered,

> Old Master pack up de wagon wid everything he can carry den, and we strike out down de big road to git out de way of any more war…
>
> Dat old Texas road just crowded wid wagons! Everybody doing de same thing we is, and de rains done made de road so muddy and de soldiers done tromp up de mud so bad dat de wagons git stuck all de time.

> De people all moving along in bunches, and every little while one bunch of wagons come up with another bunch all stuck in de mud, and dey put all de horses and mules on together and pull 'em out, and den dey go on together awhile.[41]

Many of the refugees crossed the Canadian River and continued south through the Choctaw Nation toward the Red River Valley. By early August, Stand Watie wrote that "scarcely a Southern family is left east and north of the Arkansas River."[42] Stephen Foreman observed the same conditions as he traveled south through the Canadian River Valley. After seeking shelter at a Choctaw farmstead, he wrote in his diary, "The houses were deserted, the family had evidently left in confusion. No living thing was about but some chickens, hogs, and two or three half starved dogs."[43] He eventually reached the Red River Valley and stayed there with Chickasaw governor Winchester Colbert's family. Foreman observed:

> A great many of the Creeks have also passed, on their way to some better camping place where water and grass are more abundant. Many of them are in a very destitute condition. All that they [have] now is a pony, one [or] two pot vessels, and a few old dirty bed clothes and wearing apparel. If they ever had any more it is left behind at the mercy of their enemies. But many who passed I was acquainted with and knew to be in good circumstances having an abundance of everything, now their all is put into one or two small wagons.[44]

While some refugees, such as Sarah Caroline Bell Watie, moved their families and slaves to Texas to wait out the war, others stayed on the north side of the Red River. They settled temporarily among the Choctaws and Chickasaws, who responded with typical Indian hospitality. Elizabeth Kemp, a young teenager at the time whose father was treasurer of the Chickasaw Nation, recalled, "The refugees from the Cherokee Nation came in bunches and settled near us during the war." She remembered that they collected whatever edible wild foods they could find. "Father would kill a beef and hogs and divide out among them; also let them have corn to make bread," Elizabeth said.[45]

Likewise, Martha Gibson, a Muscogee who was about fifteen at the time, fled with her family to the Choctaw Nation, where they built a simple log house, cleared ground, and put in crops. Still, she said, "We had a hard time getting anything to eat part of the time and would have starved if the Choctaws had not divided with us. But they were always willing to give us a part of anything they had that we needed."[46]

Brigadier General Samuel Bell Maxey, Confederate commander of the Indian Territory, assumed some responsibility for the refugees. In August 1864 he reported that rationing officers had supplied flour, beef, and soap to 4,823 Muscogees in the Washita River Valley, 2,906 Cherokees at Tishomingo in the Chickasaw Nation, 574 Seminoles at Oil Springs near Fort Washita, 241 Osages near Fort Arbuckle, 4,480 Choctaws, and 785 Chickasaws. That year Indian farmers produced some 1,500 bales of cotton, he reported, and it had been sent to Mexico in trade for textiles to produce much needed uniforms and clothing.[47]

Young Delia Bell's father was Colonel James M. Bell of the Second Cherokee Regiment and a niece of Sarah Caroline Bell Watie, the wife of Confederate general Stand Watie. Stand Watie Collection, Courtesy of the Oklahoma Historical Society, #16992.

Although some residents of the Muscogee and Cherokee nations refused to leave their homes, an air of desolation settled over the eastern Indian Territory. Those who stayed risked being robbed or killed by soldiers or roving bands of desperados. Malucy Bear, a child then, lived near Okemah in the western Muscogee Nation. She remembered, "We would often take to the bushes and thickets where we would stay in hiding all during the day and return to what was left of our homes during the night."[48]

Farther east some people moved close to Fort Gibson for safety, but there was little relief there either for residents who had never left the territory or Union Indians recently returned from Kansas. In May 1863 Colonel Stand Watie led a raid through the Cherokee Nation. His men took farming implements, wagons, and livestock, among other things. They also tore down fences that left the new crops vulnerable to hungry deer as well as the cattle and hogs that ranged free in the Indian nations. Watie returned to do more damage in July and August. Justin Harlan, the federal agent for the Union Cherokees, who had accompanied them back to their homeland, was as angry with the Union military as he was with Watie. Harlan wrote sourly, "3,500 men, a strong fort, and six cannon, were all required to hold Fort Gibson and the territory as far as the cannon would reach."[49] Beyond that distance, Indian civilians had to protect their property and themselves.

Nevertheless, federal officials in Kansas were eager to get the Indian Territory refugees back to their own country, and the Indians were eager to go home. In the summer of 1864, while the "wild tribes" were on the plains hunting bison, Central Superintendent of Indian Affairs William G. Coffin collected the refugee Indians remaining in the Kansas camps and set off for the Indian Territory in a wagon train six miles long.[50] Dwight D. Hitchcock, brother-in-law of Hannah Hicks and Ann Eliza Worcester Robertson, was then serving as a physician with the Union troops in the Indian Territory. Having heard that news, he wrote, "I hear with amasement [*sic*] that the refugee Indians are even now on the way back to this desolate country....I do not know what the Government means. How supplies are to reach them, and a dozen other questions, are beyond my wisdom to answer....At this juncture I do think the removal unwise and cruel."[51]

Although the journey from Fort Scott, Kansas, to Fort Gibson, Indian Territory, was fairly smooth, the arrival coincided with Brigadier General Stand Watie's capture of the *J. R. Williams*, a steamboat delivering much needed supplies from Fort Smith, Arkansas, to Fort Gibson up the Arkansas River. Watie's Indian troops ambushed the steamer and stripped it of as much of its cargo as they could carry, while the rest was lost in the Arkansas.[52] News of the loss of the boat and its cargo reached Fort Gibson at the same time as Coffin's refugee wagon train. Cherokee agent Justin Harlan, who had been trying to feed 9,000 refugees living around the fort, saw that number immediately grow to 16,000 with no increase in the amount of available supplies.[53] A month later five of the Muscogee chiefs at Fort Gibson wrote a dignified letter to the commissioner of Indian Affairs in Washington. They noted the desperation of the refugees the previous winter when, the chiefs said, "they were glad to hunt out the little corn that *fell from the horses and mules* [their emphasis] of the military." Without blaming anyone, they concluded, "We know the provisions are not here; we know that the provisions destined to relieve our present wants were destroyed by the rebels. If there were any provisions that those who have charge of us could get hold of, we should have them. They are like ourselves, helpless."[54]

In the Indian Territory, people's crops, food, and belongings were at risk, and so was something even more precious—their young sons. Kate Rackleff reported that her mother, Rebecca Ketcher Neugin, was one of several Cherokee women left alone who worked together to feed and protect their families while their men were away at war. "The boys had to be kept out of sight for the Confederates were watching for them," she explained. "If those boys were large enough to force into the army, they would be taken and perhaps killed and even the smaller boys were sometimes killed and not always by the Confederates but sometimes it was the Pin Indians who killed those boys."[55] Likewise, Annie Eliza Hendrix, who was nine when the war began, related how her mother did her best to feed and protect her children after she was widowed in 1862. Annie's brother Daniel, a Union soldier at Fort Gibson, took his twelve-year-old brother William to the fort "to protect the boy from the Confederate soldiers, as several boys near his age had been killed in homes throughout the Nation."[56] However, Brigadier General Stand Watie, on hearing that William C. Quantrill—notorious for his merciless raid on Lawrence, Kansas—had killed a little boy near Creek

Agency, wrote to his wife, Sallie, "I have always been opposed to killing women and children although our enemies have done it, yet I shall always protest against any acts of that kind."[57]

While the murder of young boys apparently happened often enough to warrant real concern, it was far less common than the theft and slaughter of the Indian nations' livestock, then their greatest asset next to their land. The Indian immigrants who arrived in the Indian Territory in the 1820s and 1830s found extensive oak forests that dropped copious acorns and natural prairies clothed in head-high bluestem grass. These fed the hogs and cattle, which were usually allowed to range free. As they multiplied over the next three decades, livestock became the wealth of the Indian nations. Civil War soldiers in the Indian Territory began killing and consuming them with impunity as early as November 19, 1861. That day, according to Sergeant George L. Griscom of the Ninth (Fourth) Texas Cavalry, they shot some cattle and enjoyed a "hearty dinner" of fresh beef while pursuing Opothle Yahola's people toward the Arkansas-Cimarron River junction.[58]

Soldiers of both sides continued the practice throughout the war. The practice was perhaps somewhat easier to understand in the case of the Confederate-allied Indian soldiers. They so rarely received supplies of any kind that foraging was necessary. However, it became so common for Union troops, too, that federal Indian Office personnel complained in official communications. Special Agent A. G. Proctor wrote in August 1863, "Cattle are yet abundant in the [Cherokee] nation, although the consumption of the army has been enormous as well as wasteful. I have known a small party of our scouts to shoot down a large fat ox, *for a few slices of steak* [his emphasis], and leave the rest for the wolves. I mention this to illustrate the reckless disregard paid by our troops to Cherokee property."[59]

During this phase of the war, the term "jayhawking" developed a new meaning different from its earlier political definition. From north of the Kansas state line, some refugee Shawnees, Delawares, and Kickapoos, along with white rustlers, raided livestock herds in the

Indian Territory. The stolen cattle, horses, and mules, still wearing the brands of their Indian owners, were herded into Kansas. There, the cattle were sold to refugee camp contractors to become food rations for the displaced Indians. These expenditures for beef rations were then charged to the Indian nations' funds held in trust by the federal government. When funds for refugees from one nation were exhausted, federal officials simply applied the charge to another Indian nation.[60] Historian Arrell Morgan Gibson estimated that by the end of the war some 300,000 head of cattle worth $5 million had been stolen from Indian Territory north of the Canadian River and herded to Kansas for sale there. This occurred while federal forces held that area, although challenged by Watie and other raiders, from mid-1863 to the end of the war. Clearly, it was not just the Indians who were being scattered like leaves—it was also their property and resources.[61]

In simple, heartfelt terms, a Cherokee girl named Emma Blythe, only six when the war began, summarized those terrible days when she and her widowed mother struggled to survive in their home near Tahlequah. "During the Civil War," Emma recalled, "our clothes was very scant as the soldiers kept the people robbed so clean....Our homes was burned. Our cattle was driven away. Our hogs was killed. Our milk cows was shot down. Our children cried for being hungry. Our bed was taken from us. Mothers set up all night to keep fires to keep from freezing. Our horses was taken out the plow. Our crops growed up in weeds. Such was the terror of war."[62]

By the time the war ended, the Indian Territory population was significantly reduced through warfare and other violence, contagious diseases such as smallpox, hunger, and other types of deprivation. Generally the Indian nations avoided taking a census of their people partly because that had in the past been associated with some outside imposition. However, estimates of population losses available for the Civil War years are as follows: The 4,500 Chickasaws enumerated in 1860 had been reduced by about 500 in 1866, or one in nine. Of possibly 15,000 Choctaws in 1861, perhaps 12,500 survived. The Seminole population dropped from about 2,500 to about 2,000 by the war's end, or a loss of one in five. There were about 22,000 Cherokees at the beginning of the war, counting slaves and white people legally residing in the nation. It is estimated there was a reduction of about 4,000 by the war's end. An 1863 enumeration of Union Cherokees revealed that one-third of the women were widows, and one-fourth of the children were orphans—with two more years of war still ahead. There were about 13,500 Muscogees at the beginning of the war. A census in 1867 revealed a twenty-four-percent decline, or about one in four dead or missing. However, the Tonkawa tribe, whose warriors had often scouted for and fought beside Texans and federal troops, probably suffered the greatest proportional loss of population. In the intertribal attack on them at Wichita Agency on October 23, 1862, only about forty men and one hundred women and children survived to reach refuge in the Chickasaw Nation.[63]

Even while the Civil War was still devastating the Indian Territory, federal officials were thinking about its future. At the time, there were several relatively new Indian reservations in eastern Kansas for tribes that once lived in the eastern United States. To some these reservations appeared to block future settlement and new transportation routes into the West. Moving these tribes to the Indian Territory to clear the way across the Great Plains seemed necessary for national progress. That would, however, involve land cessions from the Five Civilized Tribes, who had exchanged their old homelands in the southeastern United States for their new lands in the Indian Territory. The removal treaties signed in the 1830s by the United States and each of the Five Civilized Tribes guaranteed their sovereignty and ownership of their new homelands in the West forever. The Choctaws' Treaty of Dancing Rabbit Creek, the model for those that followed, promised, "no Territory or State shall ever have a right to pass laws for the government of the Choctaw Nation of Red People and their descendants; and...no part of the land granted them shall ever be embraced in any Territory or State."[64]

However, in early 1863, federal officials in Kansas approached Opothle Yahola about the sale of some Muscogee land, to which tribes in Kansas and Nebraska could be removed. That land was a triangle along the north side of the Arkansas River between the Tulsa settlement and the Three Forks near present-day Muskogee, Oklahoma. It was the "finest portion of the Creek country," according to their agent, and it was occupied by well-to-do mixed-blood Muscogees, most of whom supported their nation's Confederate alliance. He pronounced that it would be "a pleasant home for either the white or red man."[65]

That sale never occurred, as Opothle Yahola, sharp of mind and vindictive toward his enemies even when aged and frail, died not long afterward. Superintendent of Indian Affairs William G. Coffin, however, recommended that the proposed treaty be a model "for the greatly reduced and fragmented tribes in the Indian territory" and should "promote the interests of the Indians and the government, especially in view of the removal of the Indians from Kansas and Nebraska," an idea already under consideration by Congress.[66]

By early spring 1865 it was clear to the pro-Confederate forces in the Indian Territory that the war could not continue much longer. Even as the Indian nations were thinking about how to conclude hostilities with the United States, General Robert E. Lee surrendered Confederate forces at Appomattox Courthouse in Virginia. Neighboring Texas, Arkansas, Louisiana, and Missouri also surrendered before the Indian Territory nations could make their own peace. The prelude to their surrender was a large gathering of Indian Territory peoples at the Camp Napoleon Council near today's Verden, Oklahoma, in late May 1865. There they agreed to maintain unity in dealing with the federal government, but in the end the Indian nations acted individually, surrendering as circumstances allowed.[67]

The displaced residents of the Indian Territory, scattered from Kansas to Texas and from Arkansas to New York, began to make their way home. While most of the Union-allied Indians had already returned, the Confederate-allied Cherokee, Muscogee, and Seminole refugees were still mostly in the Red River Valley. They returned in 1865 with some trepidation, not knowing how they would be received by their Unionist neighbors or if there would be anything left of their property. Generally, public buildings such as churches and schools had been destroyed, and they found little or nothing left of their old home places. Surviving houses had suffered years of neglect, fields were grown up in brush, and rail fences had usually been burned in campfires.[68]

The worst loss was the missing family members, and survivors sometimes never knew what happened to them. The Robertson family, while returning to Tullahassee Mission, camped near the Flat Rock Creek battlefield in today's Wagoner County, Oklahoma. While playing, their children found the skulls of soldiers still lying unburied and forgotten on the prairie.[69] Among the returning refugees, too, were their former slaves, now freedmen and soon to be citizens of the Indian nations. While the Civil War would not be forgotten by the generation that experienced it, the coming decades would demonstrate that the Five Civilized Tribes had more to fear from the federal government than from their fellow citizens.[70]

Commissioner of Indian Affairs James W. Harlan recommended in his 1865 annual report that railroads be constructed to develop the Indian Territory's resources and its integration into the Union. This should be done as soon as possible, he said, while the Indian nations were still in a weak position relative to the United States. In line with his recommendations was the stipulation of the federal commissioners at the Fort Smith Council in September 1865: the Five Civilized Tribes must cede some of their lands for the settlement of Indian tribes from Kansas and other areas. Continuing the peace-making process in Washington DC the next summer, the federal commissioners writing the Indian nations' Reconstruction treaties required rights-of-way through each of the five Indian nations for one east-west and one north-south railroad as well as substantial cessions of land for future Indian reservations.[71]

The land cessions required of the Indian nations were significant. The Choctaw and Chickasaw nations ceded the Leased District in today's southwestern Oklahoma, which they held jointly, for $300,000. The Cherokee Nation ceded the Neutral Lands—800,000 acres between southeastern Kansas and southwestern Missouri—for $500,000. In the post–Civil War era, Neutral Lands farmer George Washington Walker did not have the money to buy the land he had once freely farmed as a Cherokee citizen. He and his neighbors moved back to the Cherokee Nation, started over, and prospered. The federal government also took control of two parcels still owned by the Cherokee Nation: the seven million acres of the Cherokee Outlet in today's northern Oklahoma and the 2.5-miles-wide Cherokee Strip along the southern Kansas border. The Cherokee Outlet could accommodate several reservations for tribes yet to be removed.[72]

The Indian nations that lost the most in the federal takeover of their lands were the Muscogees and Seminoles. Even though about half of the Muscogees and Seminoles remained loyal to the United States, fought for it, and suffered much loss for their allegiance, their nations' Reconstruction treaties were harsh. Before the arrival of Confederate-allied representatives, the Loyal Creek representatives sent to Washington DC to negotiate their Reconstruction Treaty trustingly agreed to land grants for the construction of railroads and the cession of 3,250,560 acres stretching west to the 100th meridian. For this—about half their land base—they received thirty cents per acre, or some $975,000. Of this amount, $100,000 was set aside for property losses suffered by the Loyal Creeks and freedmen.[73]

As it turned out, the Muscogee Nation was more fortunate than its neighbors, the Seminoles. About half of the Seminoles had followed Opothle Yahola, remained loyal to the Union, and fought for it. Still, they were required to cede their entire land base, about 2.17 million acres. According to the attorneys who handled the negotiations, Secretary of the Interior William Harlow believed no Indian land was worth more than fifteen cents an acre, and that was what the Seminoles received. They were then compelled to buy 200,000 acres at fifty cents per acre from the federal government for a new reservation—on lands the government had just acquired from the Muscogees for thirty cents an acre.[74]

With much of central and western Indian Territory under the control of the federal government by 1867, it had a place to move Indian peoples out of the way of non-Indian settlement and development in the aftermath of the Civil War. The Citizen Potawatomi band moved from Kansas to the former Seminole country that year, while the Sac and Fox peoples settled adjacent to them in the former Muscogee lands. In western Oklahoma in 1867, a reservation was created in the former Leased District for the Plains Apaches, Comanches, and Kiowas. Two years later, the Cheyennes and Arapahos were assigned a large reservation in western Indian Territory south of the Cherokee Outlet. It encompassed some of the ceded Seminole and Muscogee lands as well as part of the Leased District. A much smaller reservation in the former Leased District was assigned to the Wichitas and Caddos. Persuading or forcing these nomadic peoples to settle permanently on their new reservations was difficult because it meant major changes in their cultures.[75]

At the eastern end of the Cherokee Outlet, a reservation was assigned to the Osages in 1871. They chose the tall grass prairie that offered good grazing but would not entice Anglo-American farmers. The Kaws, or Kansas, the "Wind People," settled west of the Osages in 1862. The Pawnees, United States allies from the Plains Wars to this day, left the Central Plains in 1874 and settled southwest of the Osages. The Ponca Indians were forced out of Nebraska in 1876 and moved to a reservation in northern Indian Territory. The Otoes and Missourias settled together on a reservation south of them in 1882. The Iowas and the Kickapoos were assigned reservations west of the Sac and Fox lands in 1883. The Nez Perce from the Pacific Northwest came as prisoners to a small reservation in the Cherokee Outlet after conflict with settlers in their home country. They resettled west of the Poncas, but the hot dry climate of central Indian Territory took a heavy toll on them. They were allowed to return to the Pacific Northwest in 1884, and the Tonkawas, longtime allies of the United States, received the former Nez Perce reservation.

The last Indians removed to the Indian Territory after the Civil War were Geronimo's Apache followers. Sent to Fort Sill as prisoners of war in 1894, they received allotments in the former Leased District. By then, all the reservations were being allotted to individual Indians, a prelude to opening "surplus" Indian lands to homesteaders. Centered in the Indian Territory were the "Unassigned Lands," ceded by the Five Civilized Tribes but still unoccupied. They were opened for homesteading by non-Indians in the first land run in 1889 and became the nucleus of "Oklahoma Territory." As each subsequent reservation was allotted and its "surplus" lands homesteaded, it was added to "Oklahoma Territory." In 1907 it was combined with the reluctant remains of "Indian Territory" to become the state of Oklahoma.[76]

As each of these Indian nations was removed to the Indian Territory in the post–Civil War years, it vacated a homeland elsewhere in the United States. Those homelands amounted to multiple millions of acres of land that offered abundant resources—soil, timber, and minerals. As federal, state, and territorial officials and businessmen had hopefully forecasted in the 1860s, those resources helped propel the industrialization and development of the United States after the Civil War. One can argue that such national progress would have happened eventually even without the participation of the Indian Territory nations in the Civil War. That they did participate, at least partially, and officially on the losing side, certainly expedited it.

Chapter 7—Arkansas: Where One War's Edge Was Another War's Center

By Elliott West

For someone from Virginia or Pennsylvania, an essay on Arkansas in the Civil War might seem like pretty short work. The question of whether the Union or Confederacy would control the state was settled early, and despite efforts to inflate the significance of the fighting here—calling the Battle of Pea Ridge the "Gettysburg of the West," for instance—it paled in comparison to that in the East. By the crudest measure, that of blood spilled, the combined casualties of the state's two most significant battles, at Pea Ridge and Prairie Grove, were well less than half of the casualties from the Battle of Seven Pines during the Peninsula campaign three months after Pea Ridge. Those numbers in turn were less than half of Antietam's losses, which were about half of those at Gettysburg. Nor can it be credibly argued that engagements in Arkansas significantly swayed the war's outcome. So when we look back on what must surely rank as the nation's greatest tragedy and one of its two or three most consequential episodes, by the usual perspective, Arkansas appears to be much on the edge of the action, both geographically and in the weight it pulled in determining the course of events.

But what happens when we look back from something other than the "usual perspective"? Specifically, where does Arkansas stand when we consider the Civil War continentally, rethinking its causes and its consequences by pulling back and examining those awful years from a view from coast to coast? Put a bit differently, how does the story read when we allow the wider West into it—when we consider the roles of California, Oregon, and Kansas as well as those of Virginia, Pennsylvania, and South Carolina? No one can argue credibly that such a perspective boosts Arkansas's role in deciding the war's military outcome, but its place in the war's prelude, its terrible human costs, and its long-term consequences for the entire nation—in particular for America's native peoples—takes on far greater gravity. Arkansas moves from the edge of the action toward its true center.

The point is made by considering two chapters in the story. One involves events leading up to Fort Sumter, in particular the role of the West in the deepening tensions between the Northeast and the Southeast. The other involves the gathering calamity of western Native American peoples, in particular those caught in the middle of those same sectional tensions, as well as the tribal groups whose lives were convulsed by the fighting and the social chaos that came after those tensions reached their snapping point.

Connections

That the West featured prominently in the coming of the Civil War will surprise nobody, but few have recognized the place of Arkansas in the western events leading up to secession. The most obvious role of the West, of course, involved the issue that, more than any other, set Northeast against Southeast—whether African American slavery would be allowed into any of the vast country, well more than a million square miles, acquired by the United States between 1845 and 1848. The question did not apply directly to Arkansas. By the Missouri Compromise of 1820, African slavery was allowed in Arkansas, in Indian Territory, in Louisiana, and in Missouri but banned (temporarily, it turned out) north of Arkansas's northern border, as slavery was extended to what was then the nation's western boundary at the continental divide. Slavery's expansion, however, very much touched Arkansas indirectly. It did so through an issue intimately entangled with that of slavery in the West—the question of how and where to build connections from the nation east of the Mississippi River to the far West, California in particular.

Those connections included routes for overland travelers—the federal government surveyed more than 20,000 miles of roads across the West during the 1850s—and stage and postal service, notably John Butterfield's Overland Mail Company. Its long, looping "oxbow" route ran for 2,700 miles from St. Louis through northwestern Arkansas, western Texas, and the Southwest to Los Angeles and San Diego.[1] Also on the table was the more ephemeral but vital connection of the most revolutionary advance in human communication up until that time: the telegraph, which offered the virtually instantaneous transfer of information from the East to the far coast.[2] The most pressing questions around western connections, and certainly the most politically contentious, however, centered on the telegraph's partner in the era's revolution in the movement of people, things, and information: the railroad.

Although the first railroads appeared earlier, their expansion across the nation (as well as that of the telegraph) began perfectly coincident with the nation's acquisition of the far West, in the mid-1840s, as the depression begun in 1837 finally began to ease. The overlay of the two developments—expansion to the Pacific coast and the sudden momentum of rail construction—prompted immediate calls for laying an "iron road" from somewhere on the western fringe of the bulk of national population, across plains and mountains and deserts, to the new possessions at the edge of the planet's largest ocean. The discovery of gold on the American River in January 1848, plus the rapid revelation that California's gold deposits were far and away the richest in history—naturally bringing a fantastic bloom of population—all built into an urgent demand that the government take the lead in using the new technology of rail transport to bring the established America into close relation with its farthest possession, which also happened to be the most valuable place on earth.

All this raised the critical question: Where would that railroad run? More specifically, what would be its eastern terminus, the point where it would launch toward the Pacific? It was universally assumed that, at the outset, there would be only one rail line to California. The location of its eastern launching spot would be doubly propitious. First, it would be like the narrow spout of a funnel, the gathering place of all that passed between the nation's eastern half and its expanded western half. That place's whereabouts, along with its countryside and its urban sisters and cousins and its wider region, would surely feed and flourish on the commercial traffic across the continent. Second, in an increasingly divided nation, choice of terminus would go far toward determining whether the non-slave states of the Northeast or the slave states of the Southeast would dominate the movement of people and goods—and therefore of cultures, institutions, and economies—into the new America. And that linked the railroad's route to the most explosive issue of the day, whether African slavery would remain confined in the East or would be set loose across the continent.

The railroad's transition point between the Atlantic and the Pacific thus was the great prize up for grabs in the 1850s. It might be well to the north, perhaps at St. Paul, Minnesota. Or it might be more centrally located, say at St. Louis, Missouri, positioned in turn to connect into Illinois and the Great Lakes via Chicago and up the Ohio valley into Pennsylvania and New York. Or it might be farther south, through Texas and down to New Orleans and other ports on the Gulf of Mexico.

Or it might be in Arkansas. The state was already one of the prime jumping-off spots for the Southwest and beyond, with streams of travelers and the overland mail passing through Fort Smith. In 1849, perhaps five thousand travelers had chosen the southwestern route to the goldfields, from Arkansas via Santa Fe and the Gila River to southern California, and although most overland traffic after that followed the

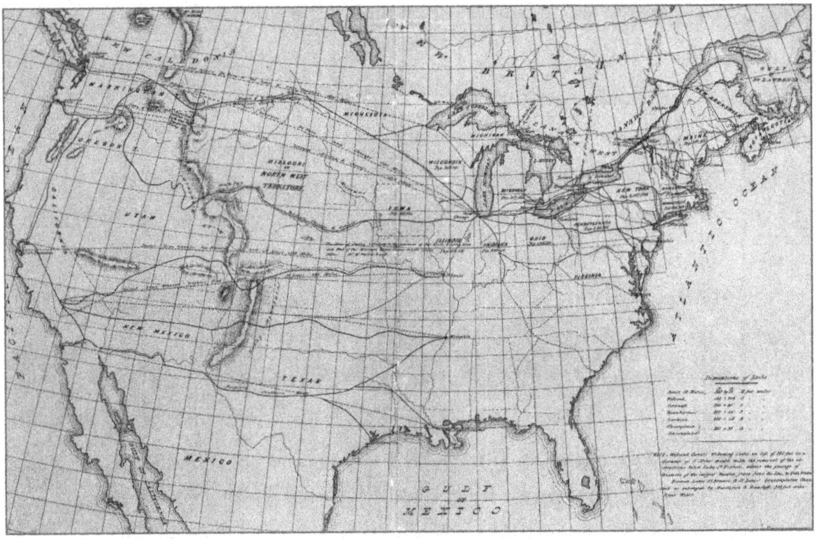

The route by which eastern railroads would find their way to the Pacific coast was one of the key questions as the United States continued its westward expansion, and Arkansas was a prime contender as a transition point. This 1853 map shows proposed routes for railroad expansion. Courtesy of the Library of Congress.

Platte River road through Nebraska and Wyoming, the more southern passage still was highly touted as a superior year-round route to California, one free from the storms that supposedly would choke off traffic across the central and northern plains during the winter months.[3] Arkansas was nicely positioned for another reason. A rail line from California could split into two branches, one angling diagonally across the state to Memphis and the other heading down to New Orleans, thus connecting the Pacific coast with the lower Mississippi and the Gulf of Mexico, and from there yet other lines might be built to the Atlantic to service the upper and deeper Southeast.

Arkansas was hailed as a splendid point of connection between the southern slave states and America's new land of promise on the Pacific coast, which made it vital to the deepening conflict between the competing visions for the nation's future. As sectional tensions tightened, southern spokesmen argued passionately that their region's interests, indeed their very way of life, depended on establishing outward connections that would allow the expansion into new lands of their culture and economic regime, both of them thoroughly enmeshed with African American slavery. Recent scholarship has stressed just how vigorously expansionist the slave states were during the 1850s, with visions of a slaveholding empire stretching across much of the middle latitudes of the Americas. The focus of this work has been mostly on hopes of a southward expansion, with an eye toward the Caribbean and even Brazil as well as northern Mexico.[4]

Southern expansionists, however, were looking westward as well as southward. They hoped to connect to California, of course, with its golden riches, growing population, and vigorous economy, but their vision went much farther. To get a full sense of their ambitions, it is important to appreciate a development that until lately has been sorely underappreciated by historians. During the twenty or thirty years before the discovery of gold, the United States and Great Britain had shown a growing interest in exploiting the resources and commerce of the Pacific basin. They cultivated a muscular trade in the skins of seals and sea otters, in native slaves, and especially in bird guano needed to fertilize European fields. The result was an increasingly elaborate web of connections binding continents and islands across fifty million square miles of seawater. Honolulu was emerging as one of the busiest ports on earth, with dozens of ships every year unloading, among other things, Italian brandy and, from one ship, fifty-one French accordions.[5] Then, just as this economic network was coming into its own, James Marshall found his glittering speck of gold in the gravel of the American River. The prodigious boom in California that followed gave a terrific jolt to trade all around the Pacific. First came a flood of imports into California from South America, Australia, and Asia, and then, remarkably soon, exports of grain and redwood from California and Oregon to markets around the Pacific rim. Commerce throughout the vast oceanic world felt a huge surge. Between 1848 and 1860, the amount of freight arriving in Hong Kong increased ten times over.

The bustling seaports on the Pacific coast fostered business with vast Asian markets and increased the desire of the eastern United States to capitalize on that trade. Shown here is the Vallejo Street wharf in San Francisco in 1866. Courtesy of the Library of Congress.

The invigorated commerce through the Pacific basin, combined with the new American presence on its eastern edge, revived the hallowed dream of tapping into the legendary Asian market. Usually the hopes of forging links to the Far East are associated with the commercial interests of the America's Northeast. Always, however, there were plenty of hopes among the slave states, which looked just as hungrily into the Pacific. As early as 1841, advocates in the Republic of Texas were proposing a system of canals, steamboats, and railroads to connect the Gulf Coast to the Gulf of California. From there, one promoter wrote, southerners could "converse with the people of China through a speaking trumpet."[6] The expansion of the 1840s, the California boom, and the quickening activity across the Pacific all amplified such southern ambitions. The great oceanographer and slavery advocate Matthew Maury, noting that the markets of the Pacific had triple the consumers of the Atlantic, in 1849 called for a rail link across Panama to make New Orleans "the thoroughfare of travel between South America, California, and China."[7] The primary focus, however, was on what seemed the most direct connection, across the nation's southwestern deserts through New Mexico Territory (including

Some argued that camels would be the most efficient means of traversing the desert southwest, and the U.S. Army experimented with a camel corps in the mid-1850s. This photo, taken in 1863 or earlier, shows a camel at the Drum Barracks at San Pedro, California. Courtesy of the Drum Barracks Civil War Museum.

present-day Arizona) to southern California. Any sort of linkage through that country seemed worth supporting. Jefferson Davis used part of his final day as U.S. senator in 1851 to argue vigorously for the army's purchase of fifty camels to secure the region, claiming they could travel at a constant twenty miles per hour, could carry small cannons, and had an advantage over railroads, as they needed less water.[8] A Californian lobbied his state legislature for support of a "speedy and secure...inter-oceanic communication" via camels. He made the astonishing promise that his fleet of dromedaries would carry mail and goods from New Orleans to Los Angeles in eight to ten days.[9]

Camel dreams aside, the slave states' essential hope was for a rail connection, an "iron road," that would secure their future by projecting their interests to California and into the Pacific world beyond. And in this transcontinental vision, Arkansas was often touted as the lynchpin. Listen to U.S. senator William Gwin, a Mississippi slaveholder and California's leading pro-South politician, arguing for construction of such a line. He proposed a rail network of 5,116 miles, more than twice the mileage of what would eventually be the first transcontinental railroad. It would run from Oregon through northern California and San Francisco down to Los Angeles, then eastward across New Mexico Territory before branching toward Memphis and New Orleans. Its forking point would be western Arkansas, specifically the town of Fulton on the Red River near the state's southwestern corner. His railroad, he said, would provide a vitalizing link from the Southeast, including the "States fronting the Gulf of Mexico," first to California, then to Hawaii, to "the Japanese Islands, soon to be unsealed," and to the ports of "Oceanica."[10] Gwin's vision, and that of many leaders of the slave states, was of a Southern capture of continental commerce, an economic boon sure to swell over the coming generations, all of it pulsing from across the Southeast through the Southwest to California, tapping from there into markets from Peru to China to Tasmania, and all of it funneling from both East and West through Fulton, Arkansas (population in 2010: 201).

Given Arkansas's place in this regional strategy, it should be no surprise that one of the state's favorite sons took the lead in pressing to make it real. Albert Pike returned from a trip to the Northeast in 1851 fairly stunned at both the pace of rail construction there and the advance of "education and knowledge as well as enterprise and comfort" that came with it. On his return, the contrast to Arkansas left him "heartsick." "A dull stupid apathy broods over the whole state like a leaden-colored cloud," he wrote in the *Little Rock Whig*. Unless Arkansas moved quickly to catch up, he warned, many of its best citizens would soon leave, and the rest would be left in even deeper poverty and ignorance.[11] Soon, Pike expanded his opinions and his efforts to the whole Southeast. "The South must not be behind in the race" to build the first rail link to the Pacific, he told a railroad convention in the state capital in the summer of 1852, and the preferred route should run from Charleston and Richmond through Memphis to Fort Smith, Van Buren, or, again, Fulton.[12]

Frustrations in finding support in Congress, plus the rising sectional tensions that threatened to undo unified support in Washington for any transcontinental line, led Pike in 1854 to present the Southern Commercial Convention in Charleston with a truly audacious proposal. On the vital question of a Pacific connection, the slave states should go their own way. They should form a corporation, provide their own land grants, negotiate for right-of-way with southwestern Indian tribes and, if necessary, Mexico, and build a railroad along the Gila River route taken by gold seekers in 1849. Any line built by Congress, he was convinced, would inevitably leave his region on the margins of the trade it would bring, while his proposed iron road, in the words of the resolution the convention eventually passed, would "secure to the South…the exclusive benefits and advantages of the commerce to the Pacific."

Addressing the Louisiana legislature the next year to ask for its support, Pike made clear that such commerce would go well beyond California, and as it did, the slave states would have a natural advantage. It was a simple matter of latitudes. However it got there, overland

Albert Pike argued in 1854 that the slave states should pursue creation of a railroad route to the West Coast on their own to "secure to the South…the exclusive benefits and advantages of the commerce to the Pacific." Courtesy of the Library of Congress.

freight arriving in California and sent off toward Asia would have to move sharply southward to catch the trade winds that would take it to Canton, then sail more southward still to reach "the great ports of Hindostan." A southern railroad thus would trim 700 to 800 miles from continental routes running from New York and Boston to San Francisco. Surely anyone with an eye for business and geography could see the lesson. "The world's route to the Indies is through the territory of the Southern States," Arkansas prime among them, Pike assured his audience: "The trade is ours, if we choose to take it."[13]

Pike's eye was on a larger goal. The profits from such trade would invigorate his region's economy and reverse what he considered an outright vassalage to the banks, mills, and factories of the free states. "From the rattle from which the nurse tickles the ear of the child born in the South to the shroud that covers the cold form of the dead," he reminded the Southern Commercial Convention of 1855, "everything comes from the North."[14] Outward connections and their infusion of capital would turn the situation around and cultivate a regional economic independence. His rhetoric occasionally hinted at an independence that was fuller and firmer, and in fact his speech in Charleston came close to anticipating what would be heard in another convention in the same city seven years later. Even if his railroad schemes should falter, he predicted, through them "the idea of a Southern Confederation…has taken root." He saw his plan as an early test to see if the slave states were "capable of combining for the accomplishment of any great work." Indeed, he sought nothing less than "a sort of declaration of independence on the part of the South." This was followed by "long-continued applause."[15]

Meanwhile, debate continued over the route of a transcontinental railroad funded by the federal government. Arkansas appeared to be in prime position. In the early 1850s, the War Department commissioned the survey of four possible paths to the Pacific coast.[16] The northernmost route crossed the Dakotas, eventually getting to Puget Sound. Another would run from St. Louis through the central Great Plains, middle Rocky Mountains, and Great Basin to San Francisco. The other two would pass through the Southwest, one roughly along the 35th parallel and the other along the 32nd. The odds seemed to strongly favor the two southern surveys. The secretary of war, who had commissioned the surveys and whose opinion would carry considerable weight in choosing one over the rest, was none other than Mississippi's Jefferson Davis. Topological difficulties with the southernmost course along the 32nd parallel had been resolved in the Gadsden Treaty (1853) with the purchase from Mexico of a largely unobstructed route through what is today southern Arizona. (The treaty's negotiator, South Carolinian James Gadsden, was arguably the most determined champion of a southern transcontinental rail line, which he considered essential for his region's expansion and the survival of African slavery and a slave-based culture. In 1851, he and others had petitioned the California legislature unsuccessfully to allow a slave colony in the state's southern reaches.) The familiar invocation of climatic dangers—the warning that winter storms would often interrupt rail passage through the Great Plains—made the choice of a southern, largely snow-free route seem all the more sensible.

Both southern routes would branch at their eastern ends. The route along the 35th parallel would pass through the Texas panhandle and Indian Territory, enter Arkansas at Fort Smith, and cross the state to Memphis. The 32nd-parallel route would enter Texas at El Paso, arc to the northeast, and would split in the north-central part of the state, with one branch turning to the south to New Orleans and the other angling to the north to Fort Smith. Therefore, each of the two leading contenders for the nation's first transcontinental line would have connected to Arkansas, and one of them (the one that, by wide consensus, had the best chance of approval) would have passed through the center of the state, presumably bringing the sort of vitalizing bounty that Albert Pike believed would save Arkansas from a slide into impoverished obscurity.

In was the near certainty of Washington choosing one of the southern routes, each with an Arkansas connection, that triggered what would likely rate as the decade's key event in setting a course toward secession and civil war. One more factor tilting the odds toward a southwestern railroad was the fact that both of the other two surveys ran through the Great Plains north of the Missouri Compromise line, country that was yet to be organized into territories. Without such elemental political structure, those lands could not be surveyed into the prevailing national grid of ranges, townships, and sections; without such a survey, Washington could not provide the grants of land that all assumed would be part of the financing of the line.

It was this fact—no territories, no surveys; no surveys, no northern route—that provoked Senator Stephen A. Douglas of Illinois to introduce the Kansas-Nebraska Bill in 1854. A railroad based out of St. Louis would assuredly connect to Chicago, which would make that city, and his state, a key connecting point between the West, the Midwest, and the Northeast. With that hope a-glimmering, Douglas proposed

In seeking to bring the benefits of a trans-continental railroad to his home state, Illinois senator Stephen A. Douglas maneuvered the Kansas-Nebraska Act through Congress in 1854 and put the United States on the path to dissolution. Courtesy of the Library of Congress.

organizing the country west of Missouri into a new territory. Passage relied on some support from congressmen from the slave states, but they declined. Given the situation, why would they vote for anything that would reduce the considerable odds favoring their region? So Douglas gave them a reason. If they would support his effort, he would call not for one new territory but two—Kansas, which presumably would quickly become a slave state, and Nebraska, which supposedly would move more slowly toward statehood without slavery. Doing that would require repealing the Missouri Compromise, and that in turn would open at least the legal possibility of more slave states carved out of the West. Calling on all of his prodigious political skills, Douglas managed to maneuver the bill through Congress and on to President Franklin Pierce's desk to be signed into law.

This is widely ranked as the costliest political blunder in American history. The Kansas-Nebraska Act led quickly to the dissolution of the already wobbly Whig Party and the birth of the Republican Party. That left only the Democrats as a truly national political presence, and thus the only party positioned to forge compromises between the sections—a thin reed of support, as it turned out. Kansas, rather than emerging quickly as a slave state, became a tussling ground between pro-slavery and free soil forces, with the latter eventually winning out, leaving pro-slave interests all the more disaffected and prone to break the bond of union. It was in Kansas, in fact, that the Civil War arguably began, if the war is defined as a fatal confrontation between factions of Americans over conflicting positions of sovereignty and sectional interest.

In the end, none of the pre-war schemes of a continental iron road bore fruit. The first transcontinental, the Union Pacific-Central Pacific, began construction after Appomattox and was finished in 1869. It followed a rough approximation of Douglas's proposal, starting in Omaha, Nebraska, and soon connected to Chicago. Its famous story, with its heroic engineering and breathtaking corruptions, tends to blur the memory that the original assumption was that the first railroad would be well to the south. We tend to forget, too, that western railroads, or rather the plans to build them, had been a proximate cause of the nation's greatest bloodletting. The competing sectional visions that clustered around each proposed route provided particular arguing points that helped drive the Northeast and Southeast apart. Those visions in turn should remind us that the slave states had grand ambitions that, again, we have largely overlooked—genuinely global aspirations of a slave-based economy and culture reaching across the continent, deep into the tropical south, and even across the wide Pacific. Those visions hinged on a rail link to California, and one of the key points of transition to a wider world was to be Arkansas, which was pictured as a gateway between the soon-to-be Confederacy and both the West and the blossoming commerce beyond it. This was no wild dream. Many considered its chances quite good—so good, in fact, that one of the nation's leading public figures, in a semi-panic, tried a political maneuver that sent events tumbling toward the disaster that left nearly three-quarters of a million Americans dead. It is not so much of a stretch to say that Stephen Douglas set the course toward the Civil War partly as an effort to prevent Fort Smith and Fulton, Arkansas, from becoming booming entrepots of global trade.

In any case, the story around Arkansas's flirtation with becoming part of what Albert Pike called "the world's route to the Indies" should remind us of the critical roles played by the opening of the far West in the onset of the Civil War. Those roles went beyond the question of African slavery's expansion into the new country. They had to do instead with the wider relationship of East to West, in particular whether and how the East's increasingly opposed sections and their ways of life would find expression in the lands of the expanded nation. In other words, they had to do with connections, and from that perspective, Arkansas and its environs stand more at the center than at the edge of one of the most critical periods of our history.

The Civil War's Neglected Tragedy

A recent re-evaluation of the combined military losses of Union and Confederate forces has upped the number of deaths from the traditional 620,000 to 750,000.[17] The figures, of course, only begin to calculate the human costs that should include shattered but surviving bodies, psychological scarring, and the disrupted lives and deep, unsolaced grief of millions of wives, children, parents, and friends of those lost to wounds and disease far from home. It was a toll the nation would bear for generations, and the collective memory is with us still today, one marked by hundreds of monuments on battlefields, town squares, and cemeteries. The remembrance of loss, as with our sense of the Civil War's legacy in general, once again bulks up in the East. And it should, given the horrific slaughter in clashes from Manassas to the Wilderness and the even greater costs from dysentery, typhus, malnutrition, malaria, yellow fever, and a long list of other maladies.

Once again, however, the sheer scale of struggle and loss in the East has obscured events to the west. Those events deserve to be part of the story simply because they happened. They also are a critical phase of an ongoing, and unsettling, theme of our national narrative—the defeat, dispossession, and cultural assault on America's Indian peoples—and they anticipate that theme's particularly tragic course during the years following the war.

The focus here is less on Arkansas than on the region often called at the time "the border," or "middle border," a rough arc stretching from eastern Nebraska and Kansas down through western Arkansas and eastern Oklahoma (Indian Territory at the time) and into northeastern Texas. By the 1840s, just as sectional tensions were beginning to mount, this country was crowded with Indian groups recently removed from the East. These included not only the so-called Five Civilized Tribes from the Southeast (Cherokees, Chickasaws, Choctaws, Muscogee/Creeks, and Seminoles) but many others—Shawnees, Iroquois, Delawares, Sauk and Fox, Pottawatomies, and more—from New York,

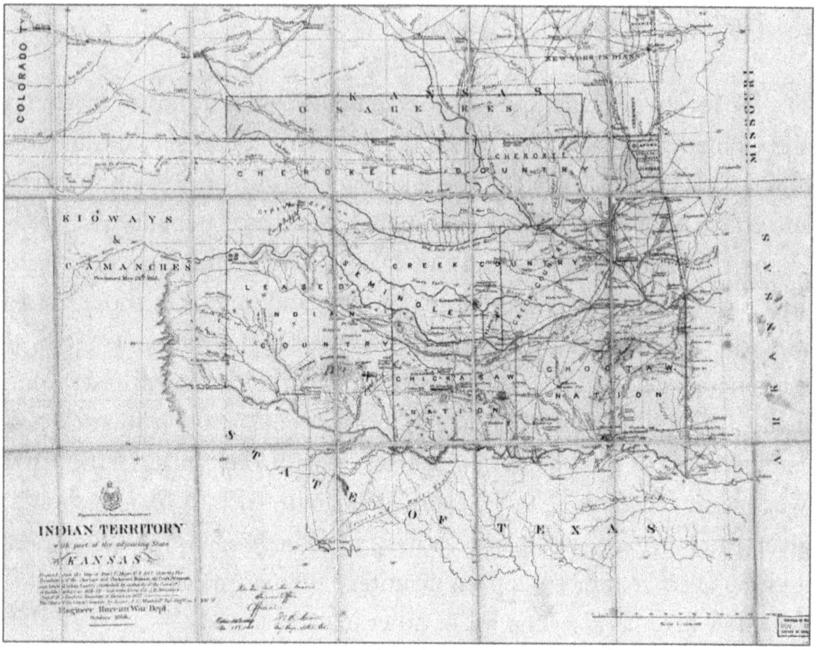

The forced removals of American Indian tribes from the eastern United States brought an estimated 100,000 Native Americans to the western territories and placed them squarely in the routes of western expansion. This 1866 map shows some of the tribes that were moved into what is now eastern Oklahoma. Courtesy of the Library of Congress.

Pennsylvania, the Ohio Valley, and the Great Lakes. In all, an estimated 100,000 Indians had been shifted westward to the border. What followed was one of grimmer ironies of the nineteenth century. The official rationale of Indian Removal was to place these varied peoples out of harm's way, shielding them from the pressures and disruptions of vigorously expanding settlement. After all, they had been taken from areas being rapidly invaded to what was then the far edge of the nation, country that supposedly had little or no lure for white pioneers. At the time, the nation's western boundary lay along the Arkansas River and up the continental divide. The semi-arid plains beyond the removed tribes would hold no interest for white farmers, while to the east a line of military posts, the "permanent Indian frontier" that included Fort Smith, would maintain a separation between native and white societies. The official hope was to buy time. Some predicted that it would be a full century before the area once again felt the pressure of white settlement—time for Indians to be fully assimilated, ready to fit comfortably into the nation's agrarian economy and into its cultural mainstream. Thus the border, including western Arkansas, was to be a vital crucible where the longstanding "Indian problem" would be faced and solved.

To understate the matter, that did not happen. First, in only three years, 1845–1848, the United States added 1.2 million square miles to its territory, annexing Texas, acquiring the Pacific Northwest in a treaty with Great Britain, and taking California and the Southwest by defeating Mexico in the Mexican War. Now the United States was a bi-oceanic, transcontinental nation, and the lands where the removed Indians had supposedly been isolated and protected now were once again squarely in the path of westward expansion—an expansion that almost immediately was immeasurably invigorated when gold was discovered in northern California. That expansion brought sectional tensions into sharp focus.

More generally, the questions involved whether African slavery would be permitted in the new country and, as already discussed, which eastern economy and culture would dominate the new West. More particularly, the tensions zeroed in on "the border," including Arkansas, the natural departure point for all those looking toward the new lands of promise and the Pacific world beyond. Sectional rivals, hoping to dominate that traffic and trade, championed one part of the border over another, which in turn led Stephen Douglas to accomplish the Kansas-Nebraska Act of 1854, which then focused the nation's attention far more hotly on the region that just a few years before had seemed remote and inconsequential.

Now the border was at the center of a terrific political contest that would help draw the nation into its most terrible bloodbath. But recall that the border was also something else: home to many thousands of Indians, most of them only recently removed from the East. They were caught doubly in the middle. They were no longer on the nation's western edge but, rather, roughly at its center, and at the staging ground for the tens of thousands gathering to cross to the Pacific. And they were caught in the middle as well of the most contentious political, economic, and cultural struggle of the era.

The result was a rarely recognized aspect of the events found in every textbook on American history. The greatest victims in the conflict spawned by the Kansas-Nebraska Act, the events of "Bleeding Kansas," were not the white advocates of either slavery or free soil. They were the Indians.

A few points are in order. When Congress created the Kansas Territory, every square foot of land along the territory's eastern edge, country certain to be the first taken by whites sure to flood into it, belonged to Indians.[18] It was organized into a series of "reserves" among nearly thirty tribes. Some, like the Kansa and Osages, were indigenous to the area; others, like the Delawares, Shawnees, and Ottawas, had been removed from the East. By law, Indian title would have to be resolved before any outsiders could settle there, but no preparations had been made to even begin the process and, apart from a small military presence, there were no authorities to stand up for Indian interests. When the first governments were organized, their officials—including the first territorial and state governors (who were at ideological poles) and the territorial secretary, attorney, and two supreme court justices—were themselves swept up in the speculations for lands and townsites. Army officers also jumped into the action, forming land associations and pursuing various schemes in blatant conflict with their charge to expel intruders and to enforce the very protections they were violating.[19] Besides that, not one square foot of that land had been surveyed. This guaranteed a chaotic scramble among squatters and speculators that worsened still more the already remote chances of the tribes salvaging much of anything.

A few officials, notably the director of the Indian Bureau, George Washington Moneypenny, tried to bring some order and minimal protection to the tribes, but to little avail. Treaties were renegotiated and reserves reduced, supposedly to put Indians in more defensible positions, but the changes did little to slow the onslaught. Indian claimants were caught in a crossfire among squatters, well-connected speculators, the army, and sometimes Washington politicians.

As a case in point, consider twenty-three sections of prime land along the Kansas River near Topeka, provided by treaty to mixed-blood children of Kansa Indians. As Territorial Governor Andrew Reeder and other officials tried to acquire some of this well-timbered acreage, more than sixty squatters were moving in, and when the Indian agent tried to get the army to evict them he was arrested for arson and later prosecuted by the territorial attorney.[20] In the end, the Kansa families lost most of the land. Matters only worsened when railroads, in an outgrowth of the competition for a transcontinental connection, entered the fray and maneuvered for land both to build westward and to sell to settlers. Newly founded towns and those along the border in Missouri competed for positions on rail lines projected west to the Rockies, north to Nebraska, southwest to New Mexico, and south to Texas. All required some Indian land, and many needed a lot.

The experience of the Delawares sums up the larger story. First their reserve was substantially reduced by a treaty in 1860. The land thus opened up, perfectly situated for a run to the west, and was acquired by the Leavenworth, Pawnee and Western for $1.28 per acre, far below what the railroad would charge in selling it, and in fact the LP&W avoided even that cost. It paid its basement price to the Delawares with its own bonds. A prominent Washington lobbyist, however, did receive $10,000 in real money for helping smooth the way. By 1866, the Delawares had lost the rest of their reserved land through similar manipulations.[21]

From early on some saw the answer as, once more, picking up the tribes and setting them down where they might be out of the way, but with the nation now on the Pacific, where might that be? If removed Indians are removed again, asked Congressman William Seward of New York, "where will it stop—the Himalayas?"[22] In the end, thousands of Indians, many arrived from the East scarcely a generation earlier, were dispossessed and shuffled onto reserves in the increasingly crowded Indian Territory, leaving only four tiny reservations in Kansas (which remain today). Fully a fourth of the state, "and by all odds the best fourth," passed from native hands to individuals, land speculators, and railroads.[23]

Meanwhile, the Indian Territory was experiencing an even more terrible time of troubles. After the unhinging of affairs in Kansas, just to the northwest of Arkansas in the years right before the Civil War, Indians in the Territory were plunged into a far bloodier disaster during the war itself. Few episodes in the nation's Indian-white relations, in fact, saw more suffering than the events across Arkansas's western border between 1861 and 1865.

In the usual, militarily centered narrative of the war, Indian Territory and western Arkansas do have some slight part. Albert Pike, having failed in his dream of a southern transcontinental railroad connecting his state to the Pacific, turned to securing Arkansas and his region for the Confederacy by courting an alliance with the "civilized" tribes. With federal troops largely withdrawn from Indian Territory, he found many of their leaders receptive, and by October 1861, the Chickasaws, Choctaws, Muscogee/Creeks, Seminoles, and Cherokees had signed treaties with Richmond.[24] Pike formed the Indian Brigade, mostly Cherokees, and joined General Earl Van Dorn's command against General Samuel Curtis at the Battle of Pea Ridge in March 1862. Following the Confederate defeat, with considerable criticism of Pike and his brigade, including reports of scalping of Union dead and wounded, the native troops withdrew to the Indian Territory. Indian troops remained part of both Union and Confederate commands, but aside from the Union victory at the Battle of Honey Springs in July of the next year, they were engaged in no other significant engagements in the area. In the larger account of the conflict, they essentially vanish until the very end, when the Cherokee Stand Watie became the last Confederate general to surrender, on June 23, 1865.[25]

The usual military narrative, however, once again obscures what Arkansas and the border has to teach us about these years and what they meant for the years ahead. In particular, we lose sight of events in Indian Territory apart from their influence on the Confederate defeat at Pea Ridge. And simply following the story of natives in alliance with the seceded states misses a point of critical consequence—the deep divisions within the tribes and their truly appalling consequences for all involved.

Significant minorities, especially among the Creeks and Cherokees, opposed an alliance with the Confederacy. An aging John Ross, the Cherokees' principal chief who had led the resistance to removal, resisted until, abandoned by Washington, he finally agreed to a treaty. Others refused to bend. In the fall of 1861, when Ross was finally coming into the secessionist fold, the elderly Creek chief Opothleyahola withdrew with his supporters to an encampment on the Canadian River.[26] Considerably more unionists from the Cherokees, Seminoles, and other groups had joined him when Confederate-Indian troops moved toward them in late November. As their caravan of horses, wagons, carriages, and people on foot retreated toward Kansas, Opothleyahola's warriors twice held off their pursuers. On the day after Christmas, however, a reinforced Confederate column routed the exhausted defenders. The panicked camp left behind virtually all conveyances and most supplies and food to flee over the Kansas line. Within hours, a vicious winter storm struck the refugees, some of them shoeless and all thinly clothed and hungry.[27]

The suffering had barely begun. Over the next weeks, many more Union sympathizers stumbled in from the south, most of them just as poorly provisioned. Conditions descended into horror. An army surgeon sent to survey their situation in late January found about 4,500 people along the Verdigris River and heard of many more scattered along other streams. It was "impossible...to depict the wretchedness of their condition," he wrote. The clothes of most were worn to shreds. Some people were wholly naked. It was bitterly cold, yet for shelter most had only "scraps and rags stretched upon switches." To help the several thousand people, the doctor had been sent boxes containing three dozen small quilts, forty pairs of socks, three pairs of pants, and assorted other items.[28] Relief supplies trickled in over the next months, but never enough, and there was the usual wartime corruption. Bacon sent from Fort Leavenworth was judged "suitable only for soap grease." The numbers of refugees kept growing—around 7,600 by April. A total of 240 among the Muscogee/Creeks alone had died during the previous two months, and a doctor reported amputating more than a hundred frozen limbs.[29] Warm weather brought its own problems. All camped along the Verdigris had to move to flee the stench from the thawed and rotting carcasses of about 200 horses.[30] Eventually most found temporary homes on lands of nearby Indians and at Forts Scott and Leavenworth.[31]

In 1863, Union forces regained control of the territory above the Arkansas River.[32] From Fort Gibson they struck periodically against Confederates to the south, but poorly supplied and hampered by squabbling commanders, they could not fully prevail. Neither, however, could their opponents, also thinly supplied and led by a succession of bickering officers. The contest degenerated into two years of grinding guerrilla attacks by Confederates, led finally by Stand Watie, with ineffectual federal response. In 1864, about 5,000 survivors of the Kansas ordeal trudged back into Indian Territory to Fort Gibson to join about 10,000 others already there. And there they stayed, penned up by the near anarchy in the country around and starved by the wholly inadequate support from distant authorities.

At war's end the Indian Territory, while on the far edge of military concern, was as devastated as the most ravaged parts of the South. An observer wrote that nearly all farms were "growing up in bushes and briars." Where there had been cattle herds, wild game now dominated and "wolves howl dismally over the land." Much of the livestock had been taken by rebels and bushwhackers, but agents reported that most by far—one estimated 300,000 head worth $4.5 million—had been rustled by white Kansans and sold at huge profits in that state.[33] The human toll was horrific. Diseases flourished, especially malaria, dysentery, and venereal disease. Many had fled southward into Texas, where some would stay as others trickled back to their wasted homes. Between deaths and those who left the Indian Territory, the Cherokee population by one estimate dropped from 21,000 to around 15,000, and a census in 1863 showed a third of their adult women were widows and a fourth of their children orphans.[34]

From the mid-1850s through the Civil War, events on the border, western Arkansas, and environs represented a watershed between one era of disaster to another among Indian peoples. This was the final, bloody winding down of the era of Indian Removal. To the north and east in Minnesota, the uprising of the eastern, or Santee, Sioux around New Ulm and the conflict that followed took the lives of more than 500 settlers and scores of Sioux. Following it, the government sent the remaining Santees and Winnebagoes (who had nothing to do with the uprising) to a desolate reserve at Crow Creek along the Missouri River in present-day South Dakota, where a quarter of their number died within a year.

This was the last of the Indian removals that had begun a half century earlier. The Five Civilized Tribes in Indian Territory had experienced their own removal thirty years before, but by 1860, they had begun to rebound from that infamous episode. Then, the next year, the whip came down again. At war's end, they were once again "desolated," wrote the head of the southern superintendency, and in fact, if census figures are accurate, the Cherokee population dropped more during these years than during the trauma of removal. And because they had allied with the Confederacy—and with Washington ignoring the fact that thousands of their numbers had resisted that alliance and had paid a horrific price for doing so—they would be forced to surrender yet more land even as they once more began the work of rebuilding.

This was one of many anticipations of the other side of the watershed, the course of Indian disaster in the generation ahead. In the 1850s, the policy of removal gave way to that of reservations, a sort of internal removal, with Indians confined to islands of territory as advancing white settlement filled the land around them. Those who resisted ultimately faced the iron fist of the military, and it was elsewhere during the Civil War that the western army developed the basic strategies of defeating western Indians, many of them highly mobile and with a well-deserved reputation for fighting prowess. The key was to wait until mobile bands were immobile and confined to winter camps, then to hit them hard, inflicting terrible losses and sending them on the run while destroying their food, supplies, and other wherewithal of survival. This was done against the Shoshones in southern Idaho in January 1863, the Navajos in Kit Carson's campaign through Arizona's Canyon De Chelly in January 1864, and the southern Cheyennes in the Sand Creek massacre in southeastern Colorado the following November. The method would be used over and over in the years ahead until all western tribes were subdued.

Along the border, then, we can see the trajectory of developments in the twenty years just ahead. In eastern Kansas and Nebraska, recently removed Indians felt the awful brunt of expansion and saw their reserves—the prototypes of reservations that even then were being founded farther west—first reduced and then dissolved. After tribes were sent from their homelands in the East into alien terrain, the press of settlers, speculators, and railroads displaced them once again, as they would tens of thousands of others across the West by 1880. They were sent now into the reduced Indian Territory to the south. Once the war began, events there anticipated the ultimate fate across the West of those native peoples who would stand against the loss of their land and independence. The calamity in the Indian Territory did not happen because of any purposeful policy; it was, rather, because it was effectively abandoned by both Washington and Richmond. The result, nonetheless, anticipated the strategy the federal government would use against resistant tribes in the generation ahead. Washington would subdue its opponents, not so much by confronting them on the battlefield, but by purposefully pursuing the fate that befell the

Cherokees, Muscogee/Creeks, and others from 1861 to 1865—by striking them where they were most vulnerable, keeping them on the move, and destroying their lives' needful things.

Arkansas: From Edge to Center

Once we pull back to a wider perspective on the Civil War and its era, those critical, awful years take on a new look, and the view is especially interesting for those drawn to the history of Arkansas and its larger neighborhood. In the years leading up the war, Arkansas and what we might call the "near West," the stretch of country from Minnesota on the north, down through Missouri, Nebraska, and Kansas, and on to eastern Texas, was the focus of national concern. The increasingly divided Southeast and Northeast saw this country as the key to their future, specifically to their chances of securing for their sections the grand benefits of the far West, with its golden possibilities and the opening world of commerce that waited beyond. In this competition, the place of Arkansas itself was seen by all sides as crucial. To champions of the slave states, it was a vital pivot point in their reach toward the Pacific, and its chances of becoming just that were, in fact, good enough to provoke free state interests to make the political move, organizing Kansas and Nebraska Territories, that tilted the nation toward civil war.

That political move, so catastrophic for the nation, was just as disastrous for the Indian peoples in those new territories, many of them only recently transplanted there from homes in the East. Overwhelmed by the chaotic scramble for land and advantage, caught up in the fight between slave and free soil advocates, they were once again displaced, now into the shrunken Indian Territory to the south. There, other removed tribes, these from the Southeast, suffered through devastation as wrenching as that of any civilian population in the East. Unlike with the war's victims in Georgia, Virginia, and Mississippi, however, the dislocations and the battered lives of Indian peoples along the border did not represent the end of a painful narrative. It was instead the start of one that would unfold in the far West over the next twenty years.

Widening our perspective on the Civil War, admitting all the expanded nation into the story and wondering what those years tell us about the West as well as the East, brings Arkansas from the edge of the action to close to the center. The story is often not a pretty one, but little around the Civil War is. This widened perspective reminds us that when that vital time of our history is seen comprehensively, the part played by our state is essential—both in grasping how the war came about and in understanding the nation the war created.

Chapter 8—Conflicting Civil War Historical Memory and Cultural Divides in Arkansas

By Carl H. Moneyhon

When considering the impact of the American Civil War on Arkansas, it is impossible not to see that it significantly altered the state's economy and society both immediately and over the long term. Many of the changes that directly affected Arkansas and its people have been of less significance as time passed, but how the war is remembered still has important implications for the state's people. The way in which we remember something is particularly important for a community, as memory, especially historical memory, helps provide the basis for a collective identity. That identity ultimately is one of the components upon which the community is based. Within Arkansas, however, competing memories of the Civil War help to create and maintain divides. Arkansans are not unique in this respect. These different historical narratives are similar to those seen elsewhere in the former Confederate states, reflecting what historian David W. Blight has called the unionist-emancipationist view of the war on the one hand and the Lost Cause perspective identified by other historians. While much the same as elsewhere, these narratives do have their own pattern of development in

Arkansas. This essay examines how these different memories came into being in Arkansas, how they have changed over time, and how they continue to exist today.

Memory emerges ultimately out of real experiences. To understand the roots of modern perceptions of the war and how these perceptions have evolved over time, an examination of what most historians consider to be the reality of the war is a critical starting point. The war obviously consisted of many different aspects—in fact, many different realities—but six questions have become central elements of the conflicting views of the Civil War that have developed over time. The first of these questions is, what caused Arkansas to secede? A second question is, what prompted young Arkansans to join the Confederate army? Additional questions are, what were the characteristics of these soldiers, how unified were Arkansans in their support of the war effort, and what role did blacks play in the conflict? A final question, and one that on first thought seems hardly debatable: What was the war's ultimate outcome?

Why secession? At the time, Arkansans who supported secession had few questions about their reasons. They seceded in order to protect slavery. The actual secession ordinance does not mention slavery per se and instead focuses on the North's intention of subordinating Arkansas's sister states following President Abraham Lincoln's call on April 15, 1861, to put down the rebellion. An examination of events preceding the passage of the ordinance, however, shows how critical slavery was to the decision. When delegates met in Little Rock on March 4 to consider how to respond to the election of Lincoln, Governor Henry Massie Rector outlined the reasons in his address, noting that "the extension of slavery is the *vital point* of the whole controversy between the North and the South." The North's position ran counter to God's will, he argued, noting that "God in his...wisdom created the cotton plant—the African slave—and the Lower Mississippi Valley" as well as a gallant race to "execute that decree." In the days that followed, the delegates passed resolutions that outlined the concerns that caused them to consider leaving the Union, emphasizing the

North's organization of a party hostile to slavery (the Republican Party), and that party's securing of the presidency. The convention adjourned without acting on April 21, but following the president's call for troops, the delegates re-assembled on May 6 and passed an ordinance of secession. While the ordinance did not mention slavery specifically, it did refer back to the resolutions passed in the previous session, citing them as among the grievances that had provoked their action. Clearly, slavery was central to the action of the state's convention.[1]

What motivated Arkansans to join the Confederate army? Were they motivated by a concern for states' rights, by the need to defend their homes, or something else? While political leaders usually called for young men to take up arms to secure independence and protect their homeland, it is not apparent that many of the men were committed to any ideological purpose when they joined.

As Arkansas voted to secede from the Union, thousands of men flocked to form units to serve the Confederacy. This May 9, 1861, Harper's Weekly *drawing depicts Arkansas troops serving in Virginia. Courtesy of the Special Collections Division, University of Arkansas Libraries, Fayetteville.*

Sir Henry Morton Stanley later recalled his days with the Dixie Grays of the Sixth Arkansas Infantry and gave possibly the most realistic assessment of the rush to enlistment in 1861. Stanley recalled that many of the men in his regiment considered the war to be something like a summer picnic, and most thought it would be over in sixty or ninety days. Their camps initially were filled with singing and drinking throughout the night, behavior that little presupposed the serious prospects they faced. Stanley concluded that, while there were some "passionate patriots" among his friends, most came for other reasons, including an "appetite for glory, the desire of applause, a fondness for military excitement, or because they were infected with the general craze, or to avoid tedious toil, or from the wildness of youth." After 1862, others came because they were forced to fight. Their only option was imprisonment. Each individual would have to find logical reasons for their actions later on, and their memoirs are full of their dedication to principles, but ideology seems to have been singularly unimportant at the time.[2]

What about the service of these Confederate Arkansans? No matter why they joined the army, did they become dedicated to the Confederate cause? Did they willingly give their lives to secure Southern freedom? Unquestionably some men were loyal Confederates, fighting to the end. Many men also served heroically through the war, although few Arkansans emerged individually to any public renown.

Junius Bragg, a surgeon with the Thirty-third Arkansas Infantry, for example, reported in the wake of General Robert E. Lee's surrender in Virginia that the Confederate dead had gone to their rest as martyrs, destined to reap the war of patriots, suffering for a righteous cause. The men who lived had pressed forward "steadily towards the promised land" of independence. A more realistic portrayal of the Confederate soldiers from Arkansas, however, is that they demonstrated a wide variety of behaviors. Their roles in the war, just like their reasons for joining the army, were complicated, and they varied from individual to individual.

There were heroes, but some failed in battle. The most notorious incident of this sort of failure took place at the Battle of Prairie Grove when an entire unit, Adams's Arkansas Infantry Regiment, broke and ran. Many of the men were conscripts, so their reluctance to fight is understandable. Some even ran to the Union lines. Many men deserted. Following the abandonment of Little Rock in September 1863, General Dandridge McRae reported that hundreds of his men left his brigade and returned home after the Confederate command refused to fight to protect the city. In the end, at least six percent of Confederate troops from Arkansas deserted. Others found ways of avoiding their duty. Augustus C. Abernathy of Crawford's Battalion reported widespread malingering in his unit, indicating that many were seeking medical discharges. In a letter to his sister he complained that "tough and abled bodied men will starve themselves, get dirty and lousy, look as bad as possible, just for an excuse to go home." Others found what soldiers called "bomb proof" jobs out of the line of fire. Clearly, all Confederate soldiers were not heroes. Ultimately, there was no *one* Arkansas Confederate soldier—there were thousands, and their experiences and conduct differed widely.[3]

How united was the Arkansas homefront behind the Confederate effort? Probably the majority of Arkansans supported the Confederacy, but many others opposed secession and then actively stood against the Confederacy. Some individuals who had opposed leaving the Union left the state but then returned to reestablish a loyal government after the fall of Little Rock in September 1863. Valentine Dell, editor of the Fort Smith *New Era*, was one such. Dell's hostility toward the Confederacy derived from his view of the war, which he saw as a plot by the slave-owning leaders of the state who sought "no other object in view than the disfranchisement and degradation of the great mass of the people of the South" motivated by their own "selfish, diabolical ambitions, covetousness and lust of power." William Fishback was another such individual, and the editorials in his *Unconditional Union* also blamed slave owners for the state's plight. Fishback looked for an end to slavery to "disperse the cloud which has heretofore hung like a pall over the people and destinies of the people of Arkansas." Others may simply have wished to stay out of any conflict, possibly the motive of the mountain men who formed the Arkansas Peace Society in 1861. Others broke with the Confederacy as the war progressed, especially after the implementation of Confederate conscription in the spring of 1862. The resistance of many who opposed conscription broke into an open rebellion in the southwestern part of the state and became problem enough that state authorities had to use force in an effort to suppress it. By the war's end, nearly 9,000 white Arkansans, motivated by this variety of reasons, enlisted in Union regiments and fought their Confederate neighbors.[4]

What was the role of the slaves in all of this? Despite white fears of insurrection, most blacks remained where they were throughout the war. Did they stay with their masters because they were loyal to them? Did they have any affinity for the Confederacy? Their actions indicated that they had little sympathy for their masters or their political cause. Whenever the Union army entered an area, the slaves quickly took their freedom. A soldier accompanying General Samuel Curtis's invasion of northeastern Arkansas in 1862 saw blacks abandoning every mansion and log cabin, carrying all their belongings, and "delirious with joy." Observing streams of blacks retreating with General Frederick Steele's unit from Camden in 1864, one soldier related, "They seem to have a thirst for freedom."[5] These runaways came to see the Union success as essential to their final liberation, and many joined the Union army.

By the war's end, approximately 5,600 African American Arkansans had served in the army. William H. Grey, a black politician from Helena, later summed up the perception of African Americans of their contribution to the war effort when he told a convention of African Americans in December 1865 that they had helped to save the Union; black soldiers were "the last feather that broke the camel's back; it was the Negro thrown into the scale on the side of the nation that broke the back of the rebellion and saved the nation."[6]

Finally, what did the war achieve? Unquestionably, it preserved the Union. President Lincoln had laid that out as his goal from the very beginning. On the other hand, goals changed as the war progressed, producing a revolution in the very character of the country's nationality. On September 22, 1862, the president signaled the beginning of this change when he issued his preliminary emancipation proclamation, warning Confederates that on January 1, 1863, he would use his war powers to emancipate the slaves in any state still in rebellion. On that day, he carried out his threat, issuing the Emancipation Proclamation and broadening the North's war goals to include bringing an end to slavery in the South. That he intended an end to slavery everywhere may have been intimated in his speech months later, on November 13, 1863, on the Gettysburg battlefield. There, he clearly stated his belief that the core of national identity lay in the Declaration of Independence with its assertion that all men were created equal and endowed with the rights to be free.

He certainly acted on this belief and pushed forward a constitutional amendment to bring an end to slavery everywhere in the United States. Before his assassination he had successfully pushed his proposed amendment through the Congress and secured its ratification by most of the northern and border states. Efforts made after his death ultimately guaranteed that those free African Americans possessed basic civil rights, rights guaranteed not by the state but by the federal government. Lincoln's actions and those carried out later by Congress meant that the war not only secured the Union, but it also brought an end to slavery and created a national citizenship.[7]

These were the realities of war, at least as perceived by contemporaries and most modern historians, but with the war's end realities faded into memory and the participants began to develop differing historical narratives as to what had happened. The differing narratives ultimately vied for acceptance as the collective memory or the public history of the war. Writing of the development of what has come to be called the Lost Cause narrative, historian William C.

Davis noted that former Confederates consciously began creating their story as soon as the war ended. The same may be said of those who advanced other narratives. It is impossible to determine what lay behind all of this revision of the war's history, but Davis provides a useful premise when he suggests that "the self-interest of participants, the defensiveness of their descendants, and the craving of all of us for a good story" nurtured the process. Further, the stories were changed to "suit political and social agendas" of the past and present. The development of the public memory of the war in Arkansas provides support for Davis's suppositions.[8]

The process of revising the story of the war in Arkansas started as Arkansans began to carry out public rituals honoring the war dead. The practice of memorializing the dead may have first started in South Carolina in 1865, when African Americans decorated the graves of the Union dead in that city. That same year, women in Richmond, Virginia, organized the first Ladies Memorial Association (LMA) to look to the burial of the Confederate dead from the Virginia battlefields, and on May 30, 1866, the LMA held a memorial service in Richmond to honor the Confederate dead. Union memorial services began to be held nationally in 1868, following an order by John A. Logan, commander of the Grand Army of the Republic, to organize ceremonies to honor the Union dead on May 30 of each year. Arkansans were slow to follow the examples set by Confederate memorial organizations elsewhere, and the first decoration ceremony did not take place until 1869 when a memorial service was held on May 10 in Little Rock. A federal ceremony, responding to the call of General Logan, was observed on May 30 that same year. These ceremonies became the birth place for rival views of what had taken place during the war.[9]

William E. Woodruff Jr., editor of the *Arkansas Gazette* and a former Confederate soldier, may have been the originator of the Little Rock ceremony, arguing for such an event the year before after hearing of those being held elsewhere. The actual decoration of the graves in 1869 was a simple event. Women gathered at Mount Holly Cemetery, and the service started with prayers and songs. There were no public addresses. After the opening proceedings, the women placed flowers on the graves of the some 2,000 Confederate dead buried there and in Oakland Cemetery. The ceremony had no overt interpretive significance in itself, but Woodruff did not hesitate to give the ceremony meaning beyond a simple remembrance of the dead. For Woodruff, the decoration of the Confederate graves was justified because these men had all died for "a cause none of us can, if we would obliterate from our mind." Woodruff believed that the Confederate cause had been a just one and that fighting for it had been an honorable endeavor. The editor did not lay out explicitly what the cause was that they had been fighting for, but it most likely was an effort to secure the rights of Southerners and for an independent nation.

Slavery, which had been central to the secession convention and the events leading up to war, was purged from the story and replaced with the rhetoric developed during the war. This revision of the past began a long-term trend in which former Confederates dismissed blacks as having any interest in the outcome of the war and also as meaningful participants in its outcome. As to the Confederate soldiers, the fact that they had fought for a worthy cause raised them as a group to heroic status. Again, the reality of the experiences of the men lying in these graves was submerged to the celebration of their heroic status as a whole.[10]

On May 30, 1869, Union veterans held their first Memorial Day in Little Rock at the new national cemetery. The men who spoke there disagreed strenuously with the views of the editor of the *Arkansas Gazette*. State Adjutant General Albert W. Bishop, a Union army veteran, offered what former Confederate general Jubal Early described as the Unionist-Emancipationist view of the war, a view that he feared would define Confederates for all time as traitors and, thus, dishonorable. Bishop's speech would have confirmed Early in his fears, for he clearly saw the South's actions as treason. He was willing to concede the bravery of individual Confederate soldiers, but he attacked the cause for which they fought. To admit, he said, "that his cause was just our presence here forbids us to concede." The South had fired upon Fort Sumter, the battle had been joined, its end had "no uncertain issue." The Union men who fought had been determined to vindicate the national honor and had destroyed the "great heresy of State's Rights." The Union was preserved and, with it, slavery had been brought to an end. The presence of members of the "Colored Society and School" at the celebration indicated even more. The war and subsequent reconstruction had raised these former slaves to full citizenship, invested in equal civil rights if not social equality.[11]

Through the early 1870s, the Confederate and Union memorial days continued much in the same pattern in Little Rock, although by the middle of that decade the ceremonies began to change. At first, the Confederate memorial services continued to center on women laying

As the years passed, veterans who fought on both sides in the Civil War joined together to honor the bravery of the individual men who served. Union and Confederate veterans united at Conway's Oak Grove Cemetery on May 30, 1890, at the grave of John D. Townsend, who served in the Seventeenth Arkansas Infantry Regiment (CS). Courtesy of the Old State House Museum.

flowers on the graves of the Confederate dead. Participants in the ceremonies refrained from any mention of the Confederate cause. Union ceremonies included speeches that continued to reflect the Unionist-Emancipationist view of the war. This began to change as early as 1873 and for a time it appeared that some common ground might be reached between the two sides, that some sort of reconciliation was possible. The basis for that reconciliation would be the disappearance of any judgment on the causes of secession or the treasonous character of the Southern cause. In addition, the role of blacks in the war even began to disappear from the Unionist-Emancipationist story. Instead, the memorial services began to focus almost exclusively on the bravery of the individual soldiers. This was a theme that was acceptable to each side. At the 1873 service at the National Cemetery, General Albert Bishop was again the main speaker. This time he advanced a reconciliationist message, saying, "I believe the time will come when those who fought for and those who fought against us will forget all the past and join in commemorating the memory of all those that fought giving to all the credit of having been inspirited by honest, though, as I believe, mistaken ideas of duty and patriotism. While believing that those to whom we opposed were wrong, we can give them credit for honesty of purpose." While not conceding the justice of the Confederate cause, Bishop went far in accepting the idea that the Confederate soldier believed that his cause was just.[12]

This spirit of reconciliation appeared to gain further traction in 1875 when veterans in Little Rock merged the Confederate and Union memorials, decorating the graves of the dead of both sides on the day now set aside as Memorial Day—the thirtieth of May. A poem read at the 1875 ceremony summed up the sentiment of reunion, its last stanza reading, "Yes! These dear boys! The warring shock, The fearful strife is past, And sweetly underneath one flag, They rest in peace at last." That the joint ceremonies did not necessarily mean a reconciliation of the warring parties was evidenced, however, in an editorial in the *Arkansas Gazette* published after the 1877 service. The editor wondered if "the memorial exercises are not fraught with more of evil than of good." He believed that many returned from the ceremonies not filled with charity and goodwill but with a recharging of bitter memories. An ex-Federal would remember all the sacrifice, blood, and tears required to preserve the Union against what he believed was treason. A former Confederate would recall the devastation, desolation, and "bitter memories of defeat" that occurred in a "cause which to him was righteous in the sight of God and man." The editor went on to suggest that rather than continued talk of the war, it needed to be forgotten. "There is one thing more than another that we need to gain," he wrote, "it is forgetfulness—an utter oblivion of the wild, fierce passions, which engendered the most fearful civil war of modern history. Time and the cultivation of a broad and magnanimous public sentiment will do more to this good end than the honors which we pay to the dead." Nonetheless, the Memorial Day remembrance in Little Rock continued as a joint ceremony until 1886. After the services that year, Confederate participation lagged in the capital city and then ceased altogether. In other towns in the state, such ceremonies took place at least until 1890.[13]

The end of the joint Memorial Day ceremonies possibly occurred because of the emergence of a variety of organizations at this time that embraced a view of the war more closely associated with the ideas William Woodruff Jr. had advanced in 1867 than with the reconciliationist version embraced in the mid-1870s. By the mid-1880s, numerous Confederate veterans across the South began to form organizations connected with their wartime units. This was as true in Arkansas as elsewhere. In 1889 many of these new associations combined to form a national organization: the United Confederate Veterans (UCV). The new organization, while not abandoning the reconciliationist view completely and especially holding to its honoring of the bravery of the individual soldier, increasingly celebrated the Confederacy itself. Among its goals was the writing of "an impartial history of the Confederate side." In Arkansas, the UCV organized its first camp in Bentonville in 1892, and thirteen camps had been formed by 1893. By the end of the decade, the UCV had spread throughout the state. The movement to memorialize the Confederate soldier and the Confederacy received even greater impetus with the formation of the United Daughters of the Confederacy (UDC) in 1895 and the Sons of Confederate Veterans (SCV) in 1896. Local units of the UDC and SCV appeared in the same years as their national organizations.[14]

The celebration of the Confederacy initiated by these groups drew heavily upon the writings of former Confederate leaders, who spent a considerable amount of time defending their actions and exonerating themselves from charges that they had fought for a dishonorable cause and had, indeed, been guilty of treason. This revisionist history owned much to the books of men such as Edward Pollard, Albert Taylor Bledsoe, and Robert L. Dabney, as well as the former vice president of the Confederacy, Alexander H. Stephens. Numerous articles appeared in Bledsoe's *Southern Review* and former Confederate general Daniel H. Hill's *The Land We Love*, later the *Southern Magazine*. Pollard, the editor of the *Richmond Examiner*, gave the name to this new interpretation in his book *The Lost Cause*.

Revisionists' history of the war years began with a view of the antebellum South as an honorable chivalric society, whose slave labor system was not only paternalistic but was a civilizing force for blacks. Secession occurred only when the North had pushed to restrict the constitutional rights of Southerners. The subsequent war was not a revolution but a war to protect the legal principle of self-government. As to the war itself, the Lost Cause interpretation insisted that Confederate commanders, especially Generals Robert E. Lee and Thomas J. "Stonewall" Jackson, were superior leaders and military tacticians, in addition to being gentlemen. As to the common soldier, the Lost Cause story portrayed them as men who fought with incomparable valor, committed to their principles and to the protection of their homeland. As to the war's result, the narrative maintained that the North had defeated the South only by overwhelming it with numbers and resources, and that the cause itself was never defeated. There were unstated parts of this new history, such as that slavery played no role in the sectional conflict. Dissent and opposition to the Confederacy within the South disappeared. The role that slaves played in the conflict, especially the contribution of the thousands who joined the Union army, was dismissed and replaced with the celebration of the faithful slave who proved the benevolent character of the slave system.[15]

Historian Gaines Foster has written of the early proponents of the Lost Cause that they had limited initial impact but became "important because their speeches and articles did help establish points that would be accepted by later veterans' movements." This was certainly true in Arkansas where the impact of their interpretation of the war began to be seen as early as 1889 when the *Arkansas Gazette* called for the renewal of the annual decoration of Confederate graves. Noting that a Confederate Memorial Day was being held elsewhere in the South and that the citizens of Helena, Arkansas, had observed such a celebration the previous year, the editor believed it was time once again to honor the Confederate dead and the remaining veterans. He clearly intended it, however, to be more than simply the honoring of former Confederates. Unlike the same paper's editorials in 1867, this time the editor advocated a celebration of the Confederate South and particularly its commitment to constitutional government. The Lost Cause narrative had clearly taken a hold, for he argued that the war unquestionably was one for the protection of the South's constitutional rights, and, in fighting for their cause, Confederates had demonstrated a heroic strength of character. Indeed, in his view, and with no apparent irony intended, this strength of character had helped the nation as a whole, giving to the American people the "grandest and greatest nation upon earth."[16]

Despite the call for a Confederate Memorial Day in 1889, a ceremony in Little Rock was not held until May 16, 1893, a year after the first camps of the UCV were organized in the state. As suggested by the *Gazette*'s editor, the ceremony was much more than one honoring the dead; it was a celebration of the Confederacy that incorporated the central components of the Lost Cause narrative. The sponsor of the event was the Ladies' Confederate Memorial Association of Little Rock, a group just formed. Prominent speakers included Rev. William Carnahan of Christ Episcopal Church; former governor Simon P. Hughes; and J. C. Marshall, a prominent local attorney. The words spoken outlined a new

Men and women gather at the Independence County Courthouse to celebrate Confederate Memorial Day in Batesville in 1900. Courtesy of the Arkansas State Archives.

view of the reality of the war. Offering a challenge to the Unionist-Emancipationist viewpoint, the speakers insisted that secession and the war had taken place because Southerners were fighting for principles. Rev. Carnahan's opening prayer praised the dead who had "defended their home and fireside [and]...battled for constitutional rights and liberties." They had possessed the "purest motives," sacrificing their lives for a "lost cause." Carnahan went on, however, to assert that their cause was not lost at all because "truth and right are eternal and the might of majorities cannot touch them." Governor Hughes joined in, insisting that "the people of the South were moved by principle," and they waged war, "only for the right of self-government." They had "offered their lives willing sacrifices to their honest convictions of right and duty." J. C. Marshall proclaimed the honored dead to be heroes and declared that he offered "no apology to friend or foe for the hallowed custom which brings us together." These men were "guilty of no treason." Indeed, he believed that ultimately history would "reverse the verdicts that had been delivered unjustly." In their speeches, these men challenged the entire Unionist-Emancipationist memory. The war had not been about slavery, they maintained. The men who fought it had been honorable, principled men. Unionist sentiment within Arkansas and the rest of the Confederacy disappeared into a mythical solid South. African Americans were purged from the state's history, both as participants in their own emancipation and as equal citizens.[17]

Obviously, the Lost Cause narrative exonerated former Confederates from charges of treason and rebellion, but in his address, Marshall indicated that it served another purpose for him and for his listeners. The revised story provided an idealized world to which white Southerners could look for roots during a time of change as Arkansans found themselves in a world being broken down by new means of communication, intrusion of the national market, political upheaval of the farmers' rebellion, and the assertiveness of a growing African American middle class. For Marshall, the antebellum South and the Confederacy offered a model for the New South. That New South had risen "phoenix like" from the ashes of the old; but it was the "old South transformed but not changed." Cherishing the traditions of their Confederate heroes, the South's youth had created a new society that was not cosmopolitan; it was a South that "preserved in its greatest purity the Anglo-Saxon blood and civilization." It was a South that had not bowed to the utilitarianism of the age. Sentiment had not been dethroned. It was a South of pure politics, especially since the "Federal drum beat" no longer "menaced the polls," and electoral reforms like the Australian ballot had eliminated the "horrid incubus of ignorant suffrage" The Lost Cause narrative created a past that not only justified the action of the men of the past, it also justified the racist white world of the present.[18]

Given the appearance of the Lost Cause interpretation of the war, the return to an emphasis on the Unionist-Emancipationist narrative at the Union memorial services could not have been an unexpected development. At the 1890 ceremony at the National Cemetery in Little Rock—taking place at the same time as the new Confederate reunions, the appearance of the UDC, and the growing popularity of the Lost Cause narrative—the principal speaker expressed his willingness to see the nation reunited, but he openly criticized the South's role in the Civil War. For him, no question existed as to why the war had been fought—the war had been fought, he insisted, "on account of the slavery question. It was to the interest of the South to perpetuate the system, and to the North to put it down." The South's cause had been immoral and when the South threatened disunion, "an appeal to arms was had, and the north victorious." There was no noble Lost Cause. As former Confederates asserted their own view of the war, those who had supported the Union once again insisted on their own.[19]

By 1900, two competing narratives of the Civil War existed—the Lost Cause view and the Unionist-Emancipationist view. At that point, a movement critical to how most Arkansans would remember the war into the twenty-first century began when the various Confederate patriotic organizations started actively working to see that their revisionist narrative was not only celebrated at their own ceremonies but that it became the civic and public memory of Arkansas. The constitutions especially of the Sons of Confederate Veterans and the United Daughters of the Confederacy were aimed at this goal. The UDC's constitution set as one of its major objectives the creation of a "truthful history of the War between the Confederate States and the United States." The SCV's constitution admonished its members to instill in their descendants "a devotion and reverence for the principles represented by the Confederate States of America, to the honor, glory and memory of our fathers who fought for the Cause." This was to be accomplished by encouraging the erection of monuments to the men and ideas of the Cause and ensuring the writing and teaching of Southern history "with impartiality." What they considered truthful and impartial in each case insisted on the Lost Cause view, linking the war to a defense of constitutional liberties. Slavery and even rebellion disappeared from the story. The Arkansas chapters of these organizations took their charge in earnest in their efforts to ensure that the Lost Cause version of Civil War history triumphed in the public arena.[20]

The initial phase of their efforts focused on the building of public monuments that celebrated the Confederacy. Possibly the earliest monument erected to the Confederate dead was that in Hempstead County honoring those killed in the Battle of Prairie D'Ane. Raised by public subscription, it was placed at the burial site in 1888. After 1900, however, the UDC and SCV were responsible for placing monuments on public grounds. Possibly the first of these monuments erected on public space was the monument placed on the courthouse grounds in Van Buren, moved there in 1906 from the Fairview Cemetery where it had been originally erected. These public monuments usually were financed at least in part with taxpayer money to erect and maintain them. The monument to Confederate mothers on the State Capitol grounds, for example, received a $10,000 appropriation from the state. The construction of Confederate monuments continued into the 1920s, with the height of the process being reached in 1910 when Confederate monuments were dedicated in Pine Bluff, Lake Village, El Dorado,

Lonoke, and Marianna. Most of these were simple shafts capped with a sculpture of a Confederate soldier, although the Marianna monument honored General Robert E. Lee and monuments on the State Capitol grounds in Little Rock paid tribute to all of the state's Confederate soldiers and to Confederate mothers. Usually unveiled with public fanfare and coverage by state and local newspapers, these monuments symbolized the acceptance of the Lost Cause narrative by public officials, thus helping to promote its acceptance not just among its Confederate adherents but among the white population in general. The proliferation of Confederate monuments also helped to push from the public view the Unionist-Emancipationist perspective as similar monuments to the Union cause were placed only at Judsonia, Little Rock, St. Charles, and Siloam Springs. No monuments were erected to memorialize African Americans in this contest for public memory.[21]

Veterans and their descendants sponsored and raised Confederate monuments across Arkansas in the late nineteenth and early twentieth centuries, such as this one placed at Camden in 1884. Courtesy of the Old State House Museum.

No event better reflected the civic triumph of the Lost Cause narrative within the state than the dedication ceremonies for the Memorial to Confederate Soldiers at the State Capitol on June 4, 1905. The unveiling of the Memorial to Confederate Soldiers proved to be a celebration of statewide proportions. The correspondent for the *Arkansas Democrat* reported the event as a great "military and civic display" with thousands coming to Little Rock to attend the dedication. Even the band of the Second Regiment of United States troops stationed at Fort Roots participated, leading a parade from Little Rock's Center Street to the State Capitol. The speakers, along with the siting of the monument on state property, indicated the political muscle of those who had backed its erection. Roy D. Campbell, the prosecuting attorney for the Sixth Circuit Court and the former state representative who had sponsored the bill funding the statue, presented the statue to the state. Governor Jeff Davis accepted the monument. U.S. senator James H. Berry presented a Confederate flag to representatives of the UDC to honor their role in raising funds for the monument. Then orations were given by Asa S. Morgan, former colonel of the Twenty-sixth Arkansas Confederate Infantry, planter, and legislator, as well as Congressman R. Minor Wallace. A final address was provided by Lieutenant General William L. Cabell, commander of the UCV's Trans-Mississippi Department. The participation of such men indicated the extent to which the UCV, the UDC, and the SCV's story had come to be accepted by those in power within the state.[22]

The speakers at the dedication iterated the various components of the Lost Cause story, with the comments of Asa Morgan offering the strongest supporting statements. His speech offered a masterly restatement of the reasons the war had happened. The roots of the war, according to Morgan, lay with the North's encroachments on the rights reserved to the states by the U.S. Constitution. These encroachments were promoted by "meddling and malevolent marplots and fanatics" who determined to use the executive branch of the national government to "prevent the plain execution of the constitution they were sworn to support." Morgan did suggest that slavery may have had something to do with this constitutional crisis, admitting that President

Abraham Lincoln had declared the nation could not be half slave, half free. Lincoln's secretary of state, William Seward, "the bitterest political leader of the north," had even declared that a conflict was inevitable. Faced with this challenge, and despite having repeatedly compromised with the North, the South found it could no longer peaceably remain in the Union. To leave, they pursued a course "contemplated in the very terms" of the constitution, and they seceded. Only the Lincoln government's decision to resist this peaceable act with military force had produced a war, forcing Southerners to defend the "God-given right of self-government." That principle was the Confederacy's cause, the cause that had "sanctified the graves of martyrs in all ages of the world." Disingenuously, considering the South's desire to protect slavery throughout the nation, Morgan insisted that the South had never intended to compel anyone else to accept the South's civilization or institutions. Its only desire was to "transmit unimpaired to our descendants the rights and franchises which had come down to us from the founders of the republic."[23]

Asa S. Morgan. From Confederate Veteran *magazine, courtesy of the Butler Center for Arkansas Studies, Central Arkansas Library System, Little Rock.*

Morgan moved forward with the Lost Cause view, insisting on the heroic character of the South's leaders. Jefferson Davis, a representative man of the South, was one "whose name will shine in undimmed lustre when the names of his detractors and calumniators are lost in obscurity." Robert E. Lee was "transcendent in his ability as a soldier, and no less conspicuous [in] his virtues as a Christian, a patriot and citizen" and represented a character "perfect and complete, upon which the gods had set their scale to give the world assurance of a man." Stonewall Jackson was "like a meteor bursting forth and illuminating its pathway through the heavens," a man who illustrated the "valor and heroism of the Confederate soldier." Mentioning Joseph Johnston, Nathan Bedford Forrest, and Patrick Cleburne as Confederate saints, Morgan summed up the role of all these leaders—"braver spirits, or more devoted, self-sacrificing patriots never guided the destinies of a nation."[24]

As to the common soldiers, Morgan viewed them as heroic in their defense of the Confederate cause. Following the basic outline of the Lost Cause narrative, Morgan praised the Confederate soldier who had espoused his "country's cause," and had fought the war with "patriotic devotion." He had borne hardships, exhaustion, and suffering, but had continued with "patience, constancy, courage and deathly endurance." For four long years, the Confederate soldier had persisted in defending his rights and his home. It was his "heroic courage that beat back from their homes and firesides the serried ranks of their ruthless and overwhelming invaders." Morgan's view paralleled that of the revised Confederate history, presenting a generalized Confederate soldier bereft of any of the shortcomings that existed in reality. Ironically, in keeping with the efforts of reconciliation, Morgan excepted from the "ruthless" invaders he condemned the man who wore the blue and "patriotically responded to his country's call." There were "Ransey Sniffels...who found their occupation in firing the northern heart, and then, at safe distance from the field of conflict, adding fuel to the flames," but the common soldiers could be honored and respected for their manliness. For the advocates of the Lost Cause, men could with honor differ on "questions of rights"—indeed, to do so was critical to the justification of their own course.[25]

Remaining in step with Confederate revisionism, Morgan went on to insist that those who remained behind were unified in their support of the Confederacy, singling out for particular praise the constancy of the women. Morgan thanked the members of the UDC present for their sacrifices in helping to fund the monument, likening it to the support their mothers had given to the men of the Confederate army. Like the men who fought for the South, the women who gave their unwavering support to these men and their cause had been "sanctified and made holy" by their actions. Morgan likened Arkansas's Confederate women to those of Sparta who had sent their sons to battle, telling them to return with honor, either with or upon their shields. It was the women who had prompted their men to "deeds of patriotism and devotion." Absent in this new history was any opposition to the cause, any wavering of support.[26]

Like Rev. William Carnahan at Little Rock's Confederate Memorial Day in 1893, Morgan went on to insist that the "Confederate cause is not a lost cause." The Confederates' resistance to Northern interference with constitutional rights had ultimately brought about change. He likened General Lee and the Confederacy to the experience of England's Oliver Cromwell and the English Commonwealth. Despite Cromwell's efforts at preventing a return of monarchy in England, the Commonwealth had failed and the monarchy was restored. But, the monarchy was modified. Despite their failure in war, the restored monarchy was one "involving all the reforms for which the chieftain had blead [*sic*]." Pointing to the decisions of the U.S. Supreme Court since the war and the end of Reconstruction, Morgan observed that the nation had returned to a community that recognized the rights of the states and limits on the power of the central government. "The wild doctrines of Thaddeus Stevens and [Charles] Sumner on these points," he insisted, "are not the law." Ignoring the new absence of slavery, Morgan concluded that, had the Southern states been sure of this conclusion, secession would never have happened."[27]

Colonel Morgan also returned to another theme from 1893, that of J. C. Marshall. The colonel believed that, in the end, the South actually had won the war, bringing the nation back to its constitutional principles. The South was back in the national fold, representing the conservative force that would hold the nation together as it faced the crises of industrialization and urbanization. The war had purified the South. The former Confederate states now brought to the councils of the nation a people "homogeneous in origin, and united in the spirit of conservativism." They now controlled the destiny of the nation. They held the balance of power. They were a compensating influence against "the spirit of radicalism, represented in the north by the admixture of its population with every known race on the face of the earth." It would be the white South, cherishing and preserving the "faith and traditions of their ancestors, as embodied in the declaration of independence," that would "control the destinies of the great republic." Rebellion had been turned into the salvation of the nation.[28]

Morgan's rhetoric was typical of the words spoken at the dedication ceremonies held across the state. Explaining the war as a defense of states' rights, celebrating the heroism and dedication of Confederate leaders and common soldiers, insisting on the unity of the homefront behind the Confederate cause, and contending that the South's cause had ultimately triumphed became the standard fare of speakers at such events. Usually implicit, although at times explicit, in these speeches was the growing insistence that not only was the Confederate cause just but that the defense of the antebellum South itself was just, as Confederates were fighting for a higher type of civilization. When saying that Confederates fought to defend their homes, these speakers were not just referring to the individual hearth and home of the soldier. Instead they were speaking of a now idealized South.

Rev. Phillip C. Fletcher of the Winfield Memorial Church in Little Rock was one of the speakers who made this point explicit. At the dedication of the monument to the Capital Guards held in Little Rock in 1911, Fletcher admonished his audience, "God forbid that we should ever forget the achievements of the old South." It was, for Fletcher, the South that had given the nation its Declaration of Independence and its first president. "Ladies and gentlemen," he went on, "the old South was the land of bravery, chivalry, romance, blue blood, cotton corn, negroes, and watermelons. Alas, there were too many negroes and not enough watermelons." Ironically, given the ultimate purpose of the Confederacy, he went on to conclude, "We are living today, thanks God, under one flag, in peace and prosperity." The irony of this thanksgiving was patent, for the very men being honored had attempted to destroy the very nation Fletcher now celebrated.[29]

The UCV, UDC, and SCV not only celebrated the Lost Cause through the erection of monuments, but they worked in a variety of other ways to make theirs the public memory of the war in Arkansas. They worked to secure public observances of Confederate heroes and events, including Confederate Decoration Day and the birthdays of Robert E. Lee, Stonewall Jackson, and Jefferson Davis. Such events received widespread coverage in the state's newspapers at least into the 1930s, coverage that put forward over and over again the basic Lost Cause narrative.

With even more effect, they labored to influence the ideas of future generations. The organizations' constitutions had all charged members with ensuring that a "correct" history of the Civil War was known and made known. As early as 1904, the historian for the Arkansas Daughters of the Confederacy, Mrs. Richard B. Willis, challenged the organization's members to insist that this acceptable history be taught in the public schools. At the annual convention that year, she asked members of the UDC to "examine and know what sort of history and history teachers are influencing our children." The members of the UDC had to guard their children from "false shame for their [forefathers'] political activities." She stopped just short of asking that they put pressure on teachers who taught the "unacceptable" story. Nine years later, Willis, still the historian, remained adamant that the Daughters must help shape what children learned in school. For Willis, the schools had fallen into unsympathetic hands, and too many of the young people of the state had been forced to hear "the apologetic, patronizing tone of men, men who feel no pride in the statesmanship of the south, no thrill of exultation of her valor. It has not been unusual for our boys to study United States History under teachers who had not and could not have any conception of the attitudes of the South in past decades." The result had been that many of these young men had "admitted a feeling of shame at what they learned of the puerile statesmanship of our ancestors and of their poor achievement in arms."[30]

The Daughters initially sought to overcome the "negative" view of the war that seemed to be appearing in the schools by increasing their involvement in the schools. They presented schools with pictures of Jefferson Davis and Robert E. Lee. On such occasions, the schools welcomed them and students received lectures on the virtues of these Confederate heroes. The UDC sponsored poetry and essay contests. In 1931, for example, the Hope Chapter offered prizes for essays on Confederate topics, all slanted in such a way as to familiarize the student with the Lost Cause story. A prize of ten dollars was awarded to the best essay on the "Glory of the Old South" and another ten dollars for the best essay on "Faithful Slaves of the Sixties." Clearly, they asked no open-ended questions.

A significant component of their educational activities was the use of David O. Dodd as an example for young Arkansans. Dodd was a young man executed in Little Rock in 1863, charged with spying for the Confederacy. The Dodd story had already emerged as a part of the Lost Cause narrative by the beginning of the twentieth century, with Dodd supposedly dying rather than surrendering the names of men who had helped him. His actions were likened to that of the iconic Revolutionary War hero Nathan Hale. His relative youth made his story one that could be empathized with by children and could be used to teach them about the goodness of the Confederate cause, the desirability of living an honorable life, and the duty of loyalty to cause and comrades. When the national organization of the UDC encouraged state

David O. Dodd, a young Confederate spy executed in Little Rock, emerged after the war as "the boy martyr of the Confederacy," inspiring such tributes as this memorial window. Courtesy of the American Civil War Museum, Richmond, Virginia.

chapters to choose someone from their state to add to the annual commemorative ceremonies for President Davis and General Lee, the Arkansas Daughters chose Dodd. Afterward, Dodd's picture was distributed along with the other heroes, and lecturers from the Daughters added Dodd to their subject matter in the schools. Dodd poetry became a standard item of their contests.[31]

In ensuring the dominance of the Lost Cause narrative before the public, the UDC may have been even more successful with its efforts at controlling the story of the Civil War that appeared in the textbooks used in the state's schools. The creation of a state school textbook commission in 1917 helped in their efforts, providing a governmental body susceptible to being lobbied. In the first year that the commission existed, the Daughters petitioned it for the right to review the history texts under consideration. The commission readily conceded to their request. From that point on, only United States and state textbooks that conformed to the Lost Cause interpretation could get through the adoption process. In 1917, the publishers of Henry Bourne and Elbert Benton's *History of the United States* actually sent page proofs to the UDC's state historian, who informed them that at least four of their paragraphs were unfair. When the state commission withheld the contract for the book, the publisher made the desired corrections and the book was approved. The revised textbook strayed little from the Lost Cause narrative. Arkansas children—black as well as white, since the same commission approved textbooks for the segregated African American schools—learned that the war was a defensive one for the South, its soldiers all fought bravely to defend constitutional rights, and African Americans played no role in the war's outcome. Bourne and Benton concluded that Southerners "believed that [the war] was a struggle for existence and for rights inherited from their fathers, especially the right to govern themselves."[32]

The UDC worked with particular industry to control what appeared in Arkansas history texts. As in the case of the American history texts, they were very successful, with their story pushing aside alternative ones into the 1960s. Generally, textbook authors avoided any lengthy discussion of what caused the war. Instead, they emphasized the state's entry into the conflict only after President Lincoln had called for troops to suppress the rebellion. This idea that the state had acted only to defend itself from invaders made the action righteous. The right of the state to secede was most explicitly asserted by Walter S. McNutt's 1932 text that labeled its chapters on the war, "The South's Struggle for Constitutional Justice." The emphasis on Arkansas secession as a response to Lincoln's attempt to subdue the other seceding states retained some viability into the 1980s in Fred Berry and John Novak's text.[33]

To avoid any discussion of divisions within the state, authors devoted the preponderance of text to a military history of the war. Details of military operations from the siege of the Little Rock Arsenal in 1861 to the Camden campaign of 1864 filled most of the war chapters. The basic unity of Arkansans behind the Confederacy also was an article of faith, although some early texts did have a sentence or two noting that a small number of Arkansans joined the Union army.

Invariably, a list of the state's wartime heroes appeared—all Confederates. The stories offered little insight into why most of these men were heroes, other than that they were leaders of Confederate Arkansas. The two most well-developed stories included those of General Patrick Cleburne, who had either the luck or the misfortune, when it came to the narrative, to be killed. The other who invariably appeared was David O. Dodd.

Completely missing from all of these textbooks was the role of the state's black population. In the approved texts, one would find little about slavery and nothing about how a large number of enslaved African Americans left their masters or that thousands of them joined the Union army. The Lost Cause story attributed their freedom only to Lincoln and the Emancipation Proclamation. None mentioned the role of the Fourteenth and Fifteenth Amendments in securing black citizens their new freedom and ensuring equal protection under the law.[34] Since these books were used in the state's black schools as well as white, generations of young African Americans grew up in a world where they were not a part of the history. Generations of white students also concluded that blacks had played no legitimate role in their state's history, a conclusion at odds with what had actually happened, a conclusion helping to support the segregated society that existed.

The UDC's influence on the textbooks also could be seen in their chapters dealing with Reconstruction, where all presented a narrative developed by contemporaries to explain the sometimes violent overthrow of Republican government in the state. For the UDC, the postwar years proved that the North's course toward the slaves had been misguided. While recognizing that slavery had been brought to an end by the war, most of the state's textbooks insisted that Reconstruction proved that the South's peculiar institution had been necessary for blacks to be meaningful participants in society and that with the end of slavery some sort of subordination of blacks was still essential. According to the textbook narratives, blacks, once free, had been easily manipulated by unscrupulous whites and had reverted to a semi-barbaric state. John H. Reynolds's *Makers of Arkansas History* portrayed a black population "spoiled" by promises of land and mules. Faith Knoop's *Arkansas* pictured a world in which black citizens, after restraints were removed, "began to get into mischief." John Moore's *School History of Arkansas* took it for granted that former masters should teach blacks to "settle down to work and live peaceably with their white friends." All of this lent further credence to the Lost Cause defense of the South, in addition to creating a stereotype of African Americans as a race that justified their treatment into the mid-twentieth century. If black residents of the state behaved in this way, then slavery was justified, suppression was acceptable. A. M. Harper's *Story of Arkansas* praised the Ku Klux Klan for getting blacks back under control, rendering "excellent work."[35]

In the end, controlling the books used in history classes assured the success of the UDC's efforts to instill the Lost Cause narrative in the youth of Arkansas. Every child who passed through the schools would have learned that interpretation as *the* history of the war. Reinforced by the UDC and SCV's memorials, the Lost Cause story came to dominate the public's, especially the white public's, view of the war and, inferentially, the character of racial relations.

The Unionist-Emancipationist narrative never completely disappeared within the state, but it seemed to have less of a hold on the public imagination. At least into the 1920s, the national Memorial Day still revolved in part around that view of the war, although following World War I the emphasis increasingly was on the dead of that conflict. In the 1960s, with the emergence of historical revisionism, the Unionist-Emancipationist story also began to be integrated into new textbooks produced by younger scholars. Their rewriting of the state's history faced little opposition from those who had controlled school texts for so long, but whether or not this view has been widely embraced is unclear, especially since many high school students receive minimal historical training.

Confederate re-enactors cross Broadway in downtown Little Rock on January 8, 2011, to participate in a memorial ceremony for David O. Dodd in Mount Holly Cemetery. Courtesy of the Arkansas Democrat-Gazette.

Even with the persistence of the Unionist-Emancipationist story of the war in the academy, the Lost Cause narrative persists in a variety of influential forums. The former editor of the *Arkansas Democrat-Gazette*, for example, has used versions of it to argue each year for the embracing of the ideas of honor and chivalry attributed to the Confederacy's leaders, especially Robert E. Lee. It is present in varying degrees among the thousands of re-enactors who gather on the battlefields of Arkansas to not only re-enact but to celebrate the heroism of the soldiers involved; few if any of them would say they are commemorating a war fought to maintain slavery. The "Voices" page of the *Arkansas Democrat-Gazette* and various websites are prominent vehicles for its continued publicity and persistence. The debates over the Confederate flag inspired one correspondent to write, "I believe true Southerners (born and raised in the South) honor and cherish it [the battle flag] for what it really symbolizes—the heroism of those who fought and died defending states' rights."[36] Another writer declared the war a "struggle for freedom and liberty," a fight against "tyranny, oppression, and injustice."[37] It also has been embraced by many who see a nation and culture under attack, who see in the Confederate experience a model for resistance to what one correspondent described as "white liberals" of both political parties and "blacks who have a hidden agenda."[38] Another saw the war as only about states' rights, a battle still to be fought with "things like marriage, health care, education and local government...being taken away from the states and put under federal control."[39]

One hundred and fifty years after the war, the fight continues, although now the fight is one of words and memory. Two major interpretations with numerous variants are a part of our perceived past, standing against each other, unreconciled. Unfortunately, this conflict denies a common history for a community, a history that can be the basis of unity, a lack of which is poisonous to that community. One view declares a generation of Arkansans guilty of fighting a war to protect an iniquitous institution, something the ancestors of those men find impossible to accept. The other view denies much of the reality of the war and especially the historical role of what was and remains an important minority of the population, accepting as fact what was essentially a racist narrative developed in the early twentieth century. In the second decade of the twenty-first century, it is unclear that either party is ready to give up its particular point of view. Perhaps resolution can come only from the continued work of historians seeking both to disprove the myths that have surrounded the nation's great Civil War and to throw a brighter light onto what actually happened.

Notes

Chapter 2—"What Is to Become of Us?": The Postwar Lives of Civil War Generals in Arkansas

By Thomas A. DeBlack

1. Talk: George S. Patton, https://en.wikiquote.org/wiki/Talk:George_S._Patton (accessed June 4, 2016).

2. Brainy Quotes: William Tecumseh Sherman, http://www.brainyquote.com/quotes/authors/w/william_tecumseh_sherman_2.html (accessed June 4, 2016).

3. "The Diary of Susan Cook," *Phillips County Historical Quarterly* 4–6 (December 1965–March 1968).

4. M. Philip Lucas, "Samuel Ryan Curtis," in *Encyclopedia of the American Civil War: A Political, Social, and Military History*, ed. David S. Heidler and Jeanne T. Heidler, vol. 1 (Santa Barbara, CA: ABC-CLIO, 2000), 533–34.

5. Ibid.

6. Ibid., 534; On Curtis's accomplishments and reputation, see William L. Shea and Earl J. Hess, *Pea Ridge: Civil War Campaign in the West* (Chapel Hill: University of North Carolina Press, 1992).

7. Terry L. Beckenbaugh, "James Gilpatrick Blunt," in *Encyclopedia of the American Civil War: A Political, Social, and Military History*, ed. David S. Heidler and Jeanne T. Heidler, vol. 1 (Santa Barbara, CA: ABC-CLIO, 2000), 246–47.

8. Thomas A. DeBlack, *With Fire and Sword: Arkansas, 1861–1874* (Fayetteville: University of Arkansas Press, 2003), 65, 67, 70–72.

9. Beckenbaugh, "Blunt."

10. Beckenbaugh, "Blunt." On Blunt's syphilis, see Mark K. Christ, *Civil War Arkansas, 1863: The Battle for a State* (Norman: University of Oklahoma Press, 2010), 221. In his footnote, Christ cites medical historian Jack Welsh, who notes that a doctor who treated Blunt at the time attributed his condition to "sunstroke with softening of the brain." When Blunt died in 1881, his immediate cause of death was listed as "paresis, three years duration." Jack D. Welsh, *Medical Histories of Confederate Generals* (Kent, Ohio: Kent State University Press 1995), 32.

11. Thomas Burnell Colbert, "Francis Jay Herron," in *Encyclopedia of the American Civil War: A Political, Social, and Military History*, ed. David S. Heidler and Jeanne T. Heidler, vol. 2 (Santa Barbara, CA: ABC-CLIO, 2000), 967–68.

12. Ibid.

13. Ibid.; Bobby Roberts, "Francis Jay Herron," Encyclopedia of Arkansas History & Culture, http://www.encyclopediaofarkansas.net/encyclopedia/entry-detail.aspx?entryID=6387 (accessed June 4, 2016); Ezra J. Warner, *Generals in Blue: Lives of the Union Commanders* (Baton Rouge: Louisiana State University Press, 1992), 228–29.

14. David Sesser, "James Totten," Encyclopedia of Arkansas History & Culture, http://www.encyclopediaofarkansas.net/encyclopedia/entry-detail.aspx?entryID=4452 (accessed June 4, 2016); "Remember Me: Captain James Totten" at http://www.littlerock.org/!userfiles/editor/docs/parks/MacArthur/learn/Remember%20Me/Capt%20James%20Totten%20Handout.pdf (accessed June 4, 2016).

15. DeBlack, *With Fire and Sword*, 21–22.

16. William Piston and Richard Hatcher II, *Wilson's Creek: The Second Battle of the Civil War and the Men Who Fought It* (Chapel Hill: University of North Carolina Press, 2004), 73.

17. James Grant Wilson and John Fiske, eds., *Appleton's Cyclopedia of American Biography* (New York: D. Appleton, 1900).

18. Cullum's Register at http://penelope.uchicago.edu/Thayer/E/Gazetteer/Places/America/United_States/Army/USMA/Cullums_Register/1083*.html (accessed June 4, 2016). On Totten's alcoholism, see Michael E. Banasik, ed., *Reluctant Cannoneer: The Diary of Robert T. McMahan of the Twenty-fifth Independent Ohio Light Artillery* (Iowa City, Iowa: Press of the Camp Pope Bookshop, 2000), 289–92.

19. Warner, *Generals in Blue*, 385–86; David S. Heidler and Jeanne T. Heidler, "Benjamin Mayberry Prentiss," in *Encyclopedia of the American Civil War: A Political, Social, and Military History*, ed. David S. Heidler and Jeanne T. Heidler, vol. 3 (Santa Barbara, CA: ABC-CLIO, 2000), 1559–60.

20. Heidler and Heidler, "Prentiss," 1559–60. On the new scholarship concerning Prentiss's role at the Hornet's Nest, see Timothy B. Smith, *Shiloh: Conquer or Perish* (Lawrence: University Press of Kansas, 2014).

21. Warner, *Generals in Blue*, 385–86; Heidler and Heidler, "Prentiss," 1559–60.

22. Gregory J. W. Urwin, "Frederick Steele," in *Encyclopedia of the American Civil War: A Political, Social, and Military History*, ed. David S. Heidler and Jeanne T. Heidler, vol. 4 (Santa Barbara, CA: ABC-CLIO, 2000), 1856–57.

23. Urwin, "Steele," 1856–57; DeBlack, 93–99.

24. Urwin, "Steele," 1856–57.

25. Thomas A. DeBlack, "Powell Clayton," in *Encyclopedia of the American Civil War: A Political, Social, and Military History*, ed. David S. Heidler and Jeanne T. Heidler, vol. 1 (Santa Barbara, CA: ABC-CLIO, 2000), 454–55.

26. DeBlack, "Clayton," 454–55. For a fuller discussion, see DeBlack, *With Fire and Sword.*

27. Carl H. Moneyhon, "Powell Clayton," Encyclopedia of Arkansas History & Culture, http://www.encyclopediaofarkansas.net/encyclopedia/entry-detail.aspx?entryID=94 (accessed June 4, 2016).

28. DeBlack, *With Fire and Sword*, 45–49.

29. Ibid., 95–96.

30. David Sesser, "James Fleming Fagan," Encyclopedia of Arkansas History & Culture, http://www.encyclopediaofarkansas.net/encyclopedia/entry-detail.aspx?entryID=3053 (accessed June 4, 2016).

31. Ibid.

32. Ibid.

33. Buck T. Foster, "Sterling Price," in *Encyclopedia of the American Civil War: A Political, Social, and Military History*, ed. David S. Heidler and Jeanne T. Heidler, vol. 3 (Santa Barbara, CA: ABC-CLIO, 2000), 1562–63.

34. Albert Castel, *General Sterling Price and the Civil War in the West* (Baton Rouge: Louisiana State University Press, 1968, 1996), 273–79.

35. Welsh, *Medical Histories of Confederate Generals*, 177; Robert E. Shalhope, *Sterling Price: Portrait of a Southerner* (Columbia: University of Missouri Press, 1971), xi, 290.

36. Castel, *General Sterling Price*, 280–83.

37. Ibid., 283.

38. Mark E. Scott, "Joseph Orville Shelby," in *Encyclopedia of the American Civil War: A Political, Social, and Military History*, ed. David S. Heidler and Jeanne T. Heidler, vol. 4 (Santa Barbara, CA: ABC-CLIO, 2000), 1745–46.

39. Mark K. Christ, "Joseph Orville Shelby," Encyclopedia of Arkansas History & Culture, http://www.encyclopediaofarkansas.net/encyclopedia/entry-detail.aspx?entryID=7017 (accessed June 4, 2016); Scott, "Shelby," 1745–46.

40. Scott, "Shelby," 1745–46.

41. Clay Williams, "Theophilus Hunter Holmes" in *Encyclopedia of the American Civil War: A Political, Social, and Military History*, ed. David S. Heidler and Jeanne T. Heidler, vol. 2 (Santa Barbara, CA: ABC-CLIO, 2000), 989–90.

42. DeBlack, *With Fire and Sword*, 64.

43. Joseph G. Dawson III, "Theophilus Holmes and Confederate Generalship," in *Confederate Generals in the Trans-Mississippi: Essays on America's Civil War*, ed. Lawrence Lee Hewitt, vol. 1 (Knoxville: University of Tennessee Press, 2013), 47.

44. Diane Neal, "Thomas Carmichael Hindman," in *Encyclopedia of the American Civil War: A Political, Social, and Military History*, ed. David S. Heidler and Jeanne T. Heidler, vol. 2 (Santa Barbara, CA: ABC-CLIO, 2000), 976–77; DeBlack, *With Fire and Sword*, 8.

45. Carl H. Moneyhon, "Thomas Carmichael Hindman," Encyclopedia of Arkansas History & Culture, http://www.encyclopediaofarkansas.net/encyclopedia/entry-detail.aspx?entryID=1672 (accessed June 4, 2016).

46. Neal, "Hindman"; DeBlack, *With Fire and Sword*, 188.

47. DeBlack, *With Fire and Sword*, 188.

48. Mike Polston, "John Sappington Marmaduke," Encyclopedia of Arkansas History & Culture, http://www.encyclopediaofarkansas.net/encyclopedia/entry-detail.aspx?entryID=6489 (accessed June 4, 2016).

49. Ibid.

50. Vaughan Motley Bryant, "John Sappington Marmaduke, '54," 2, n.d., typescript, John Sappington Marmaduke, Biographical Folder, Houghton Library, Harvard University, Cambridge, MA, 2, quoted in Helen P. Trimpi, "A 'Gallant and Prudent Commander': Major General John S. Marmaduke" in *Confederate Generals in the Trans-Mississippi: Essays on America's Civil War*, ed. Lawrence Lee Hewitt, vol. 1 (Knoxville: University of Tennessee Press, 2013), 160.

51. Polston, "Marmaduke."

52. Don Montgomery, "Thomas James Churchill," Encyclopedia of Arkansas History & Culture, http://www.encyclopediaofarkansas.net/encyclopedia/entry-detail.aspx?entryID=92 (accessed June 4, 2016).

53. Mark K. Christ, "'Not Fortunate in War': Major General Thomas James Churchill," in *Confederate Generals in the Trans-Mississippi: Essays on America's Civil War*, ed. Lawrence Lee Hewitt, vol. 1 (Knoxville: University of Tennessee Press, 2013), 167–94.

54. F. Clark Elkins, "Thomas James Churchill," in *The Governors of Arkansas: Essays in Political Biography*, ed. Timothy P. Donovan, Willard B. Gatewood, and Jeannie M. Whayne, 2nd ed. (Fayetteville: University of Arkansas Press, 1995), 74.

55. Elkins, "Churchill," 74–75.

56. Christ, "Not Fortunate in War," 188–89.

57. Carl H. Moneyhon, "Albert Pike," Encyclopedia of Arkansas History & Culture, http://www.encyclopediaofarkansas.net/encyclopedia/entry-detail.aspx?entryID=1737 (accessed June 4, 2016).

58. Ibid.

59. Ibid.

60. William L. Shea and Earl J. Hess, *Pea Ridge: Civil War Campaign in the West* (Chapel Hill: University of North Carolina Press, 1992), 274–75.

61. Moneyhon, "Pike."

62. Ibid.

63. Jeffery S. Prushankin, "Edmund Kirby Smith," in *Encyclopedia of the American Civil War: A Political, Social, and Military History*, ed. David S. Heidler and Jeanne T. Heidler, vol. 4 (Santa Barbara, CA: ABC-CLIO, 2000), 1810–11.

Chapter 3—"How Free Is Free?": A Historiographical Review of African American History in Post-Civil War and Reconstruction Arkansas

By Cherisse Jones-Branch

1. Carl H. Moneyhon, "Slavery," Encyclopedia of Arkansas History & Culture, http://www.encyclopediaofarkansas.net/encyclopedia/entry-detail.aspx?entryID=1275 (accessed June 4, 2016).

2. Kelly Houston Jones, "Bondswomen's Work on the Cotton Frontier: Wagram Plantation, Arkansas," *Agricultural History* 89, no. 3 (Summer 2015): 388–401.

3. James M. McPherson, *The Negro's Civil War: How American Blacks Felt and Acted During the War for the Union* (New York: Vintage, 2003).

4. Carl H. Moneyhon, "Race and the Struggle for Freedom: African American Arkansans after Emancipation," in *Race and Ethnicity in Arkansas: New Perspectives*, ed. John A. Kirk (Fayetteville: University of Arkansas Press, 2014), 17. See also Carl H. Moneyhon, *The Impact of the Civil War and Reconstruction on Arkansas* (Baton Rouge: Louisiana State University Press, 1994).

5. Jim Downs, *Sick From Freedom: African-American Illness and Suffering During the Civil War and Reconstruction* (New York: Oxford University Press, 2012), 45.

6. Bobby L. Lovett, "African Americans, Civil War, and Aftermath in Arkansas," *Arkansas Historical Quarterly* 42 (Autumn 1963): 329. See also

Randy Finley, "In War's Wake: Health Care and Arkansas Freedmen, 1863–1868," *Arkansas Historical Quarterly* 51 (Spring 1992): 135–63, and Gene W. Boyett, "The Black Experience in the First Decade of Reconstruction in Pope County, Arkansas," *Arkansas Historical Quarterly* 51 (Spring 1992): 119–34.

7. Randy Finley, *From Slavery to Uncertain Freedom: The Freedmen's Bureau in Arkansas, 1865–1869* (Fayetteville: University of Arkansas Press, 1996), 49.

8. Grif Stockley, *Ruled by Race: Black/White Relations in Arkansas from Slavery to the Present* (Fayetteville: University of Arkansas Press, 2009), 136. For more on black religious denominations in Arkansas, also see Calvin White Jr., *The Rise to Respectability: Race, Religion, and the Church of God in Christ* (Fayetteville: University of Arkansas Press, 2012).

9. C. Calvin Smith, *Educating the Masses: The Unfolding History of Black School Administrators in Arkansas, 1900–2000* (Fayetteville: University of Arkansas Press, 2003), 9.

10. Congress also authorized the incorporation of the Freedmen's Savings and Trust Company in 1865. The Little Rock branch operated from June 1870 until July 1874. The accounts reveal much about black organizations and institutions in Little Rock as well as African Americans' origins, occupations, ages, businesses, literacy, and wealth. See Bobby L. Lovett, "Accounts for the Little Rock, Arkansas, Freedmen's Savings and Trust Company," *Journal of Negro History* 66, no. 4 (Winter 1981–1982): 326–28.

11. Finley, *From Slavery to Uncertain Freedom*, 20–21.

12. For more on African American disfranchisement in Arkansas, see John Giggie, "Disband Him from the Church: African Americans and the Spiritual Politics of Disfranchisement in Post-Reconstruction Arkansas," *Arkansas Historical Quarterly* 60, no. 3 (Autumn 2001): 245–64.

13. Finley, *From Slavery to Uncertain Freedom*, 42–43.

14. Heather Andrea Williams, *Help Me to Find My People: The African American Search for Family Lost in Slavery* (Chapel Hill: University of North Carolina Press, 2012), 11.

15. Ibid.

16. Ibid., 154.

17. Earlier scholarship on this topic includes Joseph St. Hilaire, "The Negro Delegates in the Arkansas Constitutional Convention of 1868, A Group Profile," *Arkansas Historical Quarterly* 33 (Spring 1974): 43–69, and Horace D. Nash, "Blacks in Arkansas During Reconstruction," *Arkansas Historical Quarterly* 58 (Autumn 1989): 243–59.

18. John William Graves, *Town and Country: Race Relations in an Urban-Rural Context, Arkansas, 1865–1905* (Fayetteville: University of Arkansas Press, 1990), 17.

19. Lovett, "African Americans, Civil War, and Aftermath in Arkansas," 335. See also Carl H. Moneyhon, "Black Politics in Arkansas during the

Gilded Age, 1876–1900," *Arkansas Historical Quarterly* 54 (Autumn 1985): 222–44, and Blake J. Wintory, "African-American Legislators in the Arkansas General Assembly: 1868–1893," *Arkansas Historical Quarterly* 65 (2006): 383–484. Also see Wintory's 2005 University of Arkansas dissertation, "Environmental and Social Change in Lee County, Arkansas, and the St. Francis River Basin, 1865–1905."

20. See also Moneyhon, "Black Politics in Arkansas during the Gilded Age."

21. Moneyhon, "Race and the Struggle for Freedom," 29.

22. John William Graves, "The Arkansas Separate Coach Law of 1891," *Arkansas Historical Quarterly* 32, no. 2 (Summer 1973): 149–50.

23. Ibid., 151.

24. Ibid., 154. For a specific example of how this became manifest in the Arkansas Delta, see also Melanie Welch, "Violence and the Decline of Black Politics in St. Francis County," *Arkansas Historical Quarterly* 60, no. 4 (Winter 2001): 360–93.

25. Fon Louise Gordon, *Caste and Class: The Black Experience in Arkansas, 1880–1920* (Athens: University of Georgia Press, 1995), 4. See also Willard B. Gatewood, *Aristocrats of Color* (Fayetteville: University of Arkansas Press, 2000), and Ruth Patterson, *The Seed of Sally Good'n: A Black Family of Arkansas, 1833–1953* (Lexington: University of Kentucky Press, 1996).

26. Gordon, *Caste and Class*, 5; See Evelyn Brooks Higginbotham, *Righteous Discontent: The Women's Movement in the Black Baptist Church, 1880–1920* (Cambridge: Harvard University Press, 1994).

27. Gordon, *Caste and Class*, 4.

28. Ibid., 106–7.

29. Ibid., 110, 112.

30. Ibid., 114–15.

31. Ibid., 1, 2.

32. Story Matkin-Rawn, "The Great Negro State of the Country: Arkansas's Reconstruction and the Other Great Migration," *Arkansas Historical Quarterly* 72, no. 1 (Spring 2013): 4–5.

33. Ibid., 4–5, 22.

34. Kenneth C. Barnes, *Journey of Hope: The Back-to-Africa Movement in Arkansas in the Late 1800s* (Chapel Hill: University of North Carolina Press, 2004), 1.

35. Ibid., 2.

36. Ibid., 3.

37. Ibid., 178.

38. Jayme Millsap Stone's 2010 University of Memphis dissertation, "'They Were Her Daughters': Women and Grassroots Organizing for Social

Justice in the Arkansas Delta, 1870–1970," speaks soundly to the *longue durée* of women's activism.

39. Jeannie M. Whayne, Thomas A. DeBlack, George Sabo III, and Morris S. Arnold, *Arkansas: A Narrative History* (Fayetteville: University of Arkansas Press, 2002), 252.

40. "Royal Grand Chapter, Order of Eastern Star, Prince Hall Affiliated," http://www.arroyalgrandchapteroespha.net/royal-grand-chapter-history.html (accessed December 2, 2015).

41. Cherisse Jones-Branch, "Arkansas Association of Colored Women," Encyclopedia of Arkansas History & Culture, http://www.encyclopediaofarkansas.net/encyclopedia/entry-detail.aspx?entryID=8201 (accessed June 4, 2016).

42. Smith, *Educating the Masses*, 3.

43. Ibid., 2; Whayne et al., *Arkansas*, 254.

44. Smith, *Educating the Masses*, 5. Very little has been written about the Anna T. Jeanes Fund, also known as the "Negro Rural School Fund" or the Julius Rosenwald Fund in Arkansas. For more information, consult (among other sources) Alice Brown Smith, *Forgotten Foundations: The Role of Jeanes Teachers in Black Foundation* (New York: Vantage Press, 1997); Phyllis McClure, *Jeanes Teachers: A View into Black Education in the Jim Crow South* (Booksurge Publishing, 2009); Mary S. Hoffschwelle, *The Rosenwald Schools of the American South* (Gainesville: University Press of Florida, 2006); Peter M. Ascoli, *Julius Rosenwald: The Man Who Built Sears, Roebuck and Advanced the Cause of Black Education in the American South* (Bloomington: Indiana University Press, 2006); Stephanie Deutsch, *You Need a Schoolhouse: Booker T. Washington, Julius Rosenwald, and the Building of Schools for the Segregated South* (Evanston, IL: Northwestern University Press, 2011).

45. Mildred M. Williams, et al. *The Jeanes Story: A Chapter in the History of American Education, 1908–1968*. (Atlanta: Southern Education Foundation, 1979), 175.

46. Smith, *Educating the Masses*, 5.

47. Ralph S. Wilcox, "Rosenwald Schools," Encyclopedia of Arkansas History & Culture, http://www.encyclopediaofarkansas.net/encyclopedia/entry-detail.aspx?entryID=2371 (accessed June 5, 2016); Elizabeth Hayes Turner, *Women and Gender in the New South, 1865–1945* (Wheeling: Harland Davidson, Inc., 2009), 110.

48. Carl Moneyhon, *Arkansas and the New South, 1874–1929* (Fayetteville: University of Arkansas Press, 1997), 14.

49. Ibid., 15. For more on Scott Bond, see Ulysses S. Bond, "Highlights in the Life of Scott Bond," *Arkansas Historical Quarterly* 21 (Summer 1962): 146–152, and Willard B. Gatewood, ed. *From Slavery to Wealth: The Life of Scott Bond* (Fayetteville: University of Arkansas Press, 2008). For more on

Scipio Africanus Jones, see Tom Dillard, "Scipio A. Jones," *Arkansas Historical Quarterly* 31 (Autumn 1972): 201–19, and "Arkansas Black Lawyers," http://arkansasblacklawyers.uark.edu//lawyers/sajones.html (accessed June 4, 2016).

50. Moneyhon, *Arkansas and the New South*, 73.

51. "The Body Count: Lynching in Arkansas," http://historymatters.gmu.edu/d/5467/ (accessed June 4, 2016).

52. Vinnie Vinikas, "Specters in the Past: The Saint Charles, Arkansas, Lynching of 1904 and the Limits of Historical Inquiry," *Journal of Southern History* 65, no. 3 (August 1999): 535–64.

53. Kimberly Harper, *White Man's Heaven: The Lynching and Expulsion of Blacks in the Southern Ozarks, 1894–1909* (Fayetteville: University of Arkansas Press, 2010).

54. Guy Lancaster, "Bonanza Race War of 1904," Encyclopedia of Arkansas History & Culture, http://www.encyclopediaofarkansas.net/encyclopedia/entry-detail.aspx?entryID=6218 (accessed June 4, 2016).

55. See "The Cotter Expulsion of 1906 and Limitations on Historical Inquiry," *Baxter County History* 38 (April, May, June 2012): 26–29; "'Negroes Are Leaving Paragould by Hundreds': Racial Cleansing in a Northeast Arkansas Railroad Town," *Arkansas Review: A Journal of Delta Studies* 41 (April 2010): 3–15; "'Negroes Warned to Leave Town': The Bonanza Race War of 1904," *Journal of the Fort Smith Historical Society* 34 (April 2010): 24–29; "Nightriding and Racial Cleansing in the Arkansas River Valley," *Arkansas Historical Quarterly* 72 (Autumn 2013): 242–64; "'There Are Not Many Negroes Here': African Americans in Polk County, Arkansas, 1896–1937," *Arkansas Historical Quarterly* 70 (Winter 2011): 429–49; "'They Are Not Wanted': The Extirpation of African Americans from Baxter County, Arkansas," *Arkansas Historical Quarterly* 69 (Spring 2010): 28–44.

56. Guy Lancaster, *Racial Cleansing in Arkansas, 1883–1924: Politics, Land, Labor, and Criminality* (Lanham, MD: Lexington Books, 2014). For earlier studies, see Peggy Lloyd, "The Howard County Race Riots of 1883," *Arkansas Historical Quarterly* 59, no. 4 (Winter 2000): 353–87, and Tom Dillard, "Madness With a Past: An Overview of Race Violence in Arkansas History," *Arkansas Review: A Journal of Delta Studies* 32 (August 2001): 93–101.

Chapter 4—The Civil War's Impact on the Arkansas Economy

By Jeannie Whayne

1. Morton Sosna, "More Important than the Civil War? The Impact of World War II on the South," in *Perspectives on the American South: An Annual Review of Society, Politics and Culture*, ed. James C. Cobb and Charles R. Wilson (New York: Gordon & Breach, 1987), 145. See also S. Charles Bolton, "Turning Point: World War II and the Economic Development of Arkansas," *Arkansas Historical Quarterly* (Summer 2002): 123–51, Sven Beckert, *Empire of Cotton: A Global History* (New York: Alfred A. Knopf, 2015), and Carl Moneyhon, *The Impact of Civil War and Reconstruction on Arkansas* (Fayetteville: University of Arkansas Press, 2002).

2. For the survival of plantation agriculture and planters, see C. Vann Woodward, *The Origins of the New South, 1877–1913* (Baton Rouge: Louisiana State University Press, 1951, 1971), and Jonathan M. Weiner, *Social Origins of the New South, 1860–1885* (Baton Rouge: Louisiana State University Press, 1978).

3. Frank Uekotter, ed., *Comparing Apples, Oranges, and Cotton: Environmental Histories of the Global Plantation* (Frankfurt and New York: Campus Verlag and the University of Chicago, 2014).

4. George L. Beckford, *Persistent Poverty: Underdevelopment in Plantation Economies of the Third World* (New York: Oxford University Press, 1972), as cited by John J. Green, Tracy Greever-Rice, and Gary D. Glass Jr., "Sociodemographic Snapshots of the Mississippi Delta," in *Defining the Delta: Multidisciplinary Perspectives on the Lower Mississippi River Delta* (Fayetteville: University of Arkansas Press, 2015), 108. See also E. Valentine Daniel, Henry Bernstein, and Tom Brass, eds., *Plantations, Proletarians and Peasants in Colonial Asia* (London: Frank Cass, 1992); Charles S. Aiken, *The Cotton Plantation South since the Civil War* (Baltimore: Johns Hopkins University Press, 1998); Jay R. Mandle, *The Plantation Economy: Population and Economic Change in Guyana, 1838–1960* (Temple University Press, 1973); Jay Mandle, *The Roots of Black Poverty* (Durham: Duke University Press, 1978); Simon P. Newman, *A New World of Labor: The Development of Plantation Slavery in the British Atlantic* (University of Pennsylvania Press, 2013); M. Aso, "Profits or People? Rubber Plantations and Everyday Technology in Rural Indochina," *Modern Asian Studies* 46, no. 1 (2012): 19–45 and "From Colonial Plantations to Socialist Production: The Vietnamization of Rubber, 1956–1975," forthcoming; and Philip D. Curtin, *The Rise and Fall of the Plantation Complex* (Cambridge: Cambridge University Press, 1998).

5. Beckert, *Empire of Cotton*; Uekotter, *Comparing Apples, Oranges, and Cotton.*

6. S. Charles Bolton, *Arkansas, 1800–1860: Remote and Restless* (Fayetteville: University of Arkansas Press, 1998), 55–61, 173–76; Larry Schweikert, "Banking in Antebellum Arkansas: New Evidence, New Interpretations," *Southern Studies* 26 (1987): 188–201; Ted R. Worley, "The Arkansas State Bank: Antebellum Period," *Arkansas Historical Quarterly* 23 (Spring 1964): 65–73; Ted R. Worley, "The Control of the Real Estate Bank of the State of Arkansas, 1836–1855," *Mississippi Valley Historical Review* 27 (December 1950): 403–26; and W. B. Worthen, *Early Banking in Arkansas* (Little Rock: Democrat Printing Company, 1906). See also Carey M. Roberts, "Arkansas State Bank," Encyclopedia of Arkansas History & Culture, http://www.encyclopediaofarkansas.net/encyclopedia/entry-detail.aspx?entryID=2945 (accessed June 4, 2016) and Carey M. Roberts, "Arkansas Real Estate Bank," Encyclopedia of Arkansas History & Culture, http://www.encyclopediaofarkansas.net/encyclopedia/entry-detail.aspx?entryID=2548 (accessed June 4, 2016). And see *Statistical View of the United States, Compendium of the Seventh Census*, 1850 (New York: Norman Ross Publishing Inc., 1990), 197, 198, and *Agriculture of the United States in 1860*, Eighth Census (Washington DC: Government Printing Office, 1864), 7.

7. Cotton was marketed by the pound. Although bales varied in weight in this era, 400 pounds would be a conservative estimate. Cotton was ranging in price in 1860, with 12 cents per pound being the lower end of the scale. The arithmetic would look like the following: 400-pound bales times 367,393 bales equals 146,957,200 pounds times 12 cents per pound equals $17,634,864. Correcting for inflation, that would be $503,852,742.86 in 2015 dollars. Dave Manuel.com Inflation Calculator, http://www.davemanuel.com/inflation-calculator.php (accessed June 4, 2016).

8. Thomas DeBlack, "A Garden in the Wilderness: The Johnsons and the Making of Lakeport Plantation, 1831–1876," PhD diss., University of Arkansas, 1995, pp. 119, 167–68; *Statistical View of the United States, Compendium of the Seventh Census*, 1850 (New York: Norman Ross Publishing Inc., 1990), 197, 198; *Agriculture of the United States in 1860*, Eighth Census (Washington DC: Government Printing Office, 1864), 7.

9. C. Fred Williams, "Agriculture," Encyclopedia of Arkansas History & Culture, http://www.encyclopediaofarkansas.net/encyclopedia/entry-detail.aspx?entryID=385 (accessed June 4, 2016).

10. Ted Smith, "Slavery in Washington County, Arkansas, 1828–1860," MA thesis, University of Arkansas, 1995, p. 90; Steven Hahn, *The Roots of Southern Populism* (Oxford and New York: Oxford University Press, 1983).

11. Smith, "Slavery in Washington County," 2.

12. Ibid., 17.

13. Ibid., 36.

14. Willard B. Gatewood, "Sunnyside: The Evolution of an Arkansas Plantation, 1840–1945," in *Shadows Over Sunnyside: An Arkansas Plantation in Transition, 1830–1945*, ed. Jeannie M. Whayne (Fayetteville: University of Arkansas Press, 1993), 6.

15. Donald P. McNeill, *The Old South Frontier: Cotton Plantations and the Formation of Arkansas Society, 1819–1861* (Fayetteville: University of Arkansas Press, 2000), 126; J. Wayne Jones, "Seeding Chicot: The Isaac H. Hilliard Plantation and the Arkansas Delta," *Arkansas Historical Quarterly* 70 (Summer 2011): 173.

16. William L. Shea, "The War We Have Lost," *Arkansas Historical Quarterly* 70 (Summer 2011): 105.

17. Daniel E. Sutherland, *A Savage Conflict: The Decisive Role of Guerrillas in the American Civil War* (Chapel Hill: University of North Carolina Press, 2009), and Michael Fellman, *Inside War: The Guerrilla Conflict in Missouri during the American Civil War* (New York: Oxford University Press, 1989).

18. Michael A. Hughes, "Wartime Gristmill Destruction in Northwest Arkansas and Military-Farm Colonies," *Arkansas Historical Quarterly* 46 (Summer 1987): 171. For primary documents on Fayetteville's occupation—by one army or the other—see Mark K. Christ and Patrick G. Williams, *I Do Wish This Cruel War Was Over: First-Person Accounts of Civil War Arkansas from the* Arkansas Historical Quarterly (Fayetteville: University of Arkansas Press, 2014), 74–87.

19. Christ and Williams, *I Do Wish This Cruel War Was Over*, 168.

20. Rebecca Howard, "Civil War Unionists and Their Legacy in the Arkansas Ozarks," PhD diss., University of Arkansas, 2015, p. 108.

21. Sutherland, *A Savage Conflict*, 73; *War of the Rebellion: A Compilation of the Official Records of the Union and Confederate Armies* (*OR*), vol. X, part 2, p. 559; Frank L. Owsley Jr., *King Cotton Diplomacy: Foreign Relations of the Confederate States of America* (Chicago: University of Chicago Press, 1959); Jeannie M. Whayne, "Cotton's Metropolis: Memphis and Plantation Development in the Mississippi West, 1840–1920," in Uekotter, *Comparing Apples, Oranges, and Cotton*, 56; Sven Beckert, "Emancipation and Empire: Reconstructing the Worldwide Web of Cotton Production in the Age of the American Civil War," *American Historical Review* 109, no. 5 (December 2004): 1405–1538; and Eugene R. Dattel, "Cotton and the Civil War," *Mississippi History Now*, http://mshistory.k12.ms.us/articles/291/cotton-and-the-civil-war (accessed June 4, 2016).

22. *OR*, vol. 10, part 2, p. 559. Dan Sutherland demonstrates that the Confederacy sometimes relied on guerrillas to destroy cotton that was in dan-

ger of falling into Union hands. This could have even more disastrous results for civilians. See Sutherland, *A Savage Conflict*, 73, 151.

23. Dattel, "Cotton and the Civil War"; Dave Manuel.com Inflation Calculator, http://www.davemanuel.com/inflation-calculator.php (accessed June 4, 2016).

24. Daniel R. Doyle, "The Civil War in the Greenville Bends," *Arkansas Historical Quarterly* 70 (Summer 2011): 131, 145.

25. DeBlack, "A Garden in the Wilderness," 214.

26. Sutherland, *A Savage Conflict*, 3.

27. Gatewood, "Sunnyside," 7.

28. Kelly E. Jones, "The Peculiar Institution on the Periphery: Slavery in Arkansas," PhD diss., University of Arkansas, 2014, p. 204–5.

29. Carl Moneyhon, "From Slave to Free Labor: The Federal Plantation Experiment in Arkansas," *Arkansas Historical Quarterly* 53 (Summer 1994): 144. For the evolution of federal policy on the freedmen during the Civil War, see Willie Lee Rose, *Rehearsal for Reconstruction: The Port Royal Experiment* (Athens: University of Georgia Press, reprint, 1999).

30. Beckert, *Empire of Cotton*. For excellent treatments of the failure of Reconstruction and the implications for freedmen, see the following: Eric Foner's *Nothing but Freedom: Emancipation and Its Legacy* (Baton Rouge: Louisiana State University Press, 1983) and *Reconstruction: America's Unfinished Revolution, 1863–1877* (New York: Harper & Row, 1988); Carl H. Moneyhon, *The Impact of the Civil War and Reconstruction on Arkansas: Persistence in the Midst of Ruin, 1850–1874* (Baton Rouge: Louisiana State University Press, 1994).

31. Moneyhon, *The Impact of the Civil War*, 190–221.

32. Story Matkin-Rawn, "'The Great Negro State of the Country': Arkansas's Reconstruction and the Other Great Migration," *Arkansas Historical Quarterly* 72 (Spring 2013): 3.

33. Ibid., 1–41. Matkin-Rawn is not the first to take notice of the mass migration to the Arkansas delta—Gavin Wright has focused on the role they played in the regional labor market and Jeannie Whayne has focused on those becoming enmeshed in the plantation system. Gavin Wright, *Old South, New South: Revolutions in the Southern Economy since the Civil War* (New York: Basic Books, 1986), 82; Jeannie Whayne, *A New Plantation South: Land, Labor, and Federal Favor* (Charlottesville: University of Virginia Press, 1996), 1–2, and *Delta Empire*, 50.

34. Krista Michelle Jones, "'It was awful, but it was politics': Crittenden County and the Demise of African American Political Participation," MA thesis, University of Arkansas, 2012, pp. 33–34, 57, 67–87.

35. Pete Daniel, *Shadow of Slavery: Peonage in the South, 1901–1969* (Urbana: University of Illinois Press, 1972).

36. *Acts of the General Assembly of Arkansas*, 1868 (Little Rock: John G. Price, 1868), p. 245; *Acts of the General Assembly of Arkansas*, 1885, pp. 225–26; and *Acts of Arkansas*, 1893, pp. 228–29. See Carl Moneyhon on the 1883 law—Carl Moneyhon, *Arkansas and the New South, 1874–1929* (Fayetteville: University of Arkansas Press, 1997), 70.

37. Harold Woodman, *New South, New Law: The Legal Foundations of Credit and Labor Relations in the Postbellum Agricultural South* (Baton Rouge: Louisiana State University Press, 1995).

38. *Acts of the General Assembly of Arkansas*, 1875, p. 85.

39. *Acts of the General Assembly of Arkansas*, 1868, p. 245; *Acts of the General Assembly of Arkansas*, 1875, p. 85, as cited in Jeannie M. Whayne, *A New Plantation South*, 43–44. See also Woodman, *New South, New Law*; Woodward, *The Origins of the New South*, 184–85.

40. The historiography on Grady's vision of the New South is extensive, but a few works stand out: Edward L. Ayers, *The Promise of the New South: Life after Reconstruction* (Oxford: Oxford University Press, 1992); Harold E. Davis, *Henry Grady's New South: Atlanta, A Brave Beautiful City* (Tuscaloosa: University of Alabama Press, 1990); Paul M. Gaston, *The New South Creed: A Study in Southern Myth-Making* (New York: Knopf, 1970); and George Tindall, *The Emergence of the New South, 1913–1945* (Baton Rouge: Louisiana State University Press, 1967).

41. Woodward, *Origins of the New South*, 118; Whayne, *Delta Empire*, 48; and Moneyhon, *Arkansas and the New South*, 37–38, 102. Some of these lumber companies—like Chapman and Dewey, a St. Louis–based company that operated in Poinsett County—expanded into plantation agriculture and formed land companies. They not only sold cut-over land to prospective buyers, but they also engaged in agriculture themselves. In neighboring Mississippi County, Arkansas-born Lee Wilson founded his plantation empire on the 400 acres of timber land he inherited after the Civil War, turning it into a 50,000-acre cotton plantation by the time of his death in 1933.

42. Carl Moneyhon, *Arkansas and the New South*, 44.

43. Woodward, *Origins of the New South*, 184–85.

44. Moneyhon, *Arkansas and the New South*, 70.

45. *Twelfth Census of the United States*, 1900, vol. 5, pt. 1 (Washington DC: University Census Office, 1902), p. 60. For the Agricultural Wheel in Arkansas see Jason McCollom, "The Agricultural Wheel, the Union Labor Party, and the 1889 Arkansas Legislature," *Arkansas Historical Quarterly* 68 (Summer 2009): 157–75. Three articles by Francis Carl Elkins provide essential background on the emergence of the Agricultural Wheel: "The Agricultural Wheel in Arkansas, 1887," *Arkansas Historical Quarterly* 40 (Autumn 1982): 249–60; "The Agricultural Wheel: County Politics and Consolidation," *Arkansas*

Historical Quarterly 29 (Summer 1970): 152–75; and "State Politics and the Agricultural Wheel," *Arkansas Historical Quarterly* 38 (Autumn 1979): 248–58. See also Clifton Paisley, "The Political Wheelers and Arkansas' Election of 1888," *Arkansas Historical Quarterly* 25 (Spring 1966): 3–21, and Theodore Saloutos, "The Agricultural Wheel in Arkansas," *Arkansas Historical Quarterly* 2 (Summer 1943): 127–40.

46. *Osceola Times*, October 1 and 22, 1888. The Mississippi County Wheel's president was none other than the county judge, who ceremoniously led the burning of membership cards.

47. For excellent treatments of the process of disfranchisement in Arkansas, see John William Graves, *A Question of Honor: Election Reborn and Black Disfranchisement in Arkansas* (Charlottesville: University of Virginia Press, 1971) and *Race Relations and Urban Development in Arkansas, 1865–1905* (Fayetteville: University of Arkansas Press, 1990). See also Morgan Kousser, *The Shaping of Southern Politics: Suffrage Restriction and the Establishment of the One-Party South, 1880–1910* (New Haven: Yale University Press, 1974).

48. Steven Hahn, *A Nation Under Our Feet: Black Political Struggles in the Rural South, from Slavery to the Great Migration* (Cambridge, MA: Belknap Press of Harvard University Press, 2003).

Chapter 5—Women after the War: Profiles of Change and Continuity

By Kelly Houston Jones

1. Jeannie Whayne et al., *Arkansas: A Narrative History*, 2nd ed. (Fayetteville: University of Arkansas Press, 2013), 224–26.

2. For sources on the role of slavery in Arkansas's road to secession, see James J. Gigantino, ed., *Slavery and Secession in Arkansas: A Documentary History* (Fayetteville: University of Arkansas Press, 2015).

3. *Historical Census Browser*, University of Virginia Libraries, mapserver.lib.virginia.edu (accessed June 5, 2016).

4. Harriet would have been in her late sixties when these letters were written. If Eliza had cared for her, then Eliza was probably in her late seventies or eighties when she wrote. Margaret Jones Bolsterli, *A Remembrance of Eden: Harriet Bailey Bullock Daniel's Memories of a Frontier Plantation in Arkansas, 1849–1872* (Fayetteville: University of Arkansas Press, 1993), 31, 5 (quotation).

5. Ibid., 5–6.

6. Ibid., 6.

7. George Lankford, ed., *Bearing Witness: Memories of Arkansas Slavery* (Fayetteville: University of Arkansas Press, 2003), 150, 117.

8. Bolsterli, *Remembrance of Eden*, 102, 112, 113, 41, 49.

9. Sarah Brooke Malloy, "The Health of Our Family: The Correspondence of Amanda Beardsley Trulock, 1837–1868," MA thesis, University of Arkansas, 2005, pp. 113, 115.

10. Rebecca Howard, "Civil War Unionists and Their Legacy in the Arkansas Ozarks," PhD diss., University of Arkansas, 2015, p. 118.

11. Eliza Bradley Testimony, Sylvester Caldwell Testimony, Martha Bradley Claim, Claim # 315, Records of the Southern Claims Commission.

12. Martha Bradley Claim.

13. Lankford, *Bearing Witness*, 135. For the limits to slaves' ability to assist in their own emancipation in southwestern Arkansas, see Ryan M. Poe, "The Contours of Emancipation: Freedom Comes to Southwest Arkansas," *Arkansas Historical Quarterly* 70 (Summer 2011): 109–30.

14. Lankford, *Bearing Witness*, 56–57.

15. Whayne et al., *Arkansas: A Narrative History*, 231–33, 257–61; William L. Richter, "'A Dear Little Job': Second Lieutenant Hiram F. Willis, Freedmen's Bureau Agent in Southwestern Arkansas, 1866–1868," *Arkansas Historical Quarterly* 50 (Summer 1991): 158–60.

16. U.S. Bureau of the Census, Ninth Census of the United States, 1870, Schedule 1 (Population), Ecore Fabre Township, Ouachita County, Arkansas; Bolsterli, *Remembrance of Eden*, 34–35, 72–73.

17. Leon F. Litwack, *Been in the Storm So Long: The Aftermath of Slavery* (New York: Vintage Books, 1980), 244–46.

18. Jacqueline Jones, *Labor of Love, Labor of Sorrow*, 59; Leslie A. Schwalm, *A Hard Fight for We: Women's Transition from Slavery to Freedom in South Carolina* (Urbana: University of Illinois Press, 1997), 204–212, 268.

19. U.S. Bureau of the Census, Ninth Census of the United States, 1870, Schedule 1 (Population), Ecore Fabre Township, Ouachita County, Arkansas.

20. Ibid.

21. Ibid.

22. U.S. Bureau of the Census, Tenth Census of the United States, 1880, Schedule 1 (Population), Liberty Township, Ouachita County, Arkansas. The family had also taken on an adopted daughter, four-year-old Alsie.

23. Howard, "Civil War Unionists," 87, 98, 99; Whayne et al., *Arkansas: A Narrative History*, 222.

24. Carl H. Moneyhon, *Arkansas and the New South, 1874–1929* (Fayetteville: University of Arkansas Press, 1997), 5.

25. Moneyhon, *Arkansas and the New South*, 70–71; Whayne et al., *Arkansas: A Narrative History*, 273–74.

26. Research based on a list of twenty-four of the adult white women in the township in 1860. U.S. Bureau of the Census, Eighth Census of the United States, 1860, Schedule 1 (Population), Ecore Fabre Township, Ouachita County, Arkansas; U.S. Bureau of the Census, Ninth Census of the United States, 1870, Schedule 1 (Population), Ecore Fabre Township, Ouachita County, Arkansas.

27. U.S. Bureau of the Census, Eighth Census of the United States, 1860, Schedule 1 (Population), Ecore Fabre Township, Ouachita County, Arkansas; U.S. Bureau of the Census, Ninth Census of the United States, 1870, Schedule 1 (Population), El Dorado, Union County, Arkansas; U.S. Bureau of the Census, Ninth Census of the United States, 1870, Schedule 1 (Population), Camden, Ouachita County, Arkansas.

28. Another woman, perhaps a relative, lived with the Greens in 1870—fifty-two-year-old Harriet Gooch. U.S. Bureau of the Census, Eighth Census of the United States, 1860, Schedule 1 (Population), Ecore Fabre Township, Ouachita County, Arkansas; U.S. Bureau of the Census, Ninth Census of the United States, 1870, Schedule 1 (Population), Camden, Ouachita County, Arkansas.

29. Ibid.

30. Moneyhon, *Arkansas and the New South*, 65–66, 103–4.

31. James W. Bell, "Little Rock (Pulaski County)," Encyclopedia of Arkansas History & Culture, http://www.encyclopediaofarkansas.net/encyclopedia/entry-detail.aspx?entryID=970 (accessed June 5, 2016); Charles W. Stewart, "Fayetteville (Washington County)," Encyclopedia of Arkansas History & Culture, http://www.encyclopediaofarkansas.net/encyclopedia/entry-detail.aspx?entryID=1006 (accessed June 5, 2016); Russell E. Bearden, "Pine Bluff (Jefferson County)," Encyclopedia of Arkansas History & Culture, http://www.encyclopediaofarkansas.net/encyclopedia/entry-detail.aspx?entryID=908 (accessed June 5, 2016).

32. Moneyhon, *Arkansas and the New South*, 12.

33. Biographical material, Caroline Pynchon Breysacher Collection, box 1 file 1, Butler Center for Arkansas Studies, Little Rock; U.S. Bureau of the Census, Tenth Census of the United States, 1880, Schedule 1 (Population), First Ward Little Rock, Pulaski County, Arkansas.

34. Journal with handwritten recipes, pp. 111, 127, 9, 110, 17, Caroline Pynchon Breysacher Collection, box 1, file 4; U.S. Bureau of the Census, Tenth Census of the United States, 1880, Schedule 1 (Population), Little Rock, Pulaski County, Arkansas.

35. Julianne H. Sallee, "General Federation of Women's Clubs" Encyclopedia of Arkansas History & Culture, http://www.encyclopediaofarkansas.net/encyclopedia/entry-detail.aspx?entryID=162 (accessed June 5, 2016).

36. Whayne et al., *Arkansas: A Narrative History*, 305; Moneyhon, *Arkansas and the New South*, 48–49.

37. Howard, "Civil War Unionists," 138–39, 192; Whayne et al., *Arkansas: A Narrative History*, 238.

38. Moneyhon, *Arkansas and the New South*, 58.

39. Ben F. Johnson III, *John Barleycorn Must Die: The War against Drink in Arkansas* (Fayetteville: University of Arkansas Press, 2005), 40–41.

Chapter 6—"Scattered Like Leaves": The Impact of the Civil War on the People in the Indian Territory

By Mary Jane Warde

1. *The Indian Journal* (Eufaula, Indian Territory), May 1, 1878. The writer may have been the editor, Myron Roberts, a white man, but it could have been one of the newspaper's stockholders, all of them Muscogee citizens and some Civil War veterans. *The Indian Journal*, published in Eufaula, Oklahoma, remains the state's oldest continuously published newspaper.

2. The northeast corner was a reserve for the Senecas, Shawnees, and Quapaws. A claim by Texas to the southwestern corner was settled in 1896.

3. The pioneer historian of the Civil War in the Indian Territory was Annie Heloise Abel, whose three-volume work was published early in the early 1900s. Theda Perdue and Michael D. Green edited the Bison Book edition of Abel's work in the early 1990s.

4. Commissioner of Indian Affairs William P. Dole to Secretary of the Interior Caleb B. Smith, November 27, 1861, *Annual Reports of the Commissioner of Indian Affairs* (Washington DC: Government Printing Office, 1864), hereafter cited as AR CIA along with the year, 10. The Indian nations did not have taxation, so these monies funded their governments and schools.

5. A summary of Muscogee views on these uncertain days may be found in an article by Mrs. G. W. Grayson, "Why the Five Civilized Tribes Joined the Confederacy," *The Indian Journal*, June 6, 1913. Its author, Annie Stidham Grayson, lived through those times. She was the daughter of George W. Stidham, a prominent pro-Confederate Muscogee, and the wife of George Washington Grayson, a Muscogee Civil War veteran who served with the pro-Confederate 2nd Creek Mounted Volunteers.

6. Mary Jane Warde, *George Washington Grayson and the Creek Nation, 1843–1920* (Norman: University of Oklahoma Press, 1999), 57–58.

7. Interview of Rowland S. Bailey, 4:86–87, Indian-Pioneer History, Western History Collections, University of Oklahoma, Norman, Oklahoma

(hereafter cited as IPH WHC); Alice Robertson, "Incidents of the Civil War," box 1, 82.86, Alice Robertson Papers, Oklahoma Historical Society, Oklahoma City, Oklahoma (hereafter cited as OHS); interview of Richard Adkins, 1:280–81, IPH OHS.

8. Georgianna Stidham Grayson, untitled manuscript, Mary Hansard Knight, Okmulgee, Oklahoma; interview of Jim Tomm, 91:323–24, IPH WHC.

9. Interview of Jim Spaniard, 86:14–16, IPH WHC.

10. Angie Debo, *The Road to Disappearance: A History of the Creek Indians* (Norman: University of Oklahoma Press, 1941), 149; Gary Zellar, *African Creeks: Estelvste and the Creek Nation* (Norman: University of Oklahoma Press, 2007), 45; interview of Malucy Bear, 14: 82–85, IPH OHS.

11. Douglas H. Cooper to Lt. Col. William Potter Ross, November 10, 1861, "Creek Civil War," box 6, Grant Foreman Collection, 83.229, OHS.

12. See Lela J. McBride, *Opothleyaholo and the Loyal Muskogee: Their Flight to Kansas in the Civil War* (Jefferson, NC: McFarland & Company, Publishers, 2000). See also LeRoy H. Fischer and Kenny A. Franks, "Confederate Victory at Chusto-Talasah," *Chronicles of Oklahoma* 49 (Winter 1971–1972): 452–76. A first-person account by a Texan is found in *Fighting With Ross' Texas Cavalry Brigade, D.S.A.: The Diary of George L. Griscom, Adjutant, 9th Texas Cavalry Regiment*, ed. Homer L. Kerr (Hillsboro, TX: Hill Jr. College Press, 1976), 3–4.

13. Report of Major Elias C. Boudinot, December 28, 1861, *The War of the Rebellion: A Compilation of the Official Records of the Union and Confederate Armies, Published under the Direction of the Secretary of War* (hereafter cited as OR), series 1, volume 8, part 1, 22.

14. Report of Colonel James McIntosh, January 4, 1862, OR, series 1, volume 8, part 1, 28–29; interview of James Scott, 81:81, IPH WHC.

15. Quoted in Kevin Mulroy, *The Seminole Freedmen: A History* (Norman: University of Oklahoma Press, 2007), 169.

16. Interview of Phoebe Banks, 3, folder 2, box 25, 81.105, Federal Writers' Project Ex-Slave Narratives (hereafter cited as FWP EN), OHS.

17. Interview of James Scott, 81:81 IPH WHC.

18. Annie Heloise Abel, *The American Indian in the Civil War, 1862–1865* (Lincoln: University of Nebraska Press, 1992, Bison Book Edition), 80–81, 84–85.

19. Thomas Wildcat Alford, *Civilization and the Story of the Absentee Shawnees, As Told to Florence Drake by Thomas Wildcat Alford* (Norman: University of Oklahoma Press), 6–13.

20. "A Place to Call Home," *Texas Beyond History*, http://www.texasbeyondhistory.net/tehas/voices/place.html (accessed April 25, 2011); David La Vere, *Contrary Neighbors: Southern Plains and Removed Indians in Indian Territory* (Norman: University of Oklahoma Press, 2000), 170.

21. S. G. Colley to Commissioner of Indian Affairs William P. Dole, January 25, 1863, Report No. 57, and Dole to Colley, March 30, 1863, Report No. 58, AR CIA 1864, 135–36. They may have been prudently distancing themselves from their agency in the wake of the Tonkawa Massacre the preceding October.

22. Velma Nieberding, "Indian Home, 90, Still Stands in Craig County," *Tulsa (Oklahoma) World*, Sunday supplement, July 8, 1956, p. 36; Gary L. Cheatham, "'If the Union Wins, We Won't Have Anything Left': The Rise and Fall of the Southern Cherokees in Kansas," *Kansas History* 30 (Autumn 2007): 162, 170. There is some difference of opinion whether Rachel and her children were forced out in the first or second federal raid through Chetopa.

23. Interview of Moses Lonian, 61: 386, IPH OHS. A good discussion of Cherokee politics during this period is provided in William G. McLoughlin, *After the Trail of Tears: The Cherokees' Struggle for Sovereignty, 1839–1880* (Chapel Hill: University of North Carolina Press, 1993), 201–21.

24. Entry of July 6, 1862, F-21, Stephen Foreman Diary, WHC.

25. Muriel H. Wright, "Notes on Mrs. Hannah Worcester Hicks Hitchcock and the Park Hill Press," *Chronicles of Oklahoma* 19, no. 4 (December 1941): 351.

26. Ibid., 351.

27. Ibid., 352.

28. Interview of Mary E. Hudson James, 31:41–46, IPH OHS.

29. Warde, *George Washington Grayson*, 66–67.

30. Richard C. Rohrs, "Fort Gibson: Forgotten Glory," *Early Military Forts & Posts in Oklahoma*, edited by Odie B. Faulk, Kenny A. Franks, and Paul F. Lambert, volume 9, The Oklahoma Series (Oklahoma City: Oklahoma Historical Society, 1978), 31.

31. Ibid., 34; interview of Rochelle (Rachel) Allred Ward, 3–4, folder 4, box 28, FWP EN.

32. Surgeon A. B. Campbell to Maj. Charles G. Halpine, Fort Leavenworth, Kansas, February 5, 1862, AR CIA 1862, 151–52.

33. Superintendent Coffin to Commissioner of Indian Affairs Dole, September 24, 1863, Report No. 81 1/2, AR CIA 1863, 175.

34. Wiley Britton, *The Union Indian Brigade in the Civil War* (Kansas City, MO: Franklin Hudson Publishing Co., 1922), 204–8.

35. Ibid., 215–16; interview of Blackbird Doublehead, 22:365–77, IPH OHS.

36. Britton, *The Union Indian Brigade*, 222–23.

37. Interview of Ella Coodey Robinson, 107:451–63, 465–79, IPH OHS.

38. Entry of January 10, 1863, Stephen Foreman Diary, WHC.

39. Interview of Jim Tomm, 112:277, OHS IPH.

40. Entry of July 18, 1863, SFD WHC.

41. Interview of Lucinda Davis, 9, folder 7, box 25, FWP EN OHS.

42. Stand Watie, Principal Chief of the Cherokees, to His Excellency, the Governor of the Creek Nation, August 9, 1863, OR, series 1, volume 22, part 2, 1105.

43. Entry of August 26, 1863, SFD WHC.

44. Entry of September 5, 1863, ibid.

45. Interview of Elizabeth Kemp Mead, 64:420, IPH OHS.

46. Interview of Martha Gibson Matoy Walker, 64:420, ibid.

47. Report of Samuel Bell Maxey to Col. S. S. Scott, August 23, 1864, Samuel Bell Maxey Collection, Gilcrease Institute of American History and Art, Tulsa, Oklahoma.

48. Interview of Malucy Bear, 14:82–85, IPH OHS.

49. Agent Justin Harlan to Superintendent of Indian Affairs William G. Coffin, August 8, 1863, AR CIA 1863, 179–81.

50. Superintendent W. G. Coffin to Commissioner W. P. Dole, June 3, 1864, Report Number 169, AR CIA 1864, 340–41.

51. Dwight D. Hitchcock to "My dear friends," June 2, 1864, Alice Robertson Collection, Special Collections, McFarlin Library, University of Tulsa, Tulsa, Oklahoma.

52. For a first-person account, see W. David Baird, ed., *A Creek Warrior for the Confederacy: The Autobiography of Chief G. W. Grayson* (Norman: University of Oklahoma Press, 1988), 81–87.

53. Superintendent W. G. Coffin to Commissioner W. P. Dole, June 3, 1864, Report Number 101, AR CIA 1864, 342–43.

54. Oktahasushurgah, Kapitchafireco, Kowetamicco, Miccohutka, Tustenukechuahhikogee, and Tulladegulachapoka to the Commissioner of Indian Affairs, July 16, 1864, Report Number 172, ibid., 344.

55. Interview of Kate Rackleff, 41:114–15, IPH OHS.

56. Interview of Annie Eliza Hendricks, 41:160–64, IPH WHC.

57. Stand Watie to Sarah C. Watie, April 24, 1864, quoted in Edward Everett Dale and Gaston Litton, eds., *Cherokee Cavaliers* (Norman: University of Oklahoma Press, 1995), 156. Quantrill led his guerrilla force into the Indian Territory in 1863 to fight with Confederate allies there, which posed a moral dilemma for them. See LeRoy H. Fischer and Lary C. Rampp, "Quantrill's Civil War Operations in Indian Territory," *Chronicles of Oklahoma* 46 (Summer 1968): 155–81.

58. *Fighting With Ross' Texas Cavalry Brigade, C.S.A.: The Diary of George L. Griscom, Adjutant, 9th Texas Cavalry Regiment*, ed. Homer L. Kerr (Hillsboro, TX: Hill Jr. College Press, 1976), 5.

59. Special Agent A. G. Proctor to Superintendent of Indian Affairs William G. Coffin, August 8, Report Number 11, AR CIA 1863.

60. Superintendent W. G. Coffin, to Commissioner of Indian Affairs William P. Dole, September 24, 1863, Number 8 ½ , ibid.

61. Arrell Morgan Gibson, *Oklahoma: A History of Five Centuries* (Norman: University of Oklahoma Press, 1965, reprint 1981), 131.

62. Interview of Emma Blythe Sixkiller, 100:46–48, IPH OHS.

63. See Arrell Morgan Gibson, *The Chickasaws* (Norman: University of Oklahoma Press, 1971); Angie Debo, *The Rise and Fall of the Choctaw Republic* (Norman: University of Oklahoma Press, 1934); Morris L. Wardell, *A Political History of the Cherokee Nation, 1838–1907* (Norman: University of Oklahoma Press, 1938); Edwin C. McReynolds, *The Seminoles* (Norman: University of Oklahoma Press, 1957); Angie Debo, *The Road to Disappearance: A History of the Creek Indians* (Norman: University of Oklahoma Press, 1941); C. Ross Hume, "Historic Sites Around Anadarko," *Chronicles of Oklahoma* 16, no. 4 (December 1938): 410–24.

64. Angie Debo, *The Rise and Fall of the Choctaw Republic* (Norman: University of Oklahoma Press, 1934, second edition, 1961), 55.

65. Agent George A. Cutler to Superintendent William G. Cutler, September 5, 1863, Report No. 83, AR CIA 1863, 183.

66. Superintendent W. G. Coffin, to Commissioner of Indian Affairs William P. Dole, March 22, 1863, Report No. 98, ibid., 198–99.

67. See Brad R. Clampitt, "'An Indian Shall Not Spill an Indian's Blood': The Confederate-Indian Conference at Camp Napoleon, 1865," *Chronicles of Oklahoma* 83, no. 1 (Spring 2005): 33–54.

68. A good account of returning to the Muscogee Nation is given in Baird, ed., *A Creek Warrior for the Confederacy*, 121–22. See also the interview of Mary E. Hudson James, 31:141–46, IPH OHS, and the interview of Frank G. Audrain, 12:527–29, ibid.

69. See the interview of Mrs. Tom Rattling Gourd, 5:216, IPH OHS; Alice Robertson, "Incidents of the Civil War," Box 1, Alice Robertson Papers, 82.86, OHS.

70. The Choctaws delayed adopting their freedmen, and the Chickasaws never did adopt their freedmen, which would have made them outnumber the Chickasaws as voters. Interview of Polly Colbert, 5, folder 2, box 25, FWP EN; interview of Lucinda Davis, 7–8, folder 7, box 25, ibid; T. Lindsay Baker and Julie P. Baker, *The WPA Oklahoma Slave Narratives* (Norman: University of Oklahoma Press, 1996), 314–16.

71. AR CIA *1865*, 37. See Mary Jane Warde, *When the Wolf Came: The Civil War and the Indian Territory* (Fayetteville: University of Arkansas Press, 2013), 274–78, for a review of the negotiations at Fort Smith and in Washington DC in 1865 and 1866, respectively.

72. Daniel F. Littlefield Jr., *The Chickasaw Freedmen: A People Without a Country* (Westport, CT: Greenwood Press, 1980), 40, 45; Michael D. Green,

"Cherokee Lands in the West," in Charles Robert Goins and Danney Goble, *Historical Atlas of Oklahoma* (Norman: University of Oklahoma Press, 2006), 60–61; Nieberding, "Indian Home, 90, Still Stands in Craig County," *Tulsa (Oklahoma) World*, Sunday supplement, July 8, 1956, p. 36.

73. Debo, *The Road to Disappearance*, 167–70.

74. Statement of I. B. Luce, September 6, 1884, Grayson Family Collection, WHC; Edwin C. McReynolds, *The Seminoles* (Norman: University of Oklahoma Press, 1957), 316–17.

75. For the Cheyennes and Arapahos, suggested works include Donald J. Bethrong, *The Cheyenne and Arapaho Ordeal: Reservation and Agency Life in the Indian Territory* (Norman: University of Oklahoma Press, 1976); Jerome A. Greene, *Washita: The U.S. Army and the Southern Cheyennes, 1867–1869* (Norman: University of Oklahoma Press, 2004); and Loretta Fowler, *The Arapaho* (New York: Chelsea House Publishers, 1989). For the Kiowas and Comanches, a classic on the Plains Wars is W. S. Nye, *Carbine and Lance: The Story of Old Fort Sill* (Norman: University of Oklahoma Press, 1969). For the Caddos, see Cecile Elkins Carter, *Caddo Indians: Where We Come From* (Norman: University of Oklahoma Press, 2001).

76. The Modocs were sent as prisoners to a reservation in northeastern Indian Territory after resisting removal from their homelands in California. Michael D. Green, "Indian Territory, 1866–1889," Goins and Goble, *Historical Atlas of Oklahoma*, 98–99. See also Louis F. Burns, *A History of the Osage People* (Tuscaloosa: University of Alabama Press, 2004), 321. Additional tribal works include Mark Van de Logt, *War Party in Blue: Pawnee Scouts in the U.S. Army* (Norman: University of Oklahoma Press, 2010).

Chapter 7—Arkansas: Where One War's Edge Was Another War's Center

By Elliott West

1. W. Turrentine Jackson, *Wagon Roads West: A Study of Federal Road Surveys and Construction in the Trans-Mississippi West, 1846–1869* (Berkeley: University of California Press, 1952); Roscoe P. and Margaret B. Conkling, *The Butterfield Overland Mail, 1857–1869: Its Organization and Operation Over the Southern Route…* (Glendale, CA: A. H. Clark, 1947).

2. Alvin F. Harlow, *Old Wires and New Waves: The History of the Telegraph, Telephone, and Wireless* (New York: D. Appleton-Century Company, 1936); Robert Luther Thompson, *Wiring a Continent: The History of the*

Telegraph Industry in the United States, 1832–1866 (Princeton, NJ: Princeton University Press, 1947).

3. Patricia A. Etter, *To California on the Southern Route, 1849: A History and Annotated Bibliography* (Spokane, WA: Arthur H. Clark, 1998).

4. See for instance Robert E. May, *The Southern Dream of a Caribbean Empire, 1854–1861* (Baton Rouge: Louisiana State University Press, 2002); David C. Keehn, *Knights of the Golden Circle: Secret Empire, Southern Secession, Civil War* (Baton Rouge: Louisiana State University Press, 2013); Walter Johnson, *River of Dark Dreams: Slavery and Empire in the Cotton Kingdom* (Cambridge: Belknap Press of Harvard University Press, 2013).

5. David Igler, *The Great Ocean: Pacific Worlds from Captain Cook to the Gold Rush* (New York: Oxford University Press, 2013); Gregory T. Cushman, *Guano and the Opening of the Pacific World* (Cambridge: Cambridge University Press, 2012).

6. William Kennedy, *Texas: The Rise, Progress, and Prospects of the Republic of Texas*, Vol. II (London: R. Hastings, 1841), 395–96.

7. Quoted in Walter Johnson, *River of Dark Dreams: Slavery and Empire in the Cotton Kingdom*, 298–99.

8. *Congressional Globe*, 31st Cong., 2nd sess., March 3, 1851, 826–27.

9. *Report of the Committee on Internal Improvements, On the Use of Camels on the Plains, May 30, 1855*, California Senate Document no. 24, session 1855.

10. For Gwin's presentation of his vision, see *Congressional Globe*, 32nd Cong., 2nd sess., 280–84.

11. Walter Lee Brown, *A Life of Albert Pike* (Fayetteville: University of Arkansas Press, 1997), 281–82.

12. Ibid., 283.

13. Albert Pike, *Address on the Southern Pacific Railroad* (New Orleans: Emile La Sere, 1855), 7–8.

14. "Southern Commercial Convention at New Orleans," *De Bow's Review* 18, no. 4 (April 1855): 254.

15. "The Great Southern Convention at Charleston, No. 6," *De Bow's Review* 17, no. 5 (November 1854): 504–5.

16. On the surveys, see William H. Goetzmann, *Exploration and Empire: The Explorer and the Scientist in the Winning of the American West* (New York: Alfred A. Knopf, 1966): 265–302.

17. J. David Hacker, "A Census-based Count of the Civil War Dead," *Civil War History* 57, no. 4 (December 2011): 307–48.

18. On the scramble for Indian lands, see Craig Miner and William E. Unrau, *The End of Indian Kansas: A Study of Cultural Revolution, 1854–1871* (Lawrence: University Press of Kansas, 1978) and Paul Wallace Gates, *Fifty Million Acres: Conflicts Over Kansas Land Policy, 1854–1890* (Norman: University of Oklahoma Press, 1997).

19. Miner and Unrau, *End of Indian Kansas*, 16, 20–24; Tony R. Mullis, *Peacekeeping on the Plains: Army Operations in Bleeding Kansas* (Columbia: University of Missouri Press, 2004), 119–52.

20. For a report on this episode, see *Letter of the Secretary of the Interior...In Relation to the "Half-Breed Kaw Lands" on the Kansas River, in the State of Kansas*, S. Exec. Doc. 58, 37th Cong., 2nd sess., Serial Set 1122, vol. 5.

21. Gates, *Fifty Million Acres*, 116–21, 140–42.

22. Miner and Unrau, *End of Indian Kansas*, 11.

23. Gates, *Fifty Million Acres*, 6–7.

24. Grant Foreman, *A History of Oklahoma* (Norman: University of Oklahoma Press, 1942), 100–5; Ohland Morton, "Confederate Relations with the Five Civilized Tribes," *Chronicles of Oklahoma* 31, no. 3 (Fall 1953): 299–307; Brown, *A Life of Albert Pike*, 361–71; David A. Nichols, *Lincoln and the Indians: Civil War Policy and Politics* (Columbia: University of Missouri Press, 1978), 25–41.

25. Laurence M. Hauptman, *Between Two Fires: American Indians in the Civil War* (New York: Free Press, 1995); Annie Heloise Abel, *The American Indian in the Civil War, 1862–1865* (Lincoln: University of Nebraska Press, 1992).

26. John B. Meserve, "Chief Opothleyahola," *Chronicles of Oklahoma* 9, no. 4 (December 1931): 446–50.

27. The most thorough account of these events and the disaster that followed is Clint Crowe, "War in the Nations: The Devastation of a Removed People During the American Civil War," PhD diss., University of Arkansas, 2009.

28. A. B. Campbell to James K. Barns in *Relief to Indian refugees in southern Kansas. Letter from J.P. Usher, Assistant Secretary of the Interior, in answer to resolution of the House of 28th ultimo relative to mode and amount of relief extended to Indian refugees in southern Kansas. June 16, 1862*, H. Exec. Doc. 132, 32nd Cong., 2nd sess., Serial Set 1138, vol. 10, 5–6.

29. George W. Collamore to William P. Dole in *Message of the President of the United States to the two Houses of Congress at the commencement of the third session of the Thirty-seventh Congress. December 1, 1862*, H. Exec. Doc. 1, part 2, 37th Cong., sess. 3, Serial Set 1157, vol. 2, 301.

30. W. G. Coffin to William P. Dole in *Message of the President of the United States to the two Houses of Congress at the commencement of the third session of the Thirty-seventh Congress. December 1, 1862*, H. Exec. Doc. 1, part 2, 37th Cong., sess. 3, Serial Set 1157, vol. 2, 280.

31. For a summary account of this appalling episode, see Edmund J. Danziger, "The Office of Indian Affairs and the Problem of Civil War Indian Refugees in Kansas," *Kansas Historical Quarterly* 35, no. 3 (Autumn 1969): 257–75.

32. On the Civil War in the Territory, see Lary C. Rampp and Donald L. Rampp, *The Civil War in Indian Territory* (Austin, TX: Presidial Press, 1975); Abel, *The American Indian in the Civil War, 1862–1865*; LeRoy H. Fischer, ed., *The Civil War Era in Indian Territory* (Los Angeles: Lorrin Morrison, 1974); Fischer, *Western Territories*, 101–13; Wilfred Knight, *Red Fox: Stand Watie and the Indian Nations during the Civil War Years in Indian Territory* (Glendale, CA: A. H. Clark, 1988); Edward E. Dale, "The Cherokees in the Confederacy," *Journal of Southern History* 13, no. 2 (May 1947): 160–85.

33. J. Harlan to William G. Coffin in *Message of the President of the United States, and accompanying documents, to the two Houses of Congress, at the commencement of the second session of the Thirty-eighth Congress*, H. Exec. Doc. 1, part 5, 38th Cong., 2nd sess., Serial Set 1220, vol. 5, 453; Elijah Sells to D. N. Cooley in *Message of the President of the United States, and accompanying documents, to the two Houses of Congress, at the commencement of the first session of the Thirty-ninth Congress*, H. Exec. Doc. 1, part 2, 39th Cong., 1st sess., Serial Set 1248, no. 2, 437.

34. Morris L. Wardell, *A Political History of the Cherokee Nation* (Norman: University of Oklahoma Press, 1938), 175; Russell Thornton, *The Cherokees: A Population History* (Lincoln: University of Nebraska Press, 1990), 92–96.

Chapter 8—Conflicting Civil War Historical Memory and Cultural Divides in Arkansas

By Carl H. Moneyhon

1. *Journal of both Sessions of the Convention of the State of Arkansas* (Little Rock: Johnson & Yerkes, State Printer, 1861), 46–45 (quotation), 124.

2. Michael Dougan, *Arkansas Odyssey: The Saga of Arkansas from Prehistoric Times to Present* (Little Rock: Rose Publishing Company, Inc., 1993), 217; Dorothy Stanley, ed., *The Autobiography of Sir Henry Morton Stanley* (New York: Houghton Mifflin Company, 1909), 169.

3. Junius Bragg to My Dear Wife, April 23, 1865, in Mrs. T. J. Gaughan, ed., *Letters of a Confederate Surgeon, 1865–1865* (Camden, AR: 1960), 272; "Adams' Arkansas Infantry Regiment," Report of Major-General Hindman, Headquarters First Corps, Trans-Mississippi Army, Camp near Fort Smith, Ark., December 25, 1862, quoted by Howerton, Bryan, "mass desertion," Arkansas in the Civil War Message Board, posted February 2, 2007, http://history-sites.com/cgi-bin/bbs53x/arcwmb/webbbs_config.pl?noframes;read=14558 (accessed June 7, 2016); Battle of Fitzhugh's Woods, Near Augusta, Arkansas,

April 1, 1864, in "Minnesota in the Civil War and Indian Wars, 1861–1865," http://memory.loc.gov/service/gdc/scd0001/2003/20030908004ba/2003090800 4ba.pdf. (accessed June 7, 2016); Steven L. Warren, "Desertion (Civil War)," Encyclopedia of Arkansas History & Culture, http://www.encyclopediao-farkansas.net/encyclopedia/entry-detail.aspx?entryID=6399 (accessed June 7, 2016); August C. Abernathy to Dear Sister, Sept. 3, 1862, http://freepages.genealogy.rootsweb.ancestry.com/~bandy/kestletters.html (accessed June 7, 2016).

4. Fort Smith *New Era*, October 8, 1863 (first quotation); Little Rock *Unconditional Union*, January 28, 1864 (second quotation); Dougan, *Arkansas Odyssey*, 202–3, 222; Albert W. Bishop, *Loyalty on the Frontier; or, Sketches of Union Men of the Southwest* (St. Louis, MO: R. P. Stanley, 1863); Ted Worley, "The Arkansas Peace Society of 1861: A Study in Mountain Unionism," *Journal of Southern History* 24 (1958): 445–56; Diane Neal, "Treason or Patriotism? Union Peace Societies in Arkansas during the Civil War," *Journal of Confederate History* 1 (1988): 339–49; Carl H. Moneyhon, "Disloyalty and Class Consciousness in Southwestern Arkansas, 1862–1865," *Arkansas Historical Quarterly* 52 (Autumn 1993): 223–43.

5. H. Ankey to Wife, July 15, 1862, Florence Marie Ankeny Cox, ed., *Kiss Josey for Me* (Santa Ana, CA: Friis Pioneer Press, 1974), 73; George P. Rawick, ed., *The American Slave: A Composite Autobiography, Arkansas Narrative* (Westport, CT: Greenwood Press, 1972), Vol. 9, pt. 3, p. 24; Benjamin F. Pearson, "Benjamin F. Pearson's War Diary," *Annals of Iowa* 16 (October 1926): 439–40.

6. *Proceedings of the Convention of Colored Citizens of the State of Arkansas, Held in Little Rock, Thursday, Friday and Saturday, Nov. 30, Dec. 1 and 2, 1865* (Helena, AR: Clarion Printers, 1866); Dougan, *Arkansas Odyssey*, 227.

7. Eric Foner, *Reconstruction: America's Unfinished Revolution, 1863–1877* (New York: Harper & Row, 1988), 1–7, 66–67, 118–19, 243–47.

8. William C. Davis, *The Cause Lost: Myths and Realities of the Confederacy* (Lawrence: University Press of Kansas, 1998), x.

9. (Little Rock) *Morning Republican*, May 31, 1869; *Arkansas Gazette*, June 6, 1867, June 9, 1868; Caroline E. Janney, *Burying the Dead but not the Past: Ladies' Memorial Associations & the Lost Cause* (Chapel Hill: University of North Carolina Press, 2008), 62–63, 76–77.

10. *Arkansas Gazette*, May 11, 1869 (quotation); see also ibid., May 1, 1869.

11. (Little Rock) *Morning Republican*, May 31, 1869; David W. Blight, *Race and Reunion: The Civil War in American Memory* (Cambridge, MA: Belknap Press of Harvard University Press, 2001), 79.

12. (Little Rock) *Daily Republican*, May 31, 1873.

13. *Arkansas Gazette*, May 30, 1875 (first quotation), June 1, 1877 (second quotation), May 31, 1890.

14. "Constitution and By-Laws of the United Confederate Veterans...April 1892," https://ia800301.us.archive.org/24/items/ConstitutionAndBy-lawsOfTheUnitedConfederateVeterans/UCVcon.pdf (accessed June 7, 2016); "Organization of 1026 Camps of the United Confederate Veterans Association...1897," https://ia700406.us.archive.org/33/items/organizationof1000unit/organizationof1000unit.pdf (accessed November, 21, 2015); *Confederate Veteran*, vol. 1 (1893), p. 132; Gaines M. Foster, *Ghosts of the Confederacy: Defeat, the Lost Cause, and the Emergence of the New South* (New York: Oxford University Press, 1987), 105–14; *Arkansas Gazette*, March 28, May 1, 9, 17, 18, 21, 28, June 1, 2, 4, 16, 21, 23, 25, 30, July 3, 4, 6, 14, 18, 19, September 24, 1889; January 1, 10, 14, March 11, 14, May 1, 4, June 6, 10, July 7, 18, 19, August 22, September 12, 1890.

15. Foster, *Ghosts of the Confederacy*, 49–62.

16. Ibid., 62; *Arkansas Gazette*, May 5, 1889.

17. *Arkansas Gazette*, May 17, 1893.

18. Ibid.; Foster, *Ghosts of the Confederacy*, 79–87.

19. *Arkansas Gazette*, May 31, 1890.

20. "Constitution of the Daughters of the Confederacy," https://archive.org/details/constitutionofdaughters (accessed June 7, 2016); "Constitution of the Sons of Confederate Veterans Adopted on July 1, 1896," http://www.scv.org/pdf/SCVCON03.pdf (accessed June 7, 2016).

21. Charles Russell Logan, *"Something So Dim It Must Be Holy": Civil War Commemorative Sculpture in Arkansas 1886–1934* (Little Rock: Arkansas Historic Preservation Program), www.arkansaspreservation.com/LiteratureRetrieve.aspx?ID=133285 (accessed June 7, 2016); *Confederate Veteran*, vol. 21 (1913), 285; Stuart McConnell points to the significance of the geographic placement of monuments in reflecting the power and authority of their sponsors. Stuart McConnell, "Epilogue: A Geography of Memory," in *The Memory of the Civil War in American Culture*, ed. Alice Fahs and Joan Waugh (Chapel Hill: University of North Carolina Press, 2004), 260.

22. *Arkansas Democrat*, June 4, 1905.

23. Ibid.

24. Ibid.

25. Ibid.

26. Ibid.

27. Ibid.

28. Ibid.

29. *Arkansas Gazette*, May 18, 1911.

30. Mrs. Richard B. Willis, "History Report of Arkansas Division," *Confederate Veteran* 12 (February 1904): 74; *United Daughters of the*

Confederacy: Arkansas Division, Eighteenth Annual Convention Held in Little Rock, Arkansas, October 21, 22, 23, 24, 1913 (n.p.: 1913), 33–34. See Fred Arthur Bailey, "Free Speech and the 'Lost Cause' in Arkansas," *Arkansas Historical Quarterly* 55 (Summer 1996): 143–66 for an overview of the Daughters' efforts to control the content of history classes.

31. *Daily Fayetteville Democrat*, Nov. 2, 1915; *Hope Star*, January 28, 1930, June 13, 1931. For a discussion of the emergence of the David O. Dodd myth and its use, see Carl H. Moneyhon, "David O. Dodd, the 'Boy Martyr of Arkansas': The Growth and Use of a Legend," *Arkansas Historical Quarterly* 74 (Autumn 2015): 203–30.

32. Henry Eldridge Bourne and Elbert Jay Benton, *History of the United States* (Boston: D. C. Heath, 1913), 431. The volume cited is an earlier version.

33. Josiah Hanzen Shinn, *The History of Arkansas: A Text-book for Public Schools, High Schools and Academies* (Richmond, VA: B. F. Johnson Publishing Co., 1905), 175; Walter S. McNutt, Olin E. McKnight, and George A. Hubbell, *A History of Arkansas* (Little Rock: Democrat Printing and Litho., 1932), 142; Fred Berry and John Novak, *The History of Arkansas* (Little Rock: Rose Publishing Co., 1987), 85. See also John Hugh Reynolds, *Makers of Arkansas History* (New York: Silver Burdett, 1918, originally published in 1905); John H. Moore, *A School History of Arkansas* (Little Rock: Democrat Printing and Litho., 1924), 151; A. M. Harper, *The Story of Arkansas: With Pedagogical Aids by Dean M. McBrien* (Kansas City: The Grolier Society, 1931), 165; Walter Scott McNutt, *An Elementary History of Arkansas* (Little Rock: Democrat Printing and Lithographing Co., 1935), 193; Faith Yingling Knoop and James R. Grant, *Arkansas Yesterday and Today* (Chicago: J. B. Lippincott, 1935), 237; Hazel Presson and David Y. Thomas, *The Story of Arkansas* (Little Rock: Democrat Printing and Litho., 1942).

34. All of the books in the previous note reflect this emphasis on Confederate unity and do not touch upon the African American experience.

35. Reynolds, *Makers of Arkansas History*, 257; Knoop and Grant, *Arkansas*, 262; Moore, *School History*, 172; Harper, *Story of Arkansas*, 92.

36. Sharon Hatcher to Editor, *Arkansas Democrat-Gazette*, July 16, 2015, p. 7b.

37. Ron Springer, "Erasing history: So you want to take the flag...," *Arkansas Democrat-Gazette*, July 11, 2015, p. 9b.

38. Sharon Hatcher to Editor, *Arkansas Democrat-Gazette*, July 16, 2015, p. 7b.

39. Joe Jakonczuk to Editor, *Arkansas Democrat-Gazette*, July 11, 2015, p. 9b.

Index

CPSIA information can be obtained
at www.ICGtesting.com
Printed in the USA
BVOW03*0238130817
491443BV00002B/3/P

9 781935 106968